GREAT TRAVEL VALUES™

SPAIN

FODOR'S TRAVEL PUBLICATIONS

are compiled, researched, and edited by an international team of travel writers, field correspondents, and editors. The series, which now almost covers the globe, was founded by Eugene Fodor in 1936.

OFFICES

New York & London

Fodor's Great Travel Values: Spain

Area Editor: Hilary Bunce
Editorial Contributors: Robert Brown, Ailsa Heritage, Hilary Hughes, Lisa Marrongelli, Madeleine Nicklin
Editor: Thomas Cussans
Maps and Plans: Swanston Graphics

FODOR'S

GREAT TRAVEL VALUES

SPAIN

FODOR'S TRAVEL PUBLICATIONS, INC.
New York & London

ISBN 0-679-01486-1

MANUFACTURED IN THE UNITED STATES OF AMERICA
10 9 8 7 6 5 4 3 2 1

CONTENTS

FOREWORD

Welcome to Spain—land of white-sand beaches, historic cities, unspoiled towns, archeological treasures, spectacular scenery, and festive fiestas. All these—and more—can be enjoyed by the budget traveler at little or no cost. This guide will help to show you how.

While every care has been taken to ensure the accuracy of the information contained in this guide, the publishers cannot accept responsibility for any errors that may appear.

All prices quoted in this guide are based on those available to us at the time of writing. In a world of rapid change, however, the possibility of inaccurate or out-of-date information can never be totally eliminated. We trust, therefore, that you will take prices quoted as indicators only, and will double-check to be sure of the latest figures.

Similarly, be sure to check all opening times of museums and galleries. We have found that such times are liable to change without notice, and you could easily make a trip only to find a locked door.

When a hotel closes or a restaurant produces a disappointing meal, let us know, and we will investigate the establishment and the complaint. We are always ready to revise our entries for the following year's edition should the facts warrant it.

Send your letters to the editors of Fodor's Travel Publications, 201 E. 50th Street, New York, N.Y. 10022. European readers may prefer to write to Fodor's Travel Guides, 9–10 Market Place, London W1N 7AG, England.

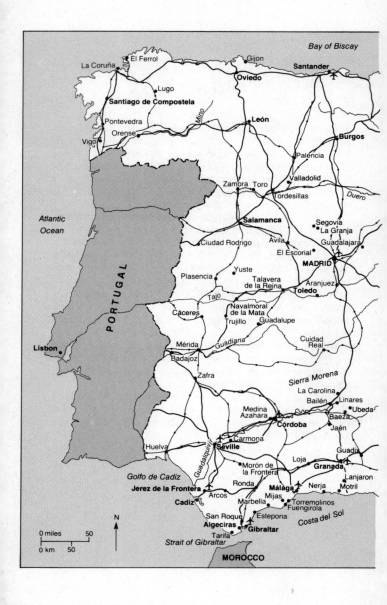

INTRODUCTION

Spain offers some of the greatest travel values in Europe: a rich brew of history, landscapes, cities, and culture at prices that are almost always affordable and often amazingly low. But don't make the mistake of thinking it's just a question of cheapness. The joy of low-cost travel in Spain is that good value is so easy to find.

The basic costs of your vacation—hotels, restaurants, and transportation—are all easily within reach. Take hotels, for example. Most people will find 3- or 2-star hotels more than adequate. They may seem a little spartan at first, with simple metal-framed beds and bare floors, but they're nearly all clean, friendly, and inexpensive. Private bathtubs or showers (the former are more expensive) are common; you won't have to plod down a dingy corridor in your robe looking for the bathroom.

Part of the reason for this affordability is the sheer number of lower-priced hotels in Spain. Healthy competition keeps hoteliers on their toes and ensures value for money. Equally, government regulations are strict, aimed at ensuring low prices and high standards (the Spanish take tourism seriously; it's one of their largest industries, pulling in around $15 billion a year). Room rates must be registered with regional tourist boards, and all hotels must have a complaint book. The latter is no mere sop to consumerism. The authorities inspect these books regularly.

Eating in Spain presents a similarly encouraging picture. The abundance of Spanish restaurants testifies to the Spanish love of eating out. Even in the smallest towns you should have no difficulty finding a reasonable place to eat. An unexpected plus is the remarkable professionalism of Spanish waiters, invariably headed by a maître d' who will show you to your table and take your order. Humble restaurants in out-of-the-way towns often have crisp linen tablecloths, silver serving dishes, and an English menu. Almost all offer a daily fixed-price menu—the *menu del día*—which at the very least ensures good value, if not always the best dishes. City restaurants—and this is especially true of Madrid, Barcelona, and Seville—are rarely inexpensive these days, but few visitors dispute their worth: a wide choice of dishes, impeccable service, and excellent food. You should remember, however, that the Spanish eat late and long. Lunch typically starts at 2 or 2:30 and dinner at 10 or 10:30. Allow yourself to get into the rhythm of the country and do as the Spanish do. Eating here is taken seriously; it's a ritual, something to savor, something to linger over.

Spanish tipping practices help keep costs down, too. The service charge is never added to the bill so there's no risk of inadvertently tipping twice. Moreover, 10% is considered generous. In more humble establishments, 5% is ample. Drink the house wine with your meals—*vino de la casa;* it's almost always good value. If you want to splurge on a good wine, ask the waiter to recommend a local one. Spanish wines have improved immeasurably in the last 10 years and there are some excellent local wines costing half the price of a name Rioja.

Public transportation in Spain is mostly excellent and low cost—if sometimes slow. If you plan to travel extensively by train, check out the InterRail and Eurail passes before you leave home (they're good for travel in the rest of Europe, too), or buy a RENFE card, the Spanish railroad go-as-you-please tourist pass. But remember that train fares here are so low that you have to put in a considerable amount of traveling before a rail pass pays its way. There are also some hidden extras on train fares. The express TALGO trains require a supplement whether you have a rail pass or not. A similar supplement is payable if you take a "couchette" or sleeping car (though again, this is hardly prohibitive, considering the fact that you're getting a modestly priced bed for the night *and* you're getting from A to B in the bargain).

Three or four people traveling together may find it advantageous to rent a car. Rates are reasonable, though you must check all the extras carefully beforehand. Insurance, tax, and "collision waiver" all add to the bill. Taking highways (*nacional* roads) rather than turnpikes (the *autopistas*) you'll avoid expensive tolls and see much more of the country. Remember, however, that as you go farther south the roads get worse. Many major highways still have just one lane in each direction and traffic is often heavy and slow. Construction is another frequent headache.

City transportation is excellent. It's reliable and cheap, and generally runs from early morning till well after midnight. Flat fares are the norm, and are a bargain compared to the New York subway, say, or the London Underground. The Madrid subway also has some excellent deals for tourists. On buses in other cities, buy a multiride *bonobus* ticket. Riding a city bus can be a great way to get acquainted with a city, a kind of budget introductory tour. Taxis are plentiful, and their meters often stop where their counterparts in U.S. or other European cities begin.

Finally, take advantage of Spain's excellent and comprehensive network of local tourist offices. They are about the best organized in Europe, and every town has one. For free up-to-the-minute information about where to stay, what to see, and upcoming events they are unbeatable.

Aspects of Spain

Most think of Spain as a land of hot dusty plains and long golden beaches. Few realize that it's also the second most mountainous country in Europe (Switzerland is the first). The Pyrenees and Sierra Nevada, the slopes of the Guadarrama near Madrid, and the alpine pastures of the Picos de Europa in Cantabria and Asturias on the north coast all provide skiing in winter and superb hiking in summer. Galicia, in the northwest, is lush and green, with mists and rain to rival Ireland's, and wild rocky scenery. Head south and east and you come to the burning plains of Castile—the *meseta*. To the west again are the orange groves and rice lagoons of Valencia; to the south are the rolling and rugged mountains of Andalusia, with regiments of olive groves marching over them. The Spanish landscape has a passionate quality—lovers of hedgerows and leafy lanes will not appreciate it. In places it's almost more African than European.

Studded about it are great cities and monuments that testify to a history as dramatic and compelling as any in Europe.

There are magnificent Roman remains in Tarragona and Seville, Mérida and Itálica. Granada and Córdoba bear witness to a later, gentler civilization, that of the Moors, which in the south held sway for 800 years before being brutally stamped out by the avenging Christian monarchs Ferdinand and Isabella in 1492. The sophistication of the Moors is made brilliantly clear by their greatest monument in Spain, the Alhambra in Granada. The proud and purposeful Christian rulers of Spain governed a country that grew to be the richest in Europe, an empire based on immeasurable riches from the New World. In the humble villages of Extremadura you can tread the same cobblestones that the first white man to land in North America knew. In Seville, you can pay homage at the tomb of Columbus; in Valladolid you can visit the house where he died. Contrast the megalomaniac palaces of the Spanish monarchs: the austerity of Philip II's Escorial; the opulence of Madrid's Royal Palace; the lavish magnificence of Pedro the Cruel's Alcázar in Seville. There are castles that recall the ghost of El Cid; glorious Gothic cathedrals; towns where the sense of the years unfolding is more vivid than almost anywhere else in Europe. And there are paintings by Spain's great painters, Velázquez, Goya, and Picasso foremost among them.

But Spain is much more than history and art. The zest and love of life of the Spanish come into their own at a *fiesta,* a local feast day. You can run into them anywhere in Spain, from large cities to tiny villages, often when you least expect them. Spaniards are masters of the art of unselfconscious enjoyment: They'll don their flamenco costumes and dance in the streets at the least provocation. The candlelit processions of Seville's Holy Week, the colorful pageants and huge bonfires of Valencia's *fallas,* the infectious merrymaking of Seville's April Fair, the crowd at the Pamplona bullring, to a man clad in white with the livid red beret and sash of the Basque national costume, provide indelible memories of Spain. Regional dances also highlight the Spanish love of spectacle and drama. In Andalusia you'll find the passionate and throbbing flamenco, in Catalonia the stately measured tread of the *sardana,* in Aragon and Castile the lighthearted *jota.* What's more, all these vastly enjoyable events are often entirely free. All you have to do is turn up.

In among all this spectacle and culture, Spain also offers terrific value for sports and beach vacations, though you should avoid the tasteless overdevelopment that has grown up around Torremolinos on the Costa del Sol. Otherwise, the sun, sea, and sand are there all summer long. There's waterskiing, Windsurfing, and sailing available all along the Mediterranean coast. If your tastes run to something less modern, visit the simple fishing villages and rugged shoreline of northern Cantabria. You can go horseback riding or hiking in many mountain areas. Spain is a paradise for golfers, with many hotels on the Costa del Sol catering exclusively for golfers. Swimming pools and tennis courts are found at most 3-star hotels along the coast; inland, tourist offices can direct you to public pools. Among spectator sports, *pelota,* or jai alai, offers the best combination of low cost and authentic atmosphere, especially in the Basque country. Some may also like to take in a bullfight, though don't go if you think you'll be upset by the gore. If you're in Seville or Ronda it's worth making an effort just to see the bullrings; they are the oldest and most beautiful in the country.

Spain can offer terrific value—go and see for yourself.

PLANNING YOUR TRIP
Before You Go

NATIONAL TOURIST OFFICES. The major source of information for anyone planning a vacation to Spain is the Spanish National Tourist Office. It can supply information on all aspects of travel to and around Spain. It also produces a wealth of extremely useful tourist literature, much of it free.

You will find the Spanish National Tourist Offices at the following addresses:

In the U.S.: 665 Fifth Ave., New York, NY 10022 (212-759-8822); 845 N. Michigan Ave., Water Tower Pl., Chicago, IL 60611 (312-944-0215); San Vicente Plaza Bldg., 8383 Wilshire Blvd., Suite 960, Beverly Hills, CA 90211 (213-658-7188); Casa del Hidalgo, Hipolita & St. George Sts., St. Augustine, FL 32084 (904-829-6460); 4800 The Galleria, 5085 Westheimer, Houston, TX 77056 (713-840-7411).

In Canada: 60 Bloor St. West, #201, Toronto, Ont. M4W 3B8 (tel. 416-961-3131).

In the U.K.: 57 St. James's St., London SW1A 1LD (01-499-0901).

ENTRY REQUIREMENTS. All visitors to Spain from the U.S., Canada, and the U.K. must have valid passports. Visas and health certificates are not required.

British Visitors' Passport. This simplified form of passport has advantages for the once-in-a-while tourist to Spain, and most European countries. Valid for one year and not renewable, it costs £7.50. Application must be made at main post offices in England, Scotland, and Wales, and in Northern Ireland at the Passport Office in Belfast. A birth certificate or medical card for identification and two photographs are needed.

BUDGET PACKAGE TOURS. There is no doubt about it: If your priority is to stick to a modest budget, then you cannot do better than to buy a package tour to Spain. Tours are numerous, however, so it is best to get expert advice from your travel agent or from the Spanish National Tourist Office nearest to you.

Among tour operators **in the U.S.** are:

American Express, 822 Lexington Ave., New York, NY 10021 (212-758-6510).

Bennet Tours, 270 Madison Ave., New York, NY 10016 (800-221-2420 or 212-532-5060) offers four-day, three-night city tours of Barcelona, Granada, Madrid, and Seville. Prices range from $200 to $550.

Cosmos/Globus Gateway, 95–25 Queens Blvd., Rego Park, New York, NY 11374 (718-268-1700) has two budget programs: ''The Best of Spain and Portugal'' (15 days, $589–$607) and ''Southern Spain, Portugal, and Morocco'' (15 days, $538–$727).

Extra-Value Travel, 437 Madison Ave., New York, NY 10022 (212-750-8800).

Flag Tours, 38 W. 38th St., New York, NY 10018 (212-921-3366).

Iberia Airlines, 97–77 Queens Blvd., Rego Park, New York, NY 10018 (718-793-3300).

TWA, 28 S. Sixth St., Philadelphia, PA 19106 (215-959-7885) offers ''The Flamenco,'' two weeks in Spain and Portugal with sightseeing in Madrid, Toledo, Córdoba, Granada, and Seville, among other cities. Costs run from $629–$729.

Remember that the prices of these tours do *not* include airfare.

In Britain there is also a huge range of tour operators to Spain. Here is just a brief selection:

Brittany Ferries, Millbay Docks, Plymouth PL1 3EW (tel. 0752-21321) offers a wide choice of automobile vacations.

Cosmos Tours, Cosmos House, 1 Bromley Common, Bromley, Kent BR2 9LX (tel. 01-637-9961) has a wide range of vacations on offer, from city tours to cruises.

Enterprise Holidays, British Airways, PO Box 10, London (Heathrow) Airport, Hounslow, Middlesex TW6 2JA (tel. 01-897-4545).

Mundi Color, 276 Vauxhall Bridge Rd., London SW1V 1BE (tel. 01-834-3492) offers a range of tours covering the Spanish fiestas.

Thomson Holidays, Greater London House, Hampstead Rd., London NW1 7SD (tel. 01-387-9321).

WHEN TO GO. As a budget traveler your main choice will be between the high season (which means high prices and plenty to see and do) or the low season (which means lower prices, and perhaps not so much in the way of spectacle but certainly fewer crowds).

The main tourist season runs from Easter through mid-October, when the weather is reliably good and the spectacular and colorful fiestas are in full swing. However, this is also when accommodations are at a premium and prices generally are at their highest. During the major festivals—Valencia's *fallas* in March, Seville's Holy Week and April Fair, Jerez's May Horse Fair and September Vintage Festival, and Pamplona's San Fermines in July, for example—hotel prices increase by as much as three times, as do costs in bars and restaurants, and even on some public transport.

Most hotels have high-season rates (usually Easter through mid-September) and low-season rates (mid-September through March); some hotels even operate midseason rates—April through mid-June and mid-September through mid-October. The exact dates when these rates come into effect vary from region to region and from hotel to hotel. Of one thing you can be sure, however: For the two-week Easter period, from mid-June through mid-September, and at major festival times hotel prices will be at their most expensive (as will airfares to Spain, too).

If economy is uppermost in your mind, then Spain's generally mild winter climate and the reduced prices may make an off-season vacation particularly attractive. Bright, sunny days are not unknown even in January and February. Good weather can't be guaranteed, of course, but you can take advantage of bargain airfares and low-season hotel rates. Many hotels offer excellent winter packages, especially those in the resort areas of the Costa Blanca or the Costa del Sol. These low-cost deals are best booked through a travel agent. Do away with the weekend supplement and fly midweek if you can, and save money this way, too.

CLIMATE. If sightseeing is your primary interest then the best months to visit are May, June, and September, when the weather is usually pleasant and sunny without being unbearably hot. In July and August, parts of Spain may be too hot for some visitors, especially in Seville and Córdoba, where many places close for the day at around 1 P.M. Madrid, too, can be unrewarding at this time: Not only are many of its citizens away on vacation, but theater and concerts shut down for the summer, and many restaurants close. If you are planning to visit Spain at this time of year then head for the coastal resorts or to the mountain regions.

The northern Cantabrian coast is the wettest and coolest region of Spain. It is also the greenest, especially in Galicia. To avoid the worst of the wet and the cold, however, visit from mid-June through August. The eastern Mediterranean coast from the Costa Brava to Cape Nao, south of Valencia, is at its best from mid-May through September. From Alicante southwards round the Costa Blanca to the southern Mediterranean coast of Costa del Sol, it can be blazing hot all summer long, and mild and balmy weather is not unknown (though nor is rain) even in January or February. Inland, in Andalusia, cities such as Granada or Ronda, lying high in the mountains, are much cooler, especially at night.

Worth remembering is that the whole of the central plateau—the Castilian *meseta*—with Madrid as its nucleus, and including the cities of Avila, Segovia, Toledo, Salamanca, and Burgos, suffers extremes of temperature: Summers are blazing, winters freezing.

Average afternoon temperatures in degrees Fahrenheit and centigrade:

Madrid	Jan.	Feb.	Mar.	Apr.	May	June	July	Aug.	Sept.	Oct.	Nov.	Dec.
F°	47	51	57	64	71	80	87	86	77	66	54	48
C°	8	11	14	18	22	27	31	30	25	19	12	9

Barcelona												
F°	56	57	61	64	71	77	81	82	78	71	62	57
C°	13	14	16	18	22	25	27	28	26	22	17	14

SPECIAL EVENTS. Fiestas are a lively and colorful Spanish spectacle; their fun and atmosphere are infectious and captivating. You are unlikely to travel far in Spain without coming across at least one fiesta. In addition to the major celebrations listed below, each region, town, and village holds its own local saint's day, and as most places have a patron saint *and* patroness, that accounts for at least two fiestas a year.

Celebrations often take place on the evening before the saint's day, rather than on the day itself. Dates given below are only an indication of when these events occur; the exact days are often not known until a few weeks before the festival, so check with the local tourist office. Remember, also, that there are 14 national holidays a year when, with the exception of restaurants, all stores, offices and businesses, and some museums and monuments will be closed.

January. Día de los Reyes, 5–6. This is the procession of the Three Kings when children all over Spain receive their Christmas presents.

February. Carnival festivities in the week leading up to Shrove Tuesday are held throughout Spain, and are particularly colorful in Cádiz.

March. The Fallas of San José is celebrated in Valencia March 12–19 with bonfires, the burning of effigies, parades, and dancing.

Easter. The most spectacular of Spain's pageants are its Holy Week celebrations, from Palm Sunday to Good Friday. They are seen at their best in Seville, Málaga, Granada, Cuenca, and Valladolid.

April. The April Fair held in Seville in the third or fourth week of the month is a riotous display of flamenco dancing, singing, cavalcades of riders, and all-night entertainment in fairground tents. The top bullfights are also held here.

May. A colorful parade of Las Cruces de Mayo—elaborate floral crosses—is held in Córdoba, Seville, and elsewhere at the beginning of the month. From May 1–12 of the month Córdoba also holds a festival of decorated patios. The week-long horse fair at Jerez de la Frontera is a fascinating exhibition of dressage competitions, horse races, flamenco, bullfights, and livestock and agricultural machinery displays. The San Isidro festivals are celebrated in Madrid in the middle of this month with 10 days of the best bullfights and fiestas in the Plaza Major.

Whitsuntide. The most famous pilgrimage in Andalusia, the Romería del Rocío, takes place at Almonte (Huelva).

Corpus Christi. Corpus Christi is celebrated throughout Spain on the second Sunday after Whitsun. There are magnificent processions in Toledo and flower-strewn parades in Sitges, near Barcelona.

June. The gardens of the Alhambra, in Madrid, make a splendid setting for the International Music and Ballet Festival which runs through mid-July. There are classical Greek and Roman drama performances in the Roman theater in Mérida through July. In Alicante, the Hogueras de San Juan is celebrated with bonfires fueled by effigies, and cavalcades and fireworks.

July. July is for jazz lovers who won't want to miss the International Jazz Festival at San Sebastián, on the Basque coast. The famous Fiesta de San Fermín is held in Pamplona with the running of the bulls through the streets, parades, dancing, fireworks, and bullfights. The festival of the Virgen del Carmen is held on July 16 in fishing villages. The Virgin's statue is borne on illuminated, flower-decked boats; especially picturesque celebrations are held on the Mar Menor in Murcia province, and in Torremolinos's Carihuela, and other Costa del Sol villages. There is a solemn pilgrimage to the tomb of St. James the Apostle at Santiago de Compostela, on July 25. At Villajoyosa, near Alicante, the festival of the Moors and Christians is celebrated with mock battles on land and sea.

August. At Elche, near Alicante, a mystery play is performed as part of the celebrations of the Assumption, which is also celebrated in many other places. At La Alberca, near Salamanca, the Feast of the Assumption is celebrated with a display of national costumes.

September. In Jerez de la Frontera, the Grape Harvest Festival is celebrated with the crowning of carnival queens, processions, and, of course, much sherry-drinking. The International Film Festival is held at San Sebastián.

October. The Fiestas del Pilar are held in Zaragoza, on October 12, in honor of the Virgin of the Pillar. There are float parades, *jota* dancing contests, and all kinds of sports.

December. At Labastida (Alava) midnight mass is celebrated on December 24, including a re-enactment of the Adoration of the Shepherds. In Madrid on December 31, people gather in the Puerto del Sol to see in the new year, eating grapes on each stroke of midnight.

WHAT TO PACK. The first principle is to travel light. The restrictions by size or weight that are imposed on air travelers are an added incentive to keep baggage within the bounds of common sense. Transatlantic passengers may take two pieces of luggage; these are subject to a size allowance, not a weight one. The total sum of the height, length, and width must not exceed 270 cms. (106 in.) and neither of the two must exceed a total of 158 cms. (62 in.) Extra pieces of luggage are prohibitively expensive.

If you are traveling to Spain on a European flight, luggage is subject to a weight allowance and you will be charged extra if your luggage weighs more than 20 kg. (44 lbs.) All travelers are entitled to one piece of hand luggage only.

Clothing. What you pack in the way of clothes will depend largely on the season. If you're visiting Spain in the summer take plenty of cool, lightweight clothes, and a sweater for the evenings. Take a combination of warm winter clothes and lighter summer garments if you're traveling in the spring or fall. Temperatures can vary tremendously from day to day and it can get quite cold at night; be sure to take a coat or a jacket.

As many of Spain's most picturesque sights involve long walks along dusty, cobbled streets a comfortable pair of low-heeled walking shoes is essential. Unless you are staying in the very top hotels or eating in the best restaurants, you won't need formal evening wear.

If you wear glasses or contact lenses take a spare pair along or the prescription. Most medicines are readily available in Spain but they will not be sold under the brand name you will know them by. Always take the prescription and a good supply of any special medicines you take regularly.

TIME ZONES. During the summer, Spain is six hours ahead of eastern standard time, seven hours ahead of central time, eight hours ahead of mountain time, and nine hours ahead of pacific time.

During the winter, Spain puts her clocks back one hour but as America does likewise the time difference remains the same. Spanish daylight saving time begins at the end of March and ends at the end of September, so there are always a couple of weeks in both spring and fall when EST is out of sync.

Similarly, Spain is one hour ahead of British summer time and during the winter, one hour ahead of Greenwich mean time. During October, Spain and Britain are on the same time.

HINTS FOR THE DISABLED. Thousands of disabled people who are physically able to travel do so enthusiastically when they know they will be able to move about in safety and comfort. A growing number of travel agents specialize in this market, with tours that generally parallel those of the nondisabled traveler. The tours are taken at a more leisurely pace, with everything checked out in advance to eliminate inconvenience, whether the traveler is blind, deaf, or in a wheelchair.

The Information Center for Individuals with Disabilities, 20 Park Plaza, Rm. 330, Boston, MA 02116 (617-727-5540) is a helpful organization.

The Society for the Advancement of Travel for the Handi-

capped, 26 Court St., Brooklyn, NY 11242 (718-858-5483) can supply a complete list of travel agents who arrange such travel.

The Travel Industry and Disabled Exchange, 5435 Donna Ave., Tarzana, CA 91356 (818-343-6339) is another possibility.

The Travel Information Center, Moss Rehabilitation Hospital, 12th St. and Tabor Rd., Philadelphia, PA 19141 (215-329-5715) offers Travel Accessibility information packages detailing travel problems and possibilities to various destinations. The cost is $5; allow a month for delivery.

Several publications are available, including the excellent *Access to the World: A Travel Guide for the Handicapped,* by Louise Weiss. It's published by Harry Holt & Co., but must be ordered through your local bookstore. *The Itinerary,* a bimonthly magazine for travelers with disabilities, is published by Whole Person Tours, PO Box 1084, Bayonne, NJ 07002 (201-858-3400).

A number of car rental companies offer cars with hand controls, including Avis (800-331-1212), Hertz (800-654-3131), and National (800-328-4567). All have European divisions.

Britain's major center for help and advice for the disabled traveler is the **Royal Association for Disability and Rehabilitation,** 25 Mortimer St., London W1N 8AB (tel. 01-637-5400). It has a library of helpful pamphlets, including the *Access* guides.

The Airline Transport User's Committee, 129 Kingsway, London WC2B 6NH (tel. 01-242-3883) publishes a useful booklet, *Care in the Air,* free, which includes advice for disabled passengers.

STUDENT AND YOUTH TRAVEL.
Student travel is a special field in itself and there are plenty of opportunities for low-cost budget travel.

Student travelers should get an International Student Identity Card (ISIC), which is usually needed to get student discounts, rail and bus passes, and European student charter flights. In the U.S. apply to the Council on International Educational Exchange, in Canada apply to the Association of Student Councils; addresses of both are given below. Passes cost $10.

All the following organizations will be helpful in finding student flights, educational opportunities, and other information. Most deal with international student travel generally, but materials of those listed cover Spain.

Council on International Educational Exchange (CIEE), 203 E. 42 St., New York, NY 10017 (212-661-1414) and 312 Sutter St., San Francisco, CA 94108 (415-421-3473) provides information on summer study, work/travel programs, travel services for college and high school students, and their free *Charter Flights Guide* booklet. Their *Whole World Handbook* ($7.95, plus $1 postage) is the best listing of both work and study possibilities.

Educational Travel Center, 438 N. Frances, Madison, WI 53703 (608-256-5551) is also worth contacting.

The Institute of International Education, 809 United Nations Plaza, New York, NY 10017 (212-883-8200) is primarily concerned with study opportunities and fellowships for international study and training. The New York office has a visitors' information center and there are satellite offices in Chicago, Denver, San Francisco, and Washington.

In Canada, contact the **Association of Student Councils** (AOSC), 187 College St., Toronto, Ont. M5T 1P7 (416-979-2604). This is a non-profit-making student cooperative, owned and run by over 50 college and university student unions. Its travel bureau provides information on tours and work camps worldwide. Try also **Tourbec,** 535 Ontario East, Montreal, P.Q. H2L 1N8 (514-288-4455).

In Britain, student travel arrangements can be made through a variety of organizations. Here are just a few useful addresses.

London Student Travel, 52 Grosvenor Gardens, London SW1W 0EB (tel. 01-730-8111); also the **Union of Student International Travel** (USIT), at the same address.

Worldwide Student Travel, 39 Store St., London WC2E 7HY (tel. 01-580-7733).

See also ''Youth Hostels'' in ''Where to Stay'' for other useful addresses. Specific information on rail and other discounts is listed in the relevant sections.

Getting to Spain

From North America

BY AIR. Iberia Airlines, 97–77 Queens Blvd., Rego Park, NY 11374 (718-793-3300) is Spain's national airline and offers services to Madrid, Barcelona, and Málaga from New York, as well as services between Montreal and Madrid.

TWA, 605 Third Ave., New York, NY 10016 (212-290-2141) also flies between New York and Madrid. Other major transatlantic airlines can also get you to Spain but you will probably have to stop off elsewhere in Europe en route.

Fares. As is so often the case with budget travel, your best hope of finding an inexpensive plane ticket is with the help of a travel agent.

Bargain fares appear and disappear with such speed that often they're not announced publicly; these are the fares only a travel agent can find for you.

The best bet for a budget traveler is not an APEX ticket on one of the major airlines serving Spain. Certain restrictions apply to APEX tickets: You have to buy them in advance, usually at least 21 days; they restrict your travel with a minimum and maximum days' stay; and they will penalize you for changes to your travel plans (voluntary or not). But if you can work around these drawbacks (and most people can), they are the best-value airline tickets available on regularly scheduled services.

Charter flights offer the lowest fares but often depart only on certain days, and seldom on time. Though you may be able to arrive at one city and return from another, you may lose all or most of your money if you cancel your ticket. Travel agents can make bookings, though they won't encourage you, since commissions are lower than on scheduled flights. Checks should as a rule be made out to the bank and specific escrow account for your flight. To make sure your payment stays in this account until your departure, don't use credit cards. Don't sign up for a charter flight unless you've checked with a travel agency about the reputation of the packager. It's particularly important to know the packager's policy concerning refunds should a flight be canceled. One of the most popular charter operators is Council Charters (800-223-7402), a division of CIEE (Council on International Educational Exchange). Other companies advertise in Sunday travel sections of daily newspapers.

Somewhat more expensive—but up to 50% below the cost of APEX fares—are tickets purchased through companies known as consolidators that buy blocks of tickets on scheduled airlines and sell them at wholesale prices. Here again you may lose all or most of your money if you change plans, but at least you will be on a regularly scheduled flight with less risk of cancellation than a charter. Once you've made your reservation, call the airline to make sure you're confirmed. Among the best known consolidators are UniTravel (800-325-2222) and Access International, 250 W. 57th St., Suite 511, New York, NY 10107 (212-333-7280). Others advertise in the Sunday travel section of daily newspapers. For a leaflet with tips for dealing with consolidators, send a request and stamped return envelope to the Metropolitan New York Better Business Bureau, 257 Park Ave. S., New York, NY 10003.

A third option is to join a travel club that offers special discounts to its members. Tickets on chartered and regularly scheduled flights are also sometimes available from ticket brokers, who buy them at the last minute from tour operators trying to fill unsold seats. These brokers include:

Discount Travel International, 114 Forrest Ave., Narberth, PA 19072 (215-668-2182).

Moments Notice, 40 E. 49th St., New York, NY 10017 (212-486-0503).

Stand Buys Ltd., 311 W. Superior, Suite 414, Chicago, IL 60610 (312-943-5737).

Worldwide Discount Travel Club, 1674 Meridian Ave., Miami Beach, FL 33139 (305-534-2082).

All ticket brokers charge a ''membership fee'' for their services, usually $35 to $45.

In early '88, an APEX ticket on the New York-to-Madrid route cost between $652 and $722 depending on season. A full-fare economy-class ticket will cost almost three times as much.

From Great Britain

BY AIR. Air travel to Spain from the whole of Europe is about to see a great upheaval. Fares will fall in the course of 1988, perhaps by as much as 30%, as greater competition is introduced. There will also be an upsurge in the number of charter companies and seat-only deals, and some charter airlines will offer scheduled services, too. The downside for the budget traveler of this new spirit of commercialism is that there are bound to be some casualties with all this new competition, especially in the charter section, so make sure you take out insurance to cover any disaster.

Iberia Airlines, Venture House, 29 Glasshouse St., London W1R 5RG (tel. 01-437-5622) has the largest number of services from London Heathrow to Alicante, Barcelona, Madrid (also from Gatwick), Málaga, Santiago de Compostela, Seville, Valencia, Palma, Mahón, and Ibiza.

British Airways, Speedbird House, PO Box 10, London Heathrow Airport, Hounslow TW6 2JA (tel. 01-897-4000) flies from London Gatwick to Barcelona, Bilbao, Gibraltar, Madrid (also from Heathrow), Málaga, and Valencia. For scheduled flights from other British cities, other than Manchester to Barcelona and Madrid four times weekly, it is necessary to make connections in London.

Fares. There has been an increase in the number of charter flight tickets from many U.K. airports to Spain. Sometimes these are sold with basic accommodations which you need not take up; sometimes as fares only. As an idea of what you can expect to pay, from Gatwick to

Málaga the round-trip fare is between £100–£175, to Palma £105–£170, to Ibiza £80–£166. Tour operators sometimes have spare, unsold seats on their flights which are sold off very cheaply, with or without accommodations. In mid-'87, a flight to Málaga could be picked up for as little as £65—even less off peak. Details are in the classified advertisements of many newspapers and magazines but use *only* those with ATOL numbers and *always* check the final price—including airport taxes, fuel surcharges, and tourist tax. The basic price quoted may not be the bargain it first appeared once these extras have been taken into account!

The economy class round-trip fare on a scheduled flight from London to Madrid is around £370. The British Airways range of Earlysaver/Eurosaver tickets—though with limited availability—can cut this to around £116 (early season, midweek) and £174 (high season, midweek). Ask your travel agent for full details or contact British Airways direct.

BY TRAIN. The rail journey to Spain can be long and tedious, involving not only a Channel crossing but also a change of station in Paris, and in many cases a change of transport at the Franco-Spanish border. If your destination is south of Madrid you can expect another change of train in the capital.

Fares. Unless you're traveling on a saver ticket such as an InterRail or Eurailpass, you are unlikely to save much money by choosing rail travel over charter flights, even if you're prepared to put up with the rather tortuous journey! The round-trip from London to Madrid costs around £165 (second class). The advantage of this is that you can break your journey en route and there are no restrictions on travel. If you are working to a very strict budget then make use of the French *Sejour* system which could bring the cost down to around £145. There are some restrictions—Sejour tickets are valid only for two months and your stay in Spain must include one Sunday. Get full details of the Sejour ticket from any French National Railway office.

Wise travelers will opt for all-inclusive tickets wherever possible, combining rail and ship fares. Get full details from the European Rail Travel Center, PO Box 303, Victoria Station, London SW1V 1JY (tel. 01-834-2345).

Ticket Bargains. Discounts available include the **InterRail Card** for those under 26 years. It costs around £140 and is valid for one month. It allows half-price travel on British Rail services, reductions on cross-Channel services (these vary according to the route taken), and unlimited second-class rail travel in 26 European countries, including Spain. InterRail Cards are available from many main-line stations in Europe and the U.K.

If you're under 26 and just going to one place, then get a **Eurotrain** or **Transalpino** ticket which offers reduced-rate rail travel. You can get more information from Eurotrain, 52 Grosvenor Gardens, London SW1W 0EB (tel. 01-730-6525) and Transalpino, 71–75 Buckingham Palace Rd., London SW1W 0QU (tel. 01-834-9656).

If you're traveling in a family group of three or more you can save money by buying a **Rail Europe Family Card.** This gives discounts of up to 50%. The card is available to a family (or a group of people) living at the same address, up to a maximum of eight people, all of whom must be named on the card. A minimum of three of the named fare-payers, at least one of whom must be an adult, must travel together throughout the journey to qualify for the reductions. The first adult pays the full ordinary fare and subsequent adults pay half fare, and children under 12 years pay half the child's reduced fare.

Senior citizens should buy a **Rail Europe Senior Card** (the price in mid-'87 was £5). This card is only issued in conjunction with a valid British Rail Senior Citizen Card. It entitles the holder to reduced-price rail travel in 19 European countries. The reductions in Spain are about 30%.

If more than six people are traveling together they will be eligible for a group discount. Full details of all these offers and the InterRail card are available from the European Rail Travel Center, address given above.

Note: If you want to be really knowledgeable about train times in Europe, then buy the *Thomas Cook Continental Timetable*. It is packed with information and is issued monthly, so make sure you get the correct issue for when you'll be traveling. It's available in the U.S. from Travel Library, PO Box 2975, Shawnee Mission, KS 66201. In the U.S. call toll-free, 800-FORSYTH; in Canada call collect, 913-384-0496. In Britain it can be ordered from Thomas Cook Ltd., Timetable Publishing Office, PO Box 36, Peterborough, Cambridgeshire PE3 6SB.

BY BUS. With the introduction of cheaper airfares to Spain, the scheduled bus services are bound to suffer. Our advice is to check with a good travel agent or with **International Express,** The Coach Travel Center, 13 Regent St., London SW1Y 4LR (tel. 01-439-9368).

At press time, early '88, the main scheduled services to Spain were run by a variety of companies grouped under the banner of Internation-

FERRY SERVICES SUITABLE FOR TRAVEL TO SPAIN FROM BRITAIN

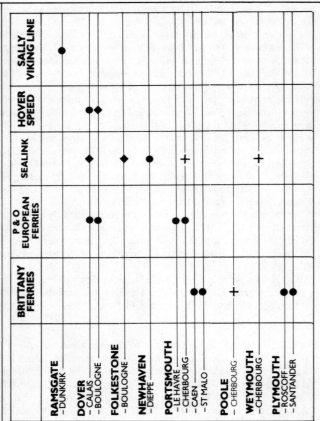

Route	SALLY VIKING LINE	HOVER SPEED	SEALINK	P & O EUROPEAN FERRIES	BRITTANY FERRIES
RAMSGATE – DUNKIRK	●				
DOVER – CALAIS		●	◆	●	
DOVER – BOULOGNE		●		●	
FOLKESTONE – BOULOGNE			◆		
NEWHAVEN – DIEPPE			●		
PORTSMOUTH – LE HAVRE				●	
PORTSMOUTH – CHERBOURG			+	●	
PORTSMOUTH – CAEN					●
PORTSMOUTH – ST MALO					●
POOLE – CHERBOURG					+
WEYMOUTH – CHERBOURG			+		
PLYMOUTH – ROSCOFF					●
PLYMOUTH – SANTANDER					●

+ Operate May-Sept only.

◆ Recommended for Rail travellers – easy rail/ship interchange.
Through services operate from Calais Maritime/Boulogne Maritime to the
South West of France/Spanish frontier during the summer months.

● Only really suitable for car-borne travellers. Several of the Operators
provide bus services between the local railway stations and the port terminal
buildings. They are only suitable for passengers with light luggage.

al Express. During the summer there is a daily service to Barcelona which leaves Victoria Coach Station at mid-evening and reaches the Catalonian capital at about 1 P.M. the following day. Three days a week this service is extended to reach Alicante, via Calpe and Benidorm. Also in the summer, there is a service to Madrid four days a week, leaving London late morning and arriving at the Spanish capital at about 5 P.M. the following day. There are no overnight stops so the journeys are not particularly restful. SSS Ltd., part of International Express, runs regular services to the northern coast of Spain, including Bilbao, Santander, Santiago de Compostela, and La Coruña.

Be sure to carry some small change in both Spanish and French currencies for refreshment stops along the way.

Fares. Fares are quite high, especially compared to air travel, at around £120 round-trip to Madrid, and £100 to Barcelona. On the plus side, journey times are surprisingly short.

BY CAR/FERRY. The only direct route to Spain is operated by **Brittany Ferries,** from Plymouth to Santander, twice weekly, year-round. The crossing takes 24 hours. The ordinary round-trip fare for a car, driver, and passenger works out at around £530. Brittany Ferries also offers a wide range of motoring packages; these are excellent value for money—especially if you travel at off-peak times.

The only other way to Spain by car is to take the short sea crossing from Dover to Calais or Boulogne, or the longer route to the ports of Brittany or Normandy, and then make the long drive through France. However, this is costly in terms of time and of money as tolls have to be paid on most French expressways and gasoline is expensive in both France and Spain.

Check with your travel agent as to the best offers available from the ferry companies and motoring packages, or contact the ferry companies direct:

Brittany Ferries, Millbay Docks, Plymouth, Devon PL1 3EW (tel. 0752-21321).

Hoverspeed Ltd., Maybrook House, Queens Gardens, Dover, Kent CT17 9UQ (tel. 0304-216205).

P&O Ferries Ltd., PO Box 5, Jamiesons Quay, Aberdeen AB9 8DL (tel. 0224-572615).

Sally Lines Ltd., Argyle Center, York St., Ramsgate, Kent CT11 9DS (tel. 0843-595522).

Sealink British Ferries, 163 Eversholt St., London NW1 1BG (tel. 01-387-1234).

For details of car rental, see "Getting Around Spain—By Car."

Getting Around Spain

BY TRAIN. Most Spanish railroads are state-owned, run by the nationalized company—RENFE. Vast improvements have been made to the service recently and Spanish trains are clean, comfortable, and efficient. They are, however, slow in comparison to other European trains, due partly to the mountainous nature of the country, partly to the fact that—incredibly—most lines are still single-track.

A plus for the cost-conscious traveler is that Spanish rail fares are inexpensive by European standards, and excellent value. Fares are determined as much by the kind of train you take as by the distance traveled.

Ticket Bargains. The **RENFE Tourist Card** is excellent value if you intend traveling extensively on the Spanish network. It gives unlimited mileage travel on all RENFE lines for eight, 15, or 22 days and costs, for second-class travel, 9,000 ptas., 15,000 ptas., and 19,000 ptas., respectively. First-class cards are also available at higher prices. The pass can be bought from RENFE's general representative in Europe at 3 ave. Marceau, 75116 Paris (tel. 47-23-52-00); from some travel agents; and, in Spain, from RENFE travel offices and from stations at Madrid, Barcelona, Port Bou, and Irun.

Días Azules (Blue Days). There are approximately 270 days in the year when you can travel at a 25% discount—these are known as *días azules* on the railway calendar. There are also favorable rates for round-trips, Madrid-to-Barcelona trips, and local suburban trips. Leaflets are available from RENFE offices and stations giving full details of the days and the offers. Be warned, some of the Blue Days bargains, such as senior citizens' 50% discounts or reduced rates for family groups, are available *only* to Spaniards or foreigners who live in Spain and have held a *residencia* permit for at least six months.

The **Eurail Pass** and the **Eurail Youthpass** are unbeatable value if you are planning on traveling extensively by train through Europe, including Spain. They give unlimited travel through western and central Europe (but *not* in the U.K. or Ireland) by train, on railway-operated bus routes, many ferries, and certain riverboat services and lake steamers—over 160,000 km (100,000 mi.) in all. The pass is available for 15 or 21 days, or one, two, or three months at $280 or $350, and $440, $620, and $760 respectively. The great advantage of the Eurail Pass, besides being amazing value for money, is that you travel in the spacious comfort of first-class compartments, so you can travel on a budget *and* in great style! Bunk beds are also available on most long-distance trains, so save money on hotel bills by traveling overnight and arriving early at your next destination.

If you can get a small group together (minimum of three in the summer, two in winter) you can get 15 days' first-class travel at a remarkable $210 each.

For those under 26 there's the Eurail Youthpass which gives unlimited second-class travel for one or two months for $310 or $400, respectively.

These passes are valid for travel on RENFE trains but *not* FEVE trains in northern Spain. You will have to pay a supplement to travel on TALGOs, TERs, and ELTs (see below). Whichever train you take you must present your pass at the ticket office *before* boarding the train.

Both these excellent money-saving passes are only available to citizens from the U.S., Canada, and South America. These passes *must* be bought *before* you leave for Europe.

In the U.S. contact: **French National Railways,** Eurail Division, 610 Fifth Ave., New York, NY 10020 (212-582-2110).

German Federal Railways, 747 Third Ave., New York, NY 10017 (212-308-3103).

Italian National Railways, 630 Fifth Ave., New York, NY 10103 (212-397-2667).

In Canada: French National Railways, 1500 Stanley St., Montreal, P.Q. H3A 1R3 (212-288-8255) or 4009 Granville St., Suite 452, Vancouver, B.C. B6C 1T2 (604-688-6707).

German National Railways, 1290 Bat St., Toronto, Ont. M5R 2C3 (416-968-3272).

Italian National Railways, 2055 Peet St., Montreal, P.Q. H3A 1V4 (514-927-7712) or 13 Balmuto St., Toronto, Ont. M4Y 1W4.

What to Look For. The most expensive train is the plush, smooth-running TALGO. Next down the line is the Electrotrén or ELT, followed by the TER. All these cost considerably more than the ordinary long-distance trains known as *rápidos* or *expresos* (which rarely live up to their names). The least expensive are the local trains, which have a variety of names: *semidirectos; ómnibuses; unidades eléctricas; ferrobuses;* and *tranvías*. Unless you like stopping at every local halt these are the ones to avoid; low cost as they are, you can waste valuable vacation time traveling on them.

Ticket Purchase and Seat Reservations. Always compare fares for the different trains going to your destination rather than just asking the fare to, say, Barcelona. By choosing your train carefully you can make considerable savings. If you're traveling by day, pay the supplements for the faster, more comfortable trains. Alternatively, if you're traveling overnight on a regular *rápido* or *expreso,* book a bunk, which will probably cost less than a night's stay in a hotel. Bunks are available on most overnight trains for around 1,200 ptas.; sleeper cars, with a two-tier price structure, are more expensive depending on how far you're traveling.

Tickets can be bought from any station (whether it is your point of departure or not), downtown RENFE offices, and travel agents displaying the blue-and-yellow RENFE sign. The latter are often better bets in high season as you can stand on line for a long time at the others. At stations buy your ticket in advance from the window marked *largo recorido, venta anticipada* (long-distance, advance sales).

Seat reservations can be made up to 60 days in advance, and are obligatory on all long-distance trains (in fact they are advisable at any time). Tickets for any unsold unreserved seats are sold two hours before the train leaves.

BY BUS. Bus routes are surprisingly numerous, and the extensive bus network excellent for reaching smaller towns not served by rail. Public bus services encompass everything from luxury, long-distance cruisers to ramshackle, bumpy old buses which ferry the locals from village to village.

Fares. There is little difference between bus and train fares, but, as a rough guide, luxury bus services may prove rather more expensive than taking the train, other than the TALGO; conversely, the regular, older buses are usually rather less expensive than the trains.

Reservations are usually only necessary for the long-distance services, such as Valencia to Seville or Madrid to Málaga; on other services extra buses will be laid on as necessary. At peak vacation times reservations may be a good idea, but are otherwise not essential.

What to Look For. For the most part, buses tend to be quicker than trains; they certainly serve a much wider range of destinations, and often you can see more of the countryside, especially in the mountainous regions where trains spend a long time in tunnels.

Bus stations tend to be more centrally located in cities than do train stations, and they also retain their luggage-checking facilities, which are useful if you have to search out your accommodations once you have arrived at your destination. All these factors make bus travel well worth considering for most trips other than long, overnight rides when you will probably be more comfortable traveling by train.

There is no national or nationwide bus company: The network is simply made up of numerous private regional bus companies. As a result, there are no all-embracing economy bus passes. Some towns have modern bus depots used by all companies but in others buses leave from all over town, depending on their destination and to which company they belong. Always check which bus leaves from where.

Remember that *días laborales* means Monday to Saturday (working days) and that *días festivos* are Sundays and public holidays, though in the case of a fiesta it is always wise to double-check times with the local tourist office.

Urban Buses. In all towns of any size buses provide the backbone of public transport, though Madrid and Barcelona also have an inexpensive subway system. There is a flat fare of between 40 ptas. and 60 ptas. for all trips, depending on the town; sometimes these prices may be on Sundays and fiestas. Some towns have "microbuses" as well as the regular buses; these are smaller, less crowded, and are often air conditioned, but also marginally more expensive.

BY CAR.

To take your car to Spain you must have your valid home driving license. Non-EEC nationals must also have a Green Card and an International Driving License; these are also advisable, though not essential, for British subjects. It is also wise to buy bail bonds to keep you out of jail if you are arrested for a motoring offense or after an accident. Spanish law also requires you to carry a spare set of bulbs for every light on your car. You must carry your driving license and car registration documents with you whenever you are driving.

Rules of the Road. Drive on the right-hand side of the road. Horns and dipped headlights must not be used in cities. City speed limits are 60 kph (37 mph); other limits are 120 kph (74 mph) on autopistas (expressways), 100 kph (62 mph) on national highways (N roads), and 90 kph (56 mph) on other roads, unless otherwise directed. The wearing of front seat belts is compulsory on highways but not in cities (except on the M30 Madrid beltway). Children may not ride in the front seats.

Gas Prices. Spanish gas prices will seem high to American drivers but they are similar to those in the U.K. At press time (early '88) a liter (see the conversion chart at the end of this section) of normal (92 octane) cost 72 ptas. and a liter of super (97 octane) cost 78 ptas. Most cars run on super. On remote country roads gas stations are few and far between; be sure not to run low. Only a few service stations accept credit cards.

Car Rental. Spanish rental rates are low by American and British standards, though this happy state of affairs has been somewhat diminished by the levying of the IVA sales tax at 12% on the total of your bill.

Avis and Hertz are well represented at all Spanish airports and in most major cities, as are Godfrey Davis/Europcar, Budget, and Ital, whose rates are often a little lower than Avis or Hertz. Many smaller local firms have special deals with hotels whereby guests can benefit from advantageous rates.

If you want unlimited kilometer rates, cars must usually be hired for a minimum of seven days; otherwise you pay by the day plus so many pesetas per kilometer. *Semana comercial* (Monday to Friday) rates are a little more advantageous than ordinary daily rates. Whatever the hire period, insurance and collision waiver cost extra, and don't forget to budget for the IVA tax, the relatively high price of gas, and the tolls for the autopistas, if you use them.

If you are thinking of hiring a car then you may be interested in a sample of the schemes on offer.

From the U.S., **Hertz,** PO Box 2692, Smithtown, New York, NY 11787 (800-654-3001), in conjunction with British Airways, operates the **Affordable Europe Scheme.** Three days' hire of a Ford Fiesta costs about $71, four days $73, five days $91, six/seven days $125, and extra days cost about $18 per day. Prices include third-party, fire, and theft insurance and unlimited mileage. Collision waiver is extra. The car must be booked 24 hours in advance and one-way rental is available.

In the U.K. **Avis's Super Value Scheme** is worth investigating. Three to six days' rental of an Opel Corsa costs about £15 per day, seven to 13 days' hire costs about £13 per day, and over 14 days' hire costs £12 per day. This again includes unlimited mileage and third-party insurance; collision waiver is extra. The car must be booked at least seven days in advance and you can pick it up from one town and leave it at another.

A more flexible way of hiring a car is to buy Avis's **Driveaway Checks.** These come in £15, £23, and £31 denominations and they are bought before you leave. One check "buys" one day's car hire. A £15 check "buys" you hire of an Opel Corsa, a £23 check a Ford Escort, and a £31 check a Ford Orion GL. Again, the price includes unlimited mileage and third-party insurance; collision damage waiver is also included. You don't have to reserve your car, though this is advisable at busy times, but you must return it to where you collected it. If you run out of checks you can extend the period of rental locally at the same rate. The advantage of this scheme is that you're not committed to a set rental period or to renting the car on consecutive days. Best of all, if you don't use all your checks, all your money will be refunded once you're back home. For more details contact

Avis, Hayes Gate House, Uxbridge Rd., Hayes, Middlesex (tel. 01-848-8733) or your local Avis branch.

Staying in Spain

CUSTOMS ON ARRIVAL. Each person aged 15 and over may import into Spain, duty free, 200 cigarettes or 50 cigars or 100 cigarillos or 250 g. of tobacco, if arriving from another EEC country; these quantities are doubled for those arriving from outside the EEC. You are also allowed one liter of alcohol over 22° proof and two liters of other wines and a quarter-liter of toilet water and 50 g. of perfume, and gifts to the value of 5,000 ptas. (or 2,000 ptas. for children under 15).

CUSTOMS ON RETURNING HOME. U.S. Residents. U.S. residents may take home $400 worth of foreign merchandise as gifts or for personal use duty free, provided they have been out of the country more than 48 hours and that they have not claimed a similar exemption within the previous 30 days. Every member of a family is entitled to the same exemption, regardless of age, and the exemptions can be pooled. For the $1,000 worth of goods a flat 10% rate is assessed.

Included in the $400 allowance for travelers over the age of 21 are: one liter of alcohol, 100 non-Cuban cigars, and 200 cigarettes. Only one bottle of perfume trademarked in the U.S. may be brought in. You may not bring home meats, fruits, plants, or other agricultural products.

Gifts valued at under $50 may be mailed to friends or to any one addressee. These gifts must not include perfumes costing more than $5, tobacco, or liquor. If you are traveling with foreign-made articles, such as cameras, watches, or binoculars that were purchased at home or on a previous trip, either carry the receipt or register them with the U.S. Customs before departure.

Canadian Residents. In addition to personal effects, and over and above the regular exemption of $300 a year, Canadian residents may import the following into Canada duty free: 200 cigarettes, 50 cigars, two pounds of tobacco, and 40 ounces of liquor, provided these are declared in writing to customs on arrival. Canadian customs regulations are strictly enforced so you are recommended to check what your allowances are and to make sure you have kept receipts for whatever you have bought abroad. Small gifts can be mailed and should be marked ''Unsolicited gifts (*nature of gift*), value under $40 in Canadian funds.'' For other details ask for the Canada Customs' brochure *I Declare*.

British Residents. There are two levels of duty-free allowance when returning to the U.K.: one, for goods bought outside the EEC or for goods bought in a duty-free shop within the EEC; two, for goods bought in an EEC country but not in a duty-free shop.

In the first category you may import duty free: 1) 200 cigarettes or 100 cigarillos or 50 cigars or 250 g. of tobacco; 2) one liter of alcohol over 22° proof and two liters of still table wine or two liters of alcohol under 22° proof, e.g., fortified or sparkling wine, or a further three liters of still table wine; 3) 50 g. of perfume and a quarter-liter of toilet water; 4) other goods to the value of £32 and no more than 50 liters of beer.

In the second category, you may import duty-free: 300 cigarettes or 150 cigarillos or 75 cigars or 400 gr. of tobacco; 2) one-and-a-half liters of alcohol over 22 proof and five liters of still table wine or three liters of alcohol under 22 proof or a further three liters of still table wine; 3) 75 gr. of perfume and 3/8-liter of toilet water; 4) goods up to a value of £250 but not more than 50 liters of beer.

CURRENCY. The unit of currency in Spain is the peseta (shortened to ptas.) Coins in circulation are 1 pta., 2 (rare), 5, 10 (rare), 25, 50, 100, and 200 ptas. Bills in circulation are 200, 500, 1,000, 2,000, and 5,000 ptas. You may also come across some of the old 100-ptas. bills which, although they are being phased out, are still legal tender.

At press time (early '88) the exchange rate was around 113 ptas. to the dollar and 198 ptas. to the pound sterling.

CHANGING MONEY. As in most other European countries the best place to change your money is in banks, where you will have to pay a small fee but you will get the best exchange rate. You can also change money at the official exchange bureaus which you will find in most major towns, train stations, and airports.

Travelers' Checks. Travelers' checks are still the best way to safeguard your money while you are traveling abroad; most companies will replace them quickly and efficiently should they be lost or stolen. Always keep a separate note of the numbers of your checks. You will also probably get a better exchange rate than you would for cash.

In the U.S. many of the larger banks issue their own travelers' checks which are almost as well recognized as those of the established firms such as American Express, Cooks, and Barclays. Many banks will carry one of these brands as well as their own.

Checks should be in dollars or pounds rather than in pesetas, as hotels and stores often refuse to change peseta checks. Note also that travelers' checks are not generally regarded as cash in Spain and that making purchases with them in small stores and restaurants is not usually possible.

When cashing travelers' checks you will probably have to show your passport. Banks charge a few pesetas' *impuestos* (tax) and a considerably larger sum in commission but bank exchange rates are often more favorable than in hotels; however, as hotels rarely take commission it's worth working out which offers the better deal. If you intend changing $100 or more in a bank always check what the rate of commission is; if it's more than 1½% go elsewhere.

Britons holding a Uniform Eurocheque card and checkbook—apply for them at your bank—can cash checks for up to £100 per day at participating banks and at some shops, hotels, and restaurants.

It is wise to bring some lose change with you to pay for telephones, buses, and taxis, etc., when you first arrive in the country. Two useful words to know are *cambio* (change) and *caja* (cash till), where you pick up your money once your counter transaction has been completed.

TOURIST OFFICES. Once you have arrived in Spain you'll find that the local tourist offices are invaluable, providing lists of accommodations and restaurants, museums, art galleries, other places of interest, and 101 other details about the area in which you are staying.

TIPPING AND TAXES. Few Spanish hotels levy service charges, especially in the budget range. If you are staying in a hotel for only a few days the only person you may want to tip is the person who carried your bags.

In restaurants, you should leave about 10% of the bill if you are satisfied, even though the check may say that service is included. In smaller restaurants and bars it is customary to round up the bill to the nearest 100 ptas., so long as this leaves at least 40 ptas. Otherwise, tip as you would at home.

ELECTRICITY. Most of Spain has been converted to 220 volts AC–50 Hz. In some older hotels and private houses you may come across 120 volts, so check before you plug *anything* in.

BATHROOMS. There are few public facilities in Spain but rest rooms are plentiful in hotels, restaurants, museums, cafés, and bars. Department stores such as Corte Inglés or Galerías Preciados always have rest rooms, usually on the top floor. Ask for *los servicios* or *los aseos,* or look for the words *señoras* (ladies) or *caballeros* (men, literally knights!)

CONVERSION CHARTS. One of the most confusing experiences for many is the first encounter with the metric system. The following quick conversion tables may help to speed you on your way.

Motor Fuel. An imperial gallon is approximately 4½ liters; a U.S. gallon about 3¾ liters.

Liters	imp. gals.	US gals.
1	0.22	0.26
5	1.10	1.32
1 0	2.20	2.64
2 0	4.40	5.28
4 0	8.80	10.56
1 00	22.01	26.42

Tire Pressure is measured in kilograms per square centimeter instead of pounds per square inch; the ratio is approximately 14.2 pounds to 1 kilogram.

Lb. per sq. in.	Kg. per sq. cm.	Lb. per sq. in.	Kg. per sq. cm.
2 0	1.406	26	1.828
2 2	1.547	28	1.969
2 4	1.687	30	2.109

Kilometers into Miles. This simple chart will help you to convert to both miles and kilometers. If you want to convert from miles into kilometers read from the center column to the right; if from kilometers into miles, from the center column to the left. Example: 5 miles = 8.046 kilometers, 5 kilometers = 3.106 miles.

Miles		Kilometers	Miles		Kilometers
0 .621	1	1.609	37.282	60	96.560
1 .242	2	3.218	43.496	70	112.265
1 .864	3	4.828	49.710	80	128.747
2 .485	4	6.347	55.924	90	144.840
3 .106	5	8.046	62.138	100	160.934
3 .728	6	9.656	124.276	200	321.868
4 .349	7	11.265	186.414	300	482.803
4 .971	8	12.874	248.552	400	643.737
5 .592	9	14.484	310.690	500	804.672
6 .213	10	16.093	372.828	600	965.606
12.427	20	32.186	434.967	700	1,126.540
18.641	30	48.280	497.106	800	1,287.475
24.855	40	64.373	559.243	900	1,448.409
31.069	50	80.467	621.381	1,000	1,609.344

WHERE TO STAY. Spanish hotels have increased their prices in leaps and bounds over the last few years; moreover they now also charge 6% sales tax—this will be added on to your bill at the end of your stay; it is not generally included in the quoted price. As a result, Spanish hotels are no longer the great bargains they once were, but accommodations are still modestly priced and of a good standard compared to those of many European countries.

Hotels are officially classified from 5-star to 1-star; hostels from 3-star to 1-star. If an ''R'' appears on the blue hotel plaque, the hotel is classified as a *residencia* and does not offer full dining services, though breakfast and cafeteria services may be available. Prices quoted are *always* per room, not per person. Breakfast is rarely included with the room; if it is, it will be charged separately. If breakfast in your hotel is an optional extra, it is usually far better value to breakfast in a nearby café.

Prices. Room rates will often vary according to season, the Spanish hotel year being divided into *estación alta* (high), *media* (mid), and *baja* (low) season. High-season rates often apply to Christmas, Holy Week, and local fiesta times, as well as to high summer.

Single rooms are usually few and far between; single occupancy of a double room is charged at 80% of the full price. An additional bed in a room is charged at 60% of the single room rate or 35% of the double room rate. If you stay more than two nights you are entitled to full-board terms, which should be the room rate plus not more than 85% of the total cost of breakfast, lunch, and dinner charged separately.

All hotels' and hostels' prices should be displayed at reception. A useful book is the *Guía de Hoteles,* which lists hotels, prices, and facilities. Published in March every year, it costs about 500 ptas. and is available from bookstores and major department stores. Though most Spanish hotels offer good, if modest, accommodations, it is not unknown for an impressive lobby to belie shabby rooms upstairs. If, at the end of your stay, you have a complaint, enter it in the hotel's complaint book, kept for this purpose; report it to the local tourist office; or put it in writing to the Dirección General de Política Turística, Sección de Reclamaciones, María de Molina 50, 28006 Madrid.

If you intend paying your bill by credit card, check that your hotel accepts it. Displaying a credit-card sign does not always guarantee acceptance in Spain!

Though it is always difficult to give a clear guide to hotel prices, as a general indication our Moderate (M) category usually covers 2-star and some 3-star hotels, and 3-star hostels; prices range from 3,000–4,000 ptas. for a double room without breakfast. Our Inexpensive (I) category covers 1-star and some 2-star hotels, and 1- and 2-star hostels; prices range from 2,000–3,000 ptas. for a double room, again without breakfast. In Madrid, Barcelona, and Seville at Holy Week or *feria* time, you can expect to pay slightly higher rates, say (M) 3,500–4,500 ptas., and (I) 2,500–3,500 ptas. ⊖ = Highly Recommended.

YOUTH HOSTELS. There are so many inexpensive pensions in Spain that youth hosteling isn't as popular as in other European countries. Additionally, many of Spain's 55 youth hostels are located too far from major centers to be reached by public transport. However, if you plan to stay in youth hostels, get the *International Youth Hostel Handbook,* published annually; it lists all the hostels in Spain. Youth hostels in Spain are signposted AJ *(albergue juvenil).*

The Red Española de Albergues Juveniles (Spanish Youth Hostel Association) has its headquarters at Ortega y Gasset 71–3A, 28006 Madrid (tel. 401-1300/9461) and is open mornings only. You'll also find plenty of information about youth hosteling from: **American Youth Hostels, Inc.,** PO Box 37613, Washington, DC 20013.

In Canada, write **The Canadian Hosteling Association National Office,** Tower A, 333 River Rd., 3rd Fl., Ottawa, Ont. K1L 8H9.

In Britain, write **The Youth Hostels Association,** 14 Southampton St., London WC2E 7HY.

RENTALS. A group renting a villa can be a very economical way of staying in Spain. A villa for six can be rented for around $375 a week off season, and $475 a week in July and August. **At Home Abroad, Inc.,** 405 E. 56th St., New York, NY 10022 (212-421-9165) has properties in Spain, Portugal, Mallorca, and Tangiers, as well as six other countries. **Rent-a-Villa Ltd.,** 422 Madison Ave., New York, NY 10017 (212-262-2600) operates on the Mediterranean coast of Spain. **Villas International,** 71 W. 23rd St., New York, NY 10010 (212-929-7585) has a number of properties along the Mediterranean coast of Spain.

In the U.K., try **Arrowsmith Ltd.,** Royal Buildings, Mosley St., Piccadilly, Manchester M2 3AB (tel. 061-236-2361); **Halsey Villas, 22 Boston Pl., Dorset Sq., London NW1 6HZ (tel. 01-723-6043); Meon Villa Holidays,** Meon House, Petersfield, Hants. GU32 3NJ (tel. 0730-66561); **Palmer and Parker Villa Holidays,** 63 Grosve nor St., London W1X 0AJ (tel. 01-493-5725); and **Star-**

villas, 25 High St., Chesterton, Cambridgeshire CB4 1ND (tel. 0223-311990).

CAMPING. There are over 500 state-run campsites in Spain. Most have good facilities and their own food stores and restaurants. You will find most campsites along the Mediterranean coast, especially from the Costa Brava to the Costa Blanca, and along the northern coast. There are fewer sites inland.

The camping season is April through mid-October though some sites are open year-round. You will have to show your passport when registering, and although camping *carnets* (books of tickets) are not essential they are nonetheless recommended. Reservations are not generally needed, though they are recommended for the most popular sites in the high season.

The Spanish National Tourist Office will give you a map and a list of campsites; or get information from local tourist offices once in Spain. The annual *Guía de Campings* gives full details of sites and fees, and can be bought from bookstores in Spain.

WHERE TO EAT. Spanish restaurants are officially graded from 5-forks to 1-fork. The vast majority of restaurants fall into the 2-fork category; for modestly priced eating, this is the category to look for. You may feel that it is worth splashing out on a 3-fork restaurant for that extra ambience or more varied menu, but 1-fork restaurants, if you can find them, can offer great value for money.

Spaniards eat out a great deal and restaurants are often crowded, especially at Sunday lunchtimes. Expect to find some city restaurants closed on Saturday or Sunday, as well as for a month in summer, usually July or August.

Restaurant prices have risen considerably since Spain joined the EEC in 1986 and unless you stick to the fixed-price menus offered by many restaurants, dining out can run away with a large portion of your vacation budget.

If the menu states *IVA no incluído,* then expect 6% to be added onto your bill. You will always be charged for mineral water and bread, whether you eat it or not, but neither a cover nor a service charge is added to your check, so you can control that part of your spending.

Restaurant Prices. The cost of a meal will obviously depend on what dishes you order, but as a rough guide expect a three-course *à la carte* meal for two with a bottle of *vino de la casa* (house wine) to cost around 3,500–4,500 ptas., in our Moderate (M) category, and a similar meal in our Inexpensive (I) category to probably cost around 1,800–3,450 ptas. The symbol ● in our listings means Highly Recommended.

If you want to keep your costs down, go for the *menu del día* (menu of the day) or *menu turístico* (tourist menu). These are fixed-price meals consisting of a soup or appetizer, main course, bread, and dessert. A small quantity of wine or mineral water is sometimes included, but never Coke or coffee. This may be an unexciting way to eat, but it will work out far less expensive than choosing *à la carte*. Prices vary, but 700–1,000 ptas. per person is fairly average.

Platos combinados are an excellent budget bet and are served in *cafeterías* and low-cost restaurants. There is usually a choice of six to 10 different *platos;* each consists of a mixture of any of the following: chicken, fried squid, *merluza* (white fish), omelet, *paella,* fried egg, sausage, *chorizo* (spicy sausage), Russian (potato) salad, asparagus, lettuce, and tomato. Prices range from around 400–700 ptas. *Platos combinados,* while rarely the most exciting food you'll eat, are good value for money for all that.

TAPAS AND RACIONES. *Tapas,* a peculiar and wonderful Spanish delicacy, are savory snacks served in cafés and bars as an appetizer. The variety is infinite, from every imaginable combination of seafood through salami, cheese, chunks of *tortilla* (Spanish omelet), down to the humble olive. In the evenings many Spaniards go bar-hopping trying different *tapas* in each instead of sitting down to a full meal. Be warned, though, *tapas* are only a budget option if you limit your selection; if you choose ham, for example, ask how much it is first! Some bars will only serve larger portions, known as *raciones;* these can be expensive.

RESTAURANTES ECONÓMICOS. These are inexpensive, usually family-run restaurants in the back streets of larger cities. The decor is often unexciting and the food fairly basic, but they are usually clean and offer great value for money. Though they can be difficult to find, they are worth seeking out. We have named a few in our Madrid and Barcelona listings. They cater largely to workers at lunchtime and are always crowded; they are often closed on weekends.

CAFETERÍAS. *Cafetería* is the Spanish word for a café or coffeehouse and does not mean the self-service establishment of the U.S. They are common throughout Spain and serve tea, coffee, alcohol, breakfast, sandwiches, *tapas, platos combinados,* cakes, and pastries. They are

open long hours during the day and are ideal for affordable snacks and light meals.

FAST FOOD AND PIZZAS. American fast food has caught on rapidly in Madrid and, to a lesser extent, in Barcelona. Most other Spanish cities and towns have resisted this invasion. A few take-out joints exist, especially in the coastal resorts, but generally speaking bars and cafeterias are the best places for a quick, low-cost, and filling meal.

OPENING AND CLOSING TIMES. Shops. Shops in Spain open in the morning between 9 and 10 to either 1:30 or 2. In the afternoon they open from around 4 to about 7 in winter, and 5 until 8 in summer. In some cities, especially in summer, shops may close on Saturday afternoons. Tourist shops in seaside resorts and branches of the *Corte Inglés* and *Galerías Preciados* department stores mostly stay open through the siesta.

Banks and Post Offices. Banks are open 9 to 2, Monday to Friday, and 9:30 to 1 on Saturday.

Post offices normally open 9 to 2, though there are exceptions. They often close early on Saturdays and, except for Madrid and Barcelona, main post offices are closed on Sundays.

Places of Interest. Opening times of museums, art galleries, and other places of interest change constantly. As a rough guide, museums are open in the mornings between 9:30 and 1, and some open again in the afternoon between 4 and 7, or 5 and 8. Most museums shut one day a week, usually Sunday or Monday.

Churches and cathedrals are generally open to sightseers during much the same hours as museums. It is, of course, best to check with the local tourist office for the latest details to avoid disappointment and wasted trips.

National Holidays. There are numerous national holidays when shops, businesses, museums, and monuments close. January 1 (New Year's Day); January 6 (Day of the Three Kings or Epiphany); Holy Thursday (some cities); Good Friday; Easter Monday (some cities); May 1 (Labor Day); Corpus Christi (second Thursday after Whitsun); July 25 (Santiago); August 15 (Feast of the Assumption); October 12 (El Pilar); November 1 (All Saints); December 8 (Immaculate Conception); December 25 (Christmas Day).

MAIL AND TELEPHONES. As we go to press, airmail rates are as follows: to the U.S., letters up to 15 g. cost 68 ptas., postcards 58 ptas.; to the U.K. and the rest of Europe, letters up to 20 g. cost 48 ptas., postcards 14 ptas. These rates usually change each year in mid-summer, so check before you mail anything.

Buzones (mailboxes) are yellow with red stripes; there are plenty around. They usually have two or three slits. If you're sending mail out of Spain, put it in the slit marked *extranjero;* the other two are for local and provincial mail.

If you need a post office look for the *correos* sign. If you need stamps ask for *sellos.* You can have your mail sent either to your hotel or you can collect it from the local post office by simply having it addressed *lista de correo* and the name of the town where you'll collect it. You must take along your passport or other means of identification to claim your mail.

Public pay phones are silver-gray and are found on city streets and at stations and airports: They are rarely found in hotel lobbies, bars, or cafés as in many other European countries. If you want to use the phone in a bar or café, ask the barman; he will usually let you use his phone and charge you afterwards.

Pay phones take five-, 25-, 50-, and 100-ptas. coins; 10 pesetas is the minimum charge for a short local call; long-distance calls eat up many more coins, so have plenty ready. Place several coins in the groove at the top of the phone, lift the receiver, and dial your number. Coins then fall into the machine as needed. International calls can be made from public pay phones but far and away the best method of making long-distance calls, both within Spain and abroad, is to go to the *telefónica* (telephone exchange), which is usually open from 9 A.M. to 10 P.M. in major cities, 9 to 2 elsewhere.

Calls made from your hotel will *always* cost far more than from a pay phone or telefónica. Be warned that even if you make a collect call home, many Spanish hotels will make a service charge for this, about 450 ptas. to the U.S. and 250 ptas. to the U.K.

MADRID

By European terms, Madrid is an upstart capital. In a land bursting with ancient historic cities, it is odd that Madrid should have taken Philip II's fancy in 1561 as he cast around for a new capital: It stands on no great river, nor on any important medieval trade route. But catch his eye it did, possibly due to its central position at the heart of the Iberian peninsula, or simply because its dry, bracing climate was good for his gout. Whatever the reason, in just over 400 years Madrid has become one of Europe's liveliest and most exciting capitals.

Somewhat short on great sights, and with no real cathedral or beautiful churches to speak of, Madrid is a city of museums, boasting one of the world's best art collections in its Prado Gallery. The Plaza Mayor, created by the Hapsburgs for their newly chosen capital, is one of Europe's great squares, the Royal Palace of the Bourbons among Europe's most lavish royal residences. Madrid is graced by a string of neo-Classical monuments—the Puerta de Alcalá, Cibeles fountain, and the church of San Francisco, to name a few—commissioned from architects Sabatini and Ventura Rodríguez by Charles III and Charles IV. Works by Goya and Velázquez adorn the city, as do reminders that Golden Age talents like Lope de Vega and Cervantes once lived and worked here. But if sights seem few by the standards of other European capitals, don't be disappointed, for Madrid is ringed by ancient cities—Toledo, Avila, and Segovia—all easily accessible on a day's outing.

Madrid owes its name to the small Moorish settlement called after an insignificant stream, the Majrit, which ran beneath the present Calle Segovia. After its Reconquest in 1083, an inconsequential Castilian town grew up on the two hills where the Royal Palace and Vistillas Park now stand. The

MADRID

0 Miles   ¼
0 Kilometers   ¼

Points of Interest

1 Atheneum
2 Biblioteca Nacional
3 Casa Cisneros
4 Casa de Lope de Vega
5 Casa de la Villa (City Hall)
6 Casón del Buen Retiró
7 Centro de Arte Reina Sofía
   (Queen Sofia Arts Center)
8 Fuente de la Cibeles
   (Cibeles Fountain)
9 Monasterio de la Descalzas Reales
10 Monasterio de Ja Encarnación
11 Municipal Museum
12 Museo Arqueológico
13 Museo des Artes Decorativas
14 Museo Carruajes (Coach Museum)
15 Museo de Cera (Wax Museum)
16 Museo Cerralbo
17 Museo del Ejército (Army Museum)
18 Museo Etnología
19 Museo Lázaro Galdiano
20 Museo Naval
21 Museo del Prado
22 Museo Romántico
23 Museo Sorolla
24 Palacio de Liria
25 Palacio Real
26 Puerta de Alcalá
27 Puerta del Sol
28 Real Academia de Bellas Artes de
   San Fernando
29 Real Fábrica de Tapices (Royal
   Tapestry Workshops)
30 San Antonio de la Florida
31 San Francisco el Grande
32 San Ginés
33 San Jerónimo el Real
34 San José
35 Teatro Español
36 Teatro Real (Opera House)
37 Teatro Zarzuela
38 Templo de Debod
39 Torre de Lujanes
40 Torre de Madrid

i   Information
✉   Post Office
Ⓜ   Metro Station

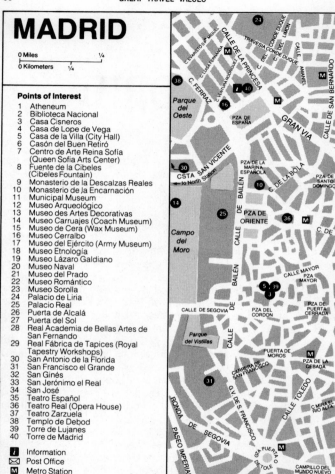

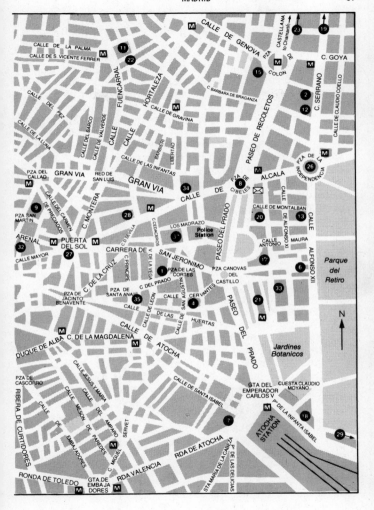

Catholic monarchs, Ferdinand and Isabella, added to the old Moorish *alcázar,* but it was their great-grandson, Philip II, who rescued Madrid from eternal insignificance.

The city has seen its share of unrest in the course of its years as capital, the most memorable incident being the uprising on May 2, 1808 against Napoleon's attempted abduction of the Spanish royal family, which, though swiftly and ruthlessly suppressed, fast became a *cause célèbre,* immortalized by Goya, and remembered to this day on the annual May 2 holiday celebrated throughout the Community of Madrid (Madrid province). The Franco era spelled death to Madrid's cultural and intellectual life, though the city expanded in other ways, its population doubling to just under four million in the 20 years from 1960–80. Together with the huge influx of migrant workers, who flocked to Madrid as part of Franco's centralization policy, came dreary concrete suburbs, shantytowns, and a vast featureless northward expansion. On the cultural front, Madrid had long played second fiddle to Barcelona, but since the early '80s all that has changed. While in no way denigrating Barcelona's considerable cultural achievements, Madrid has finally picked up the reins of leadership, politically and economically as well. Trees have been planted, new parks established. The paltry Manzanares, once an apology for a river, has been cleaned up and beautified. More recently still, Madrid opened its doors to the Reina Sofía Center, one of Europe's liveliest art houses, and to the avant-garde La Vaguada shopping mall in the Barrio del Pilar. Few months pass without a festival of some kind—international cinema in March, classical music in October, and jazz in November, to name a few. *La Movida,* or "Madrid on the Move," became the catchphrase of the early '80s as Madrid rejoiced in its new-found freedom and flung off all restraints, its citizens reveling in its all-night discos, sporting the creations of its outrageous fashion designers, flocking to view the works of previously banned or frowned-upon artists, and eagerly returning to the city's concert halls and theaters.

These exciting new trends have in no way diminished the colorful Madrid of old: The atmospheric taverns are still as popular as ever, the crowds still throng the streets at all hours of day and night, and Madrid still boasts more restaurants, and keeps later hours, than any other European city. The Madrileños themselves have no doubt that theirs is the liveliest and most creative city in Europe. Whether or not you agree with this piece of local chauvinism, only you can decide.

PRACTICAL INFORMATION
How to Get There

FROM THE AIRPORT. The least expensive means of travel from the airport to the city center is the yellow airport bus to the Plaza Colón terminal on the Castellana, a 20-minute journey. Buses leave the National and International Terminals of Barajas Airport about every quarter of an hour, and the fare, including luggage, was 175 ptas. at press time. The Colón terminal is underground, taxis meet the buses, and it is then only a short ride to most Madrid hotels.

Taxi fares into central Madrid are not prohibitive; the average ride will cost about 900–1,100 ptas. If you are heading for a hotel in northeast Madrid, on the airport side of town, or for Chamartín Station, take a cab; it will cost only a little more than the combined airport bus and cab ride.

BY TRAIN. Madrid has three main train stations. The newest, Chamartín, is in the north, out beyond the Plaza Castilla at the end of the Castellana, and covers the north and northeast, including Barcelona. Atocha (or Mediodia) Station (on Glorieta del Emerador Carlos V at the far end of Paseo del Prado) is a departure and arrival point for Andalusia, Extremadura, and Lisbon services. Finally, Norte (or Príncipe Pío) Station, on Paseo de la Florida below Plaza de España, covers services to and from Salamanca, Santiago de Compostela, La Coruña, and all other Galician cities and towns.

For train information call: 91-733-3000/2000, or go to the central RENFE ticket office on Alcalá 44 (open Mon. to Fri. 8:30–2:30 and 4–5, Sat. 8:30–1:30).

BY BUS. The city's two main bus stations are: Estación del Sur (Canarias 17, tel. 91-468-4200), covering points in the south, including Alicante; and Auto-Res (Pza. Conde de Casal 6, tel. 91-251-6644), with buses to and from Badajoz, Cáceres, Cuenca, Salamanca, Valladolid-Palencia, Valencia, and Zamora.

For further information, check with the tourist office.

Facts and Figures

USEFUL ADDRESSES. Tourist Offices. The main tourist office of the

Community of Madrid is on the ground floor of the Torre de Madrid in the Plaza de España near the beginning of Calle Princesa (tel. 91-241-2325). Also at the International Arrivals Hall of Barajas Airport (tel. 91-205-8656), and in the central hall of Chamartín Station near Gate 14 (tel. 91-215-9976). All three supply tourist information on Madrid, the Community of Madrid, and the whole of Spain. They do not provide a hotel booking service, however, though they can supply lists of hotels and hostels.

The Municipal Tourist Office—which provides lots of useful information on the city of Madrid only, and organizes walking and bus tours of the city—is at Pza. Mayor 3 (tel. 91-226-5477).

Consulates. U.S.: Serrano 75 (tel. 91-276-3600); **U.K.:** Fernando el Santo 16 (tel. 91-419-1528/0208).

Emergencies. Ambulance, tel. 91-230-7145 or 91-734-4794 (Red Cross); police, tel. 091; municipal police, tel. 092; fire, tel. 080.

Pharmacies. For 24-hour prescription service, look in the daily newspaper (*El País*) under *Farmacias de Guardia*.

Police. Calle de los Madrazo 9 (tel. 91-221-9350).

Main Post Office. Pza. de Cibeles. Open for stamps Mon. to Fri. 9 A.M.-10 P.M., Sat. 9-8, Sun. 10-1. Open for telephones, telex, and telegrams Mon. to Fri. 8 A.M.-midnight, Sat. and Sun. 8 A.M.-10 P.M.

Main Telephone Exchange. Corner of Gran Vía and Fuencarral, entrance on Fuencarral 3.

Getting Around

BY SUBWAY. The subway is the easiest and quickest way of traveling round Madrid. There are 10 subway lines, operating from 6 A.M. to 1:30 A.M. Subway maps are available from ticket offices, some hotel receptions, and tourist offices. The main subway station, good for information, is at Puerta del Sol. Many ticket booths close at 10 P.M. so you will need change for the automatic machines at night (5, 25, or 50 ptas.) or to be in possession of a *taco* (see below).

A flat fare system is used: A ride cost 50 ptas. in 1987. Savings can be made by buying a *taco* of 10 tickets for 410 ptas., or by purchasing a tourist card called *Metrotour,* which allows unlimited metro travel for three days at 575 ptas., or five days at 850 ptas. (1987 prices).

BY BUS. City buses are red and mostly run from 6 A.M. to midnight (some stop earlier). Again there is a flat fare system, 50 ptas., or 60 ptas. for a transfer (*correspondencia*). Yellow microbuses are air-conditioned, and cost 60 ptas. Plans of the routes are displayed at

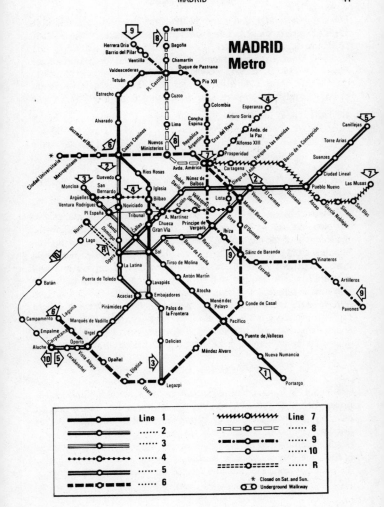

MADRID
Metro

bus stops *(paradas)*, and a map of the entire system is available from EMT *(Empresa Municipal de Transportes)* booths on Cibeles, Callao, or Puerta del Sol.

Savings can be made by buying a **bonobus,** good for 10 rides on red buses; available from EMT booths for 310 ptas., or at any branch of the Caja de Ahorros de Madrid. Books of 20 tickets valid for yellow microbuses cost 1,150 ptas. (All prices quoted are for 1987.)

BY TAXI. There are over 15,500 taxis in Madrid, and fares are low by New York or London standards; the average city ride comes to 300-400 ptas. Cabs available for hire display a *libre* sign during the day and a green light at night. Cab stands are numerous, or you can hail cabs on the street. Always check that the driver puts his meter on when you start your ride. Tip 10% of the fare. For a radio cab, call 91-247-8200, 404-9000, or 445-9008.

ON FOOT. Madrid is a fairly compact city, and most of the main sights are close enough to be reached on foot. If you have a hotel in the modern part of the city off the Castellana or much to the north of Gran Vía, however, you will have to resort to the subway or buses. The main north-south axis is the Castellana—its length is deceptive and will defeat all but the hardiest walker, if the roar and fumes of the traffic don't get to you first; the main east-west axis is Calle Alcala and Gran Vía. Walking anywhere in the center of Madrid is always a delight (apart from heavy traffic pollution) as there are plenty of sights, and shops, bars, and cafés line your way. Arm yourself with a good map if you're taking anything but the most major streets.

Where to Stay

HOTELS. Few European capitals can boast such a wealth of moderately priced hotels and hostels as Madrid. Furthermore, nearly all are centrally located and within convenient walking distance of the principal sights. Rooms can be hard to come by over Easter and in the height of summer, so the earlier you arrive, the better. At the lower end of the scale, few hostels take bookings; finding a room entails turning up when someone else has just vacated one—late morning is a good time.

Tourist offices supply lists of places to stay but do not make reservations. If you arrive by plane or train, however, there are hotel booking agencies at Barajas Airport and at Chamartín and Atocha train stations, or call the hotel booking agent **La Brujula** (tel. 91-248-9705), open 9–9.

Moderate

Aresol, Arenal 6 (tel. 91-232-2427). 12 rooms, all with bath-rooms. A small, spanking-clean, 3rd-floor boarding house just down from Puerta del Sol, with a more intimate ambience than most.

Atlántico, Gran Vía 38 (tel. 91-222-6480). 62 rooms. On the north side of Gran Vía between Callao and Red San Luis, this stylish, 3-star hotel has recently been redecorated, and though the location can be noisy, standards are good if you have a room on the front.

☛**Inglés,** Echegaray 10 (tel. 91-429-6551). 58 rooms. Don't let the shabby street deter you. The Inglés is a long-standing budget favorite once patronized by Virginia Woolf; rooms are comfortable with good facilities, and the location is conveniently close to inexpensive restaurants and Puerta del Sol.

Madrid, Carretas 10 (tel. 91-221-6520). 71 rooms. Its convenient setting and comfortable, old-fashioned appeal make this 3-star hotel a pleasant base from which to explore the city. Breakfast only.

☛**París,** Alcalá 2 (tel. 91-221-6496). 114 rooms. This real Madrid old-timer on the Puerta del Sol still has a dining room, one of the few moderate hotels in the capital to do so. A delightful place, chock-full of old-fashioned charm, it's sure to please.

Inexpensive

Americano, Puerta del Sol 11 (tel. 91-222-2822). 43 rooms. An ideal choice for those who like to be in the center of things, the attractive Americano lies in the heart of town between the shopping streets of Preciados and Carmen. Well decorated, and offering extremely modest rates.

☛**Cliper,** Chinchilla 6 (tel. 91-231-1700). 52 rooms. People interested in ideal low-cost accommodations should be delighted with the simple, friendly Cliper, on a quiet side street to the south of Gran Vía.

Ducal, Hortaleza 3 (tel. 91-221-1045). 42 rooms, most with bathrooms. This comfortable, 3-star hostel is set in a well-decorated, old-fashioned house just off the Red San Luis, and has long been a sound budget bet.

☛**Metropol,** Montera 47 (tel. 91-221-2935). 62 rooms. This delightful hostel, next to McDonald's on the Red San Luis, is without doubt one of the city's most pleasant budget bargains. It has recently been redecorated and refurbished, and meals are served.

Regente, Mesonero Romanos 9 (tel. 91-221-2941). 124 rooms. The 3-star Regente has seen better days, but though its rooms are nothing to rave about, they are clean and perfectly adequate. It has the advantage of a full hotel reception service and a very convenient central location near the Gran Vía.

Roma, Travesía de Trujillos 1 (tel. 91-231-1906). 23 rooms. The Roma has long been recognized as another of Madrid's best budget deals, being both colorful and friendly, and extremely inexpensive, to boot.

Where to Eat

RESTAURANTS. Madrid is packed with restaurants to suit all pocketbooks, serving every kind of cuisine, though if economy is a major consideration, you'd best stick to traditional Spanish fare. Most restaurants display a menu with prices in their windows, so gauge the situation before going in. As a general rule, if there's no price list in the window, go elsewhere. Restaurants are required to offer a *menu del día*, though many don't. The 6% IVA tax is usually included, but it's worth checking. Many restaurants close for a month in summer, usually between July and September, and most close one day a week, so telephone first if you are making a special journey.

Moderate

La Bola, Bola 5 (tel. 91-247-6930). Closed Sun. This atmospheric little spot has belonged to the same family since the early 1800s and oozes plenty of old-world charm. Choose from lots of local specialties.

El Buda Feliz, Tudescos 5 (tel. 91-232-4475). The Happy Buda, just above Pza. Callao, is one of the best-known Chinese restaurants in town. Prices are very reasonable and there is an excellent-value *menu del día*.

El Callejón, Ternera 6 (tel. 91-222-5401). In an alley just off the top part of Calle Preciados, this excellent restaurant serves good seafood and was a favorite of Ernest Hemingway.

Carmencita, Libertad 16 (tel. 91-231-6612). Dating back to 1850, this is a charming old Madrid favorite serving both new and traditional dishes. Decor is simple but pretty, and numerous famous people have dined here, among them García Lorca and Pablo Neruda.

Casa Botín, Cuchilleros 17 (tel. 91-266-4217). One of Madrid's most famous restaurants, Casa Botín figures in Hemingway's *Death in the Afternoon.* Located at the back of the Pza. Mayor in a well-preserved 17th-century house, its specialty is suckling pig (*cochinillo*) served on blackened earthenware platters, as well as roast lamb (*cordero asado*) and roast kid (*cabrito asado*). There are two sittings for dinner, at 8 and 10:30; reservations are a must.

Casa Ciriaco, Mayor 48 (tel. 91-248-0620). A good old-fashioned standby, well known to Madrileños, and the kind of restaurant rarely found nowadays. In the Pza. Mayor area.

Casa Gallega, Bordadores 11 (tel. 91-241-9055). An old-fashioned Galician restaurant, behind the San Ginés church on Calle Arenal, specializing in seafood.

Casa Paco, Puerta Cerrada 11 (tel. 91-266-3166). This busy and hugely atmospheric old-time favorite is well known for its thick, juicy steaks, though there's also a good choice of fish dishes. Prices are on the high side, but it's worth it.

Los Galayos, Botoneras 5 (tel. 91-266-3028). On the corner of the Pza. Mayor, this restaurant in an early 19th-century building has a stylish decor, and is an ideal initiation spot into the pleasures of Spanish food.

●**Goyamar,** Ventura de la Vega 11 (tel. 91-429-7581). One of the smartest restaurants on this street packed with budget eating places. Decor is pleasant, the service friendly, and the prices amazingly reasonable. There's a very good inexpensive *menu de la casa* too.

El Luarqués, Ventura de la Vega 16 (tel. 91-429- 6174). Closed Sun. evening, Mon., and Aug. *Fabada asturiana* and *arroz con leche* are among the Asutrian specialties on the menu of this popular restaurant. It's always packed with appreciative Madrileños, so get there early.

Mesón San Javier, Conde 3 (tel. 91-248-0925). Tucked away behind the Ayuntamiento (City Hall), Mesón San Javier offers a good choice of roast pork and lamb dishes, as well as other tasty local fare.

Taberna da Queimada, Echegaray 15. This colorful Galician restaurant serves huge *paellas* and delicious Galician specialties like *lacón con grelos* (ham and turnip tops) and *pulpa gallega* (octopus), accompanied by Riberio wine. It's extremely popular with locals and tourists alike, and fills up quickly at lunchtime, especially on Sundays.

Terra Nosa, Cava San Miguel 3 (tel. 91-247-1175). This Galician bistro, just off the Pza. Mayor overlooking the covered market, has attractive decor and serves up hearty helpings of Galician food and wine.

Inexpensive

●**La Argentina,** corner of Gravina and Válgame Dios (tel. 91-221-3763). The setting is unpretentious and the food comes in simple but hearty portions at this good-value spot in the Chueca district.

Casa Gades, Conde de Xiquena 4. This is actually two eateries right next door to each other. The café is trendy and serves inexpensive pasta and pizzas; the restaurant is smarter and serves more expensive meat dishes as well as pasta. In the Chueca area.

Casa Mingo, Paseo de la Florida 2 (tel. 91-247-7918). This Asturian tavern, at the back of the Norte Train Station, is a Madrid institution. It's near the Goya Pantheon and convenient for anyone arriving at the station or by bus from Segovia. Long famous for its Asturian cider, goat's cheese, and Galician *empanadas*.

➌ La Caserola, Echegaray 3 (tel. 91-463-0316). This atmospheric tavern is one of the best-known budget eateries on this street, itself a haven for cost-conscious diners. As well as its regular menu, it also serves *bocadillos* (sandwiches) and *platos combinados*.

La Choza, Echegaray 11 (tel. 91-429-6329). Prices are unbeatable at this authentic old *económico*, which is far less touristy than many, and therefore less crowded. The decor is of no interest whatsoever but the menu is wider than most, with a good choice of vegetable dishes.

El Criollo, Barbieri 21. Behind a rather scruffy bar is a top-value *económico* whose rock-bottom prices are hard to beat: the *menu de la casa* is only 500 ptas.!

Fosters Hollywood, Tamayo y Baus 1 (tel. 91-231-5115). Almost opposite the María Guerrero theater, this American-style restaurant serves inexpensive hamburgers and good old U.S. favorites like spare ribs. Great if you're feeling homesick.

El Inca, Gravina 23 (tel. 91-232-7745). Closed Sun. evening and Mon. lunch. Opposite La Argentina (see above), this inexpensive restaurant specializes in dishes from Peru.

➌ Pagasarri, Barco 7. This authentic hole-in-the-wall above the Gran Vía offers little in the way of decor, but fills up rapidly at lunchtime with locals who appreciate its sheer value for money. Get there early as lines form outside long before it opens at 1 P.M.

Las Palmeras, Costanilla de los Angeles 8. Very popular at lunchtime with local workers, this *económico* lies just off Arenal and is convenient to the Preciados stores. Decor is plain, the food fairly basic, and the service swift if lacking polish, but the prices are right.

La Quinta del Sordo, Sacramento 10 (tel. 91-248-1852). A restaurant of long-standing reputation, named after Goya's house—the House of the Deaf Man—which stood across the river. It's famous for its baked chicken, Goyaesque (!) soup, and a good choice of Castilian specialties. Near the Pza. Mayor.

Tienda de Vinos, Augusto Figueroa 35, near Barbieri. More often known by its nickname "El Comunista," this is a real Chueca hangout. It's colorful and practically reeks atmosphere, and you can eat extremely well at laughably low prices. It can be daunting, however, if you don't speak Spanish and are unfamiliar with Spanish menus since you'll rarely be given a printed menu.

BARS AND CAFÉS. Café Comercial, Glorieta de Bilbao 7. This café has changed little over the last three decades: It's always crowded, and has long been a political meeting point.

Café Gijón, Paseo de Recoletos 21. The best and most famous of the old guard. It's still a hangout for writers and artists, a tradition dating back to the turn of the century. There are tables outside on the main avenue in summer.

Cervecería Alemana, Pza. Sta. Ana 6. A great favorite with Ernest Hemingway (who used to stay in the nearby Victoria Hotel), this popular beer hall was founded by Germans over 100 years ago and is still going strong.

El Elhecho, Huertas 56. Calle Huertas is the heart of one of Madrid's most popular nighttime areas, and this cozy wine bar with turn-of-the-century decor and lots of potted ferns is one of the favorites. It's always crowded, and most evenings there is live chamber or piano music.

Los Gabrieles, Echegaray 17. A magnificent old bodega with four bars and superb ceramic decoration, in the heart of old Madrid.

La Mallorquina, Puerta del Sol, between Calle Mayor and Arenal. You can purchase pastries and a quick cup of coffee on the ground floor, or relax in the tea salon upstairs with superb views over Puerta del Sol. The incredible tea ritual between 6 P.M.–7 P.M. is something to see.

La Trucha, Manuel Fernández y González 3. Colorful and atmospheric, with strings of garlic and giant hams hanging from the ceiling, this ancient bar is ideal for just a drink or a typical meal. Its specialties are *trucha navarra* (trout stuffed with ham) and *rabo de toro* (bull's tail). Though long established, it's very popular with Madrid's fashionable young set.

Viva Madrid, Manuel Fernández y González 7. Just off the Pza. Sta. Ana, this beautiful old bar is currently one of Madrid's most popular meeting places. Piano music often accompanies your drinking.

Exploring Madrid

SAFETY WARNING. Take extra care at all times when walking through Madrid. There have been numerous reports of muggings, so don't carry purses or flaunt obviously expensive jewelry in the street. Carry your cash in your pockets or hidden on your person, and take just one credit card with you. Leave the rest, along with any travelers' checks, locked in your hotel safe (some hotels charge for this, but it's worth the expense). You can be mugged *anywhere* at any time of day, but take extra care in the following places: on Calle Preciados; at the Sunday morning Rastro street market (notorious for thefts); on the streets of Old Madrid below (south) Calle Atocha (the Embajadores district); and the Malasaña district around the Pza. Dos de Mayo—it's colorful and crammed with fascinating cafés and bars, but is the drug-peddling center of Madrid. If you have your wallet or passport stolen, report it within 24 hours to the police station at Calle de los Madrazo 9 (tel. 91-221-9350).

The Prado and the Retiro

The Paseo del Prado, part of the city's main north-south axis, was planned and laid out in the reign of Charles III (1759–88). Running from Cibeles Fountain, one of Madrid's great landmarks, to the Glorieta de Atocha, this once-elegant tree-lined promenade is now choked with roaring traffic, and pedestrians take their lives in their hands when crossing from one side to the other. The central walkway with its trees, benches, and coffee stands provides a kind of haven in summer—if you can shut out the traffic roar—and walking its length will take you past two of Madrid's leading hotels, the Ritz and the Palace, as well as the Prado Museum. At the bottom end, the newly revamped Glorieta de Atocha—still undergoing extensive remodeling after the demolition of an unsightly overpass—offers the choice of an exhibition in the exciting new Reina Sofía Art Center, a stroll around the Botanical Gardens, or a browse among the 30 secondhand bookstalls on the slopes of the Cuesta Moyano. When intensive sightseeing and ceaseless traffic fumes get the better of you, head for the oasis of the nearby Retiro Park, whose shady trees, calm lakes, and delightful baths provide a much needed refuge from the hurly-burly.

MAJOR ATTRACTIONS. Centro de Arte Reina Sofía (Queen Sofia Center of Art), *Santa Isabel 52, off Pza. Atocha. Open 10 A.M.–9 P.M.; closed Tues*. This vast, quadrangular building, six stories high, was built by Francisco de Sabatini at the end of the 18th century as a city hospital. In the early years of the century it became Madrid's Medical School, and in 1986 it underwent a further dramatic internal conversion to house Madrid's new art center. The center has become the symbol of the great cultural revolution that has gripped Madrid in the '80s, and, when completed, should rank among the most dynamic art centers anywhere in the world. Exhibits already hosted include the works of the Mexican muralist Diego Rivera, Venice Biennale prizewinner Frank Auerbach, and the legacy bequeathed to the Spanish people by Joan Miró.

Museo del Prado. *Open Tues. to Sat. 9–7, Sun. 9–2; closed Mon.* The Prado is Madrid's uncontested number-one sight, and, ever since its opening in 1823, has competed fiercely with Granada's Alhambra as the country's major tourist attraction. To view the Prado's vast collection properly would take weeks, but the most popular standouts are the El Greco, Velázquez, Goya, and Bosch galleries. The greatest treasures are on the second floor. A visit is best begun at the Goya (north) entrance opposite the Ritz. The main gallery and adjoining rooms contain El Grecos, Riberas, Titians, Murillos, and the works of one of the most highly regarded of Spanish painters, Diego Velázquez. Be sure to see the *Surrender of Breda, The Drunkards,* his disturbing portraits of court dwarfs, and *Las Meniñas,* perhaps his most enigmatic work. It has been placed in a room by itself, with a strategically placed mirror to help you appreciate its ambiguities and complexities.

For many, the Prado provides a unique opportunity to pay homage to Goya, the 19th century's most provocative painter. His works are exhibited in several adjacent rooms at the far end of the upper gallery. Among the highlights are portraits of the royal family, including the superb *Family of Charles IV,* individual portraits of *Queen María Luisa* and *Carlos IV,* and the beautiful *Marquesa de Santa Cruz.* In an adjacent room hang the disturbing *Naked Maja* and *Clothed Maja,* for which the 13th duchess of Alba is rumored to have posed. Next door are: *The 2nd of May,* depicting the uprising of the Spaniards in 1808 against the French, and the *Fusillade of Moncloa,* or *3rd of May,* which depicts the execution of patriots by a French firing squad.

Downstairs are paintings from Goya's "Black Period," the most startling of which are the *Pilgrimage to San Isidro, Meeting of Witches,* and *Saturn Eating His Children.* Most of the ground floor is given over to the Flemish School, notably Rubens, Van Dyck, and Brueghel, and to a sizable collection of late medieval religious paintings, mostly by Spanish artists. Don't miss the astounding collection of Hieronymus Bosch (El Bosco in Spanish), displayed to the side of the lower Goya entrance, which includes his most famous works, *Garden of Earthly Delights,* and the triptych *The Hay Wagon.*

Parque del Retiro (Retiro Park). The Retiro, Madrid's prettiest park, originally formed the grounds of a magnificent palace built for Philip IV in the 17th century. (The palace was largely destroyed in the Peninsular War, and the **Salón de Reinos** (Army Museum) and the **Casón del Buen Retiro** (Prado Annex) are all that remain.) This once royal retreat (*retiro*) is embellished with statues and fountains, and a beautiful rose garden (La Rosaleda). The central lake, El Estanque, is overlooked by the vast statue of Alfonso XII (1874–86) on horseback by Mariano Benlliure. Other statues include Victorio Macho's 1919 sculpture of Benito Pérez Galdós, the Spanish Dickens, and Ricardo Bellver's *Monument to the Fallen Angel*. (Unusually dedicated to the Devil, it won first prize in the Paris Exhibition of 1878.) The park is at its loveliest on Sunday mornings with band concerts, puppet shows, and stately *sardanas* danced by Madrid's Catalan colony. Outdoor plays are staged in summer, and art exhibitions are held in the Palacio de Velázquez and the 19th-century glass-and-iron Crystal Palace.

OTHER ATTRACTIONS. Casón del Buen Retiro, *Felipe IV. Open Tues. to Sat. 9–7, Sun. 9–2; closed Mon. Admission by same ticket as the Prado.* Once the ballroom of Philip IV's palace, the Prado annex houses a fairly undistinguished collection of 19th-century Spanish paintings. But displayed separately (entrance around the back on Alfonso XII) is Picasso's *Guernica*, the haunting expression of the artist's anguish and outrage at the German bombing of a small Basque town in April 1937. The work was brought to Spain in 1981 from the Museum of Modern Art in New York to which it had been loaned, at Picasso's wish, till freedom was restored to Spain. Its arrival in Madrid was the highlight of the centenary celebrations of Picasso's birth, and was recognized by most Spaniards as a symbolic acknowledgement of the restoration of Spanish democracy.

Casa de Lope de Vega, *Cervantes 11. Open Tues. and Thurs. 10–2; closed mid-July through mid-Sept.* The house where the great playwright lived from 1610 till his death in 1635 has been skillfully restored. His contemporary, Cervantes, also lived nearby; though his house no longer stands, the great novelist is buried in the Convento de las Trinitarias on Lope de Vega 27.

Museo de Artes Decoratives, *Montalbán 12. Open Tues. to Fri. 10–3, Sat. and Sun. 10–2; closed Mon. and July to Sept.* This display of household ornaments and utensils from throughout the ages includes ceramics, gold and silver ornaments, glass, textiles, embroidery, furniture, and a lovely 18th-century Valencian kitchen.

Museo del Ejército (Army Museum), *Méndez Núñez 1. Open*

Tues. to Sun. 10–2; closed Mon. The Army Museum houses over 27,000 trophies, weapons, flags, and military regalia from Spain's wars in Europe and America. Highlights are bits of armor worn by the *conquistadores;* the cross carried by Columbus when he landed in the New World; *Tizona,* the sword of El Cid; and letters written by Napoleon, Nelson, and the duke of Wellington.

Museo Naval, *Montalbán 2. Open Tues. to Sun. 10:30–1:30; closed Mon.* In the Navy Museum are models of ships including Columbus' *Santa María,* nautical instruments, and rooms dedicated to the Battle of Lepanto (1571) and the discovery of America. Its most famous exhibit is Juan de la Cosa's chart dating from 1500, which shows the American shoreline for the first time.

Puerta de Alcalá. This grandiose archway, one of three remaining gateways into the city, was built by Francisco Sabatini in 1779 for Charles III. A customs station originally stood beside the gate, as did the old bullring until it was moved to its present site at Ventas in the 1920s. At the beginning of this century, the Puerta de Alcalá marked the eastern limits of Madrid.

Real Fábrica de Tapices, *Fuenterrabia 2. Open Mon. to Fri. 9:30–12:30; closed Aug.* The Royal Tapestry Workshops were founded by Philip IV (1621–65) and have created many of the priceless tapestries that now adorn the walls of the Royal Palace, the Escorial, and numerous other royal residences around Madrid. Some of their most famous tapestries were based on designs by Goya, and are now exhibited in the Prado.

San Jerónimo el Real, *Ruíz de Alarcón and corner of Academia just behind the Prado.* One of the oldest churches in Madrid, this monastery began as a royal foundation in the early 16th century, though it was only completed in its present form in 1854. It has witnessed many great events in Spanish history: parliaments and royal weddings were held here, it has served as both hospital and barracks, and the princes of Asturias—from Philip II to Prince Felipe, son of Juan Carlos—have been sworn in here as heirs to the throne of Spain.

Puerta del Sol to Gran Vía

The area between the bustling Puerta del Sol and Madrid's principal avenue, the Gran Vía, is the real heart of the city. Though there are few sights or museums in this downtown area, the district is packed with cafés, restaurants, and shops. While traffic roars around Puerta del Sol and along the Gran Vía, the main shopping streets of Carmen and Preciados are pleasantly traffic-free, and you can happily browse for hours. In addition, the Gran Vía is home to most of Madrid's movie theaters, and most of the flamboyant billboards advertise the same Hollywood blockbusters which are playing back home. When you tire of shopping, head off into the narrow streets to the west of Preciados and explore some of the colorful *mesones* around the Postigo de San Martín, the Cuesta Santo Domingo or Calle de la Bola, all offering moderately priced food in atmospheric surroundings. Finally, there's that main hive of activity, the Puerta del Sol, where you can watch, or take part in, the ritual *paseo,* or evening stroll.

MAJOR ATTRACTIONS. **Monasterio de las Descalzas Reales,** *Pza. de las Descalzas Reales 3. Open Tues. to Thurs. and Sat. 10:30–12:30 and 4–5:15, Fri. 10:30–12:30, Sun. and fiestas 11–1:15; closed Mon.* Princess Juana de Austria, daughter of Charles V, founded this Franciscan convent of Poor Clares in 1559 in the palace in which she was born. For the next 200 years it was inhabited by the daughters of royalty, and to this day cloistered nuns still inhabit a part of the convent. *One section is open to visitors (guided tours only),* so you can admire its enormous wealth of jewels and religious ornaments, its statues by Pedro de Mena, its famous Flemish tapestries based on designs by Rubens, and the paintings by Zurbarán, Titian, Rubens, and Brueghel the Elder. Your entrance ticket also entitles you to visit the Monasterio de la Encarnación (see below).

　　Puerta del Sol. The Puerta del Sol—its name means Gate of the Sun, though the old gateway disappeared in the 16th century—is the heart of Madrid, indeed of all of Spain. Kilometer distances throughout the nation are measured from the marker in front of the police headquarters. Moreover, this is also the meeting place of no less than 10 of the city's principal streets as well as most major bus routes and subway lines. The Puerta del Sol has witnessed many stirring events in Spanish history. The most famous incident was the uprising of Spanish patriots against the French in 1808, vividly depicted in Goya's *El Dos de Mayo* (2nd of May). Though the cafés, where generations of intellectuals once argued over the burning issues of the day, have moved elsewhere, the Puerta del Sol remains the epicenter of the Spanish capital. There is no better place to experience Madrileño life, and no better vantage point than the upstairs tearoom of the old Mallorquina pastry shop between Arenal and Mayor.

OTHER ATTRACTIONS. **Monasterio de la Encarnación,** *Pza. de la Encarnación 1. Open Mon. to Sat. 10:30–1:30 and 4–6, Sun. and* *fiestas 10:30–1:30 only*. Founded in 1611 by Margaret of Austria, wife of Philip III, this convent contains a vast array of works of art, including two painted wooden statues by Gregorio Fernández, the 17th-century sculptor.

Real Academia de Bellas Artes de San Fernando, *Alcalá 13. Open Tues. to Sat. 9–7, Sun. and Mon. 9–2*. This recently refurbished art gallery ranks second only to the Prado in the richness of its valuable collection. The works of art on show are mainly Spanish: Velázquez, Murillo, Zurbarán, Ribera, and Goya.

San Ginés, *Arenal 13*. San Ginés is one of the oldest churches in Madrid, and dates originally from 1465, but was largely rebuilt between 1642–45. Two of its best paintings are Francisco de Rizi's *Martyrdom of San Ginés* and El Greco's *Expulsion of the Moneylenders from the Temple*.

Old Madrid and the Palacio Real

To the south of Calle Mayor lies Old Madrid, a warren of narrow streets, silent churches, and small squares. It's an ideal area for the wanderer, its twisting 16th-century alleyways more like a medieval Moorish medina than the capital city of 16th-century Europe's most powerful nation. The Hapsburgs soon embellished the Old Town, however, commissioning both the magnificent new Plaza Mayor, still the city's great architectural showpiece, and the Casa de la Villa, still the City Hall. Just over a century later the Bourbon monarchs erected the sumptuous Palacio Real here on the site of the Moorish *alcázar,* so that today Madrid's two greatest monuments, bar the Prado, lie just 10 minutes' walk apart.

Old Madrid has suffered little from the development fever which has gripped the rest of the capital. You will come across old market buildings on the Plaza San Miguel and Puerta Cerrada, while colorful taverns and traditional mesones line the Cava San Miguel and Cuchilleros and ancient palaces now serve as government buildings. Curious old shops line the streets to the east of the Plaza Mayor, and the famous Sunday morning flea market—the Rastro—spills over the slopes to the south. Just follow your footsteps, for getting lost in this most charming of the city's *barrios* is very much part of its appeal.

MAJOR ATTRACTIONS. Palacio Real, *Pza. de Oriente. Open Mon. to Sat. 9:30–12:45 and 4–6; 3:30–5:15 winter; Sun. and fiestas 9:30–1:30; closed when in use for official functions*. Philip V, Spain's first Bourbon king, built this magnificent granite and limestone palace in 1737, the first in a chain of royal residences erected in and around Madrid by Bourbons emulating the opulence of Versailles. The building was completed in 1764, by which point Charles III had moved in. For the next 167 years the palace provided a glamorous residence for Spanish monarchs, until the coming of the Second Republic in 1931, when Alfonso XIII left for exile in Italy. Today, King Juan Carlos, who lives in the far less ostentatious Zarzuela Palace outside Madrid, uses it for official state functions.

Visits are by guided tour only—in English as well as Spanish—and take the best part of two hours, so go early. You can visit the **Salones Oficiales** (state apartments); otherwise, buy an all-inclusive ticket which is good for the endless sumptuous salons (the palace has some 2,800 rooms), and for the **Royal Library,** the **Royal Armory,** and the **Royal Pharmacy.**

Plaza Mayor. This elegantly serene arcaded square was built by architect Juan Gómez de Mora between 1617–19 for Philip III. Eight days of merrymaking followed its completion in 1620, and the square has been the setting of Madrid's leading celebrations and seasonal activities ever since. 1623 saw the canonization here of San Isidro, patron of Madrid, as well as mystic San Ignacio de Loyola, San Francisco Xavier, Santa Teresa de Jesús, and San Felipe Neri. It also saw the celebrations that greeted the arrival of the Prince of Wales, the future Charles I of England, who came to inspect the king's sister with a view to taking her for his bride (he went home empty-handed). Bullfights were held here throughout the 17th century, as were masked balls, firework displays, and *autos da fé,* the burnings of heretics condemned by the Inquisition.

In the early '70s the plaza was closed to traffic, and the cobblestones and equestrian statue of Philip III were replaced. With several colorful restaurants and an array of ancient curiosity shops nearby, the Plaza Mayor is a must for every visitor to Madrid, and its sidewalk cafés provide a perfect setting for a relaxing drink.

OTHER ATTRACTIONS. Museo de Carruajes (Royal Carriage Museum), *in Campo del Moro gardens, entrance on Paseo Vírgen del Puerto. Open Mon. to Sat. 9:30–12:45 and 4–6; 3:30–5:15 winter; Sun. and fiestas 9:30–1:30.* Visit on either an individual or the all-inclusive Palace ticket. Located in an old greenhouse in the Campo del Moro beneath the Palace's western facade, the Royal Carriage Museum houses a collection of 17th- and 18th-century carriages, including the litter which bore Charles V to his retirement in Yuste (though another at Yuste claims the same honor), and the coronation carriage of Fernando VII, badly damaged in 1906 when a bomb disguised as a bouquet was thrown at the wedding procession of Alfonso XIII and Victoria Eugenia, granddaughter of Queen Victoria.

Plaza de Oriente. The plaza unfortunately serves as a parking lot for tour buses, but when these have departed it gives the city's best view of the impressive facade of the Royal Palace. Across from the palace, the 19th-century **Teatro Real** is Madrid's main concert hall. The figure on the prancing horse in the plaza's center, designed by Velázquez, is Philip IV; it is considered Madrid's finest statue. The numerous other statues in the plaza are of kings and warriors of medieval Spain; 108 of these were originally destined for the palace roof, but their weight was so great it was deemed more prudent to place them here and in the Retiro Park.

Plaza de la Villa, *off Calle Mayor.* This notable cluster of buildings just west of Plaza Mayor are some of Madrid's oldest houses. The **Casa de la Villa,** the Madrid City Hall, was built in 1644 by Juan Gómez de Mora, architect of the Plaza Mayor, and once served as the city prison and the mayor's home. An archway joins it to the **Casa Cisneros,** built in 1537 for the nephew of Cardinal Cisneros, archbishop of Spain and infamous Inquisitor General. Across the square the **Torre de Lujanes,** one of the oldest buildings in Madrid, is all that remains of the medieval home of the Lujanes family. Francois I of France, archenemy extraordinaire of the Emperor Charles V, was imprisoned here after his capture at the battle of Pavia in Italy in 1525.

San Francisco El Grande, *Pza. de San Francisco.* Madrid's largest church, the Basílica de San Francisco, was built between 1761–84 as part of Charles III's rebuilding of Madrid, but the church is more impressive for its size than its beauty. Its **dome** is larger than St. Paul's in London, and its **chapels** were painted by Goya, Claudio Coello, and Lucas Jordán. The 50 carved choir stalls came from El Paular Monastery in the Guadarrama mountains. The fine English organ dates from 1882.

Plaza de España to Parque del Oeste

On the western fringes of Madrid, this section is not so much a clearly defined area of the city as a grouping of sights worth a visit if you have time left over after viewing the more famous monuments. Insofar as there is a unifying feature, it is that these sights are either in or near the Parque del Oeste, a shady hillside garden alongside the Paseo de Rosales on the edge of the Argüelles district.

ATTRACTIONS. Ermita de San Antonio de la Florida and Panteón de Goya, *Glorieta de San Antonio de la Florida. Open summer 10–1 and 4–7; winter 11–1:30 and 3–6; Sun. and fiestas mornings only; closed Wed.* Tucked away alongside the railroad sidings of Norte station, this hermitage was built in the 1790s by order of Charles IV, and was decorated by Goya in a highly original manner. In the **dome,** the scene of St. Anthony of Padua performing a miracle seems at first glance a conventional religious painting, though a further look reveals onlookers who are anything but—respectable court officials hobnob with some very much less respectable ladies. The church was deconsecrated in 1927 and is now a museum to Goya's memory. The artist died in Bordeaux in 1828; later, his body—mysteriously minus its head—was exhumed and returned to Spain, where it was buried in 1919.

Museo Cerralbes, *Ventura Rodríguez 17 on the corner of Ferraz. Open Tues. to Sat. 10–2 and 4–7, Sun. 10–2; closed Mon. and Aug.* Visiting this mansion built by the Marqués de Cerralbo in 1876 is akin to paying a call on a nobleman's private quarters at the turn of the century. The house is crammed full of paintings (El Greco's *St. Francis in Ecstasy* hangs in the chapel), furniture, chandeliers, splendid mirrors, personal mementos, and some lovely old porcelain.

Templo de Debod. *Located in the pleasant Parque del Oeste just beneath the Calle Ferraz,* this ancient Egyptian temple was a gift to Spain from the Egyptian government as a thank-you for Spanish help in moving monuments that would have been flooded during the building of the Aswan Dam. The temple, dedicated to Amon, was built in 4 B.C. by order of Azakleramon, King of Meroe, and was transported to Madrid from the Aswan flood site.

Paseo de la Castellana and the Barrio Salamanca

The reign of Isabel II saw a lot of new development in Madrid, and in the 1860s the old city walls were torn down to make way for this expansion. The area northeast of Cibeles, the Barrio de Salamanca, is one of Madrid's most elegant districts, its streets lined with expensive boutiques, art galleries, and high-priced apartment buildings. Inhabitants are recognized as some of Madrid's most traditional and conservative citizens, and this smart neighborhood has been the scene of several Basque separatist terrorist attacks in recent years. A walk up the elegant Calle Serrano will take you past boutiques, department stores, art galleries, the U.S. embassy, the residence of the British ambassador, and two of Madrid's leading museums. If you feel up to a return stroll down the Paseo de la Castellana, Madrid's multilaned north-south axis, a good many sights will reward your efforts. Few of the noble palaces remain, but every now and again, tucked away between the glass and concrete structures of this ultramodern thoroughfare, you will catch a glimpse of the splendors of yesteryear. On the Castellana's lower reaches, along the Paseo de Recoletos, some 50 or so rather pricey sidewalk cafés line the central promenade in summer, among them the Café de Gijón, longtime meeting place of intellectuals and literary giants.

MAJOR ATTRACTIONS. **Museo Arqueológico** (Archeological Museum), *Serrano 13. Open Tues. to Sun. 9–1:30; closed Mon.* This admirable archeological collection includes some particularly fine Greek vases, Egyptian mummies, Roman mosaics, over 180,000 coins, jeweled Visigoth crowns and crosses, and Moorish and medieval Christian art and furniture. The museum's uncontested highlight is the lovely **Dama de Elche,** an Iberian statue found at Elche, near Alicante, thought to date from between the 3rd and 5th centuries B.C. Outside in the garden, you can visit a convincing replica of the famous Altamira Caves near Santander, complete with ocher and rust wall-paintings of prehistoric bison and bulls.

Museo Lázaro Galdiano, *Serrano 122 on the corner of María de Molina. Open Tues. to Sun. 10–2; closed Mon.* Housed in the former private villa of José Lázaro Galdiano, writer, journalist, and great antique collector of the early 20th century, this museum holds a splendid array of *objets d'art*—clocks, watches, armor, weapons, jewels, furniture, tapestries, and enamels. Its magnificent collection of paintings includes Spanish masters El Greco, Zurbarán, Velázquez, and Goya, as well as a number of English masters like Constable, Turner, and Reynolds; it also has one of the best displays in Europe of medieval ivory and Limoges enamels.

OTHER ATTRACTIONS. **Biblioteca Nacional,** *Paseo de Recoletos near Pza. Colón. Open Mon. to Sat. 9–1:30 and 4:30–7; closed Sun.* Housed in the same building as the Archeological Museum, the National Library is home to Spain's most valuable collection of books, including a first edition of *Don Quixote.*

Museo de Cera, *Paseo Recoletos 41. Open 10:30–2 and 4–9.* One of Europe's leading wax museums displays figures of all the great names of Spanish history. There's a special gallery of Spanish kings, queens, and heads of state, and foreign personalities ranging from Gary Cooper to President Kennedy.

Museo Sorolla, *Gen. Martínez Campos 37. Open Tues. to Sun. 10–2; closed Mon.* On the opposite side of the Castellana from the Salamanca district, this house was home to the Valencian painter Joaquín Sorolla (1863–1923). If you enjoy paintings with a turn-of-the-century flavor—girls in white frocks and wasp-waisted ladies—folk art, and period furniture, this museum will reward a visit.

Escorted Tours

Tours of Madrid are run by: **Pullmantur,** Pza. de Oriente 8 (tel. 91-241-1807); **Trapsatur,** San Bernardo 23 (tel. 91-266-9900); **Julia Tours,** Gran Vía 68 (tel. 91-270-4600). All three offer the same tours at the same prices and there is little to choose between them. In high season, all tours (except those taking in bullfights) operate daily; in low season, tours are often shared out among the three companies.

Tours are given in English as well as Spanish. Make reservations directly with the operators at the addresses above, at any travel agent, or at your hotel. Departure points are from the addresses above, though in some cases you can be collected from your hotel.

Shopping

Madrid's central shopping area lies around the Puerta del Sol, the Calles Preciados, Carmen, and Montera, and along the Gran Vía. Here you'll find the main branches of the country's leading department stores—**El Corte Inglés** (on Preciados just above Sol) and **Galerías Preciados** (off Pza. Callao on Gran Vía)—as well as a vast range of boutiques, shoe stores, bookshops, and leather, craft, and porcelain dealers. Most are open Mon. to Sat. 9:30–1:30 and 5–8; the two department stores are open 10 A.M.-8 P.M.

For a traditional Spanish keepsake, you may be interested in the pale-hued Lladro porcelain which, while not cheap, costs far less here in Spain than when exported elsewhere; **Original Hispana,** at Maestro Guerrero 1 behind the Hotel Plaza on the Plaza de España, has a vast display. If brightly colored ceramics are more your thing, try **Cántaro,** on **Flor Baja** just off the Gran Vía.

While Old Madrid is not primarily a shopping area, the **Calle Mayor** and the rabbit warren of narrow streets around the **Plaza**

Mayor hold a fascinating amalgam of tiny shops straight out of the 19th century. You'll find an array of curiosities ranging from religious objects to tools, and military regalia tucked behind dark wooden counters in shops run by the same family for 100 years or more. Madrid's flea market, the **Rastro,** is held along the Ribera de Curtidores from 9–2 each Sunday, where junk of every description is sold alongside some rather nice antiques. Don't expect bargains, and beware of pickpockets—the market is riddled with them.

If you have a sweet tooth, or know someone who does, there's an outstanding candy shop in the Paseo del Prado area, **Casa Mira** (Carrera San Jerónimo 30), which dates from 1855. Its gift-boxed goodies make ideal presents, and the shop's elegant interior is worth a trip in itself.

Finally, shopping mall addicts may enjoy a visit to **La Vaguada** (also called **Madrid 2**) in the northern suburbs. There are over 350 shops, two department stores, several movie theaters, and lots of restaurants and cafés to choose from.

Entertainment and Nightlife

For information about what's on in Madrid, try the weekly *Guía del Ocio,* available from newsstands for around 60 ptas. It gives a complete rundown of movies, music, discos, art exhibitions, and concerts, as well as listing restaurants, cafés, and bars. The tourist office also publishes a monthly bulletin, *En Madrid,* listing concerts, exhibitions, and special events in both Spanish and English.

MUSIC AND OPERA. Madrid's main concert hall is the **Teatro Real,** Pza. de Oriente (tel. 91-248-3875) opposite the **Palacio Real.** Weekly concerts are held here from Oct. through Apr., and opera and ballet performances are given as well (Oct. through June). Ticket prices vary, but are inexpensive by U.S. or U.K. standards.

The city's other concert venue is the **Teatro Lírico Nacional de la Zarzuela,** Jovellanos 4 (tel. 91-429-8216), whose ground plan is identical to Milan's famous *La Scala.* Opera and ballet performances are held here regularly as are *zarzuelas,* a uniquely Spanish extravaganza combining operetta and folk dance.

THEATER. Most theaters have two performances, at 7 and 10:30 P.M., and close one day a week, usually Mon. Tickets are inexpensive and easy to obtain; it's not unusual to buy them on the night of the performance. Obviously you need to speak good Spanish to enjoy a visit to the theater, but as a brief guide, some leading venues are: **Círculo de Bellas Artes,** Alcalá 42 (entrance on Marqués de Casa

Riera 2) (tel. 91-231-7700); **Centro Cultural de la Villa de Madrid,** beneath the Pza. de Colón; and **Teatro María Guerrero,** Tamayo y Baus 4 (tel. 91-419-4769).

FILM. Most foreign films shown in Spain are dubbed into Spanish, but there are around half a dozen cinemas in Madrid showing films in their original language with Spanish subtitles. Consult the local press, *El País,* or *Guía del Ocio,* for listings marked "v.o." for *versión original. El País* also lists cinemas showing subtitled films. For movies in English, the following are often good bets, and are just off the Pza. de España; Alphaville Cinemas, Martín de los Heros 14 (tel. 91-248-7233); Cines Renoir, Martín de los Heros 12 (tel. 91-248-5760); and Cine Torre, Princesa 1 (tel. 91-247-1657).

FLAMENCO. Madrid offers the widest choice of flamenco in Spain, though the connoisseur may be disappointed at the extent to which shows are aimed at the tourist market. Dining at the various *tablaos* is mediocre and vastly overpriced, so opt for a drink (*consumición*) only; this often means going around 10:30 or 11:30 **P.M.** The entrance price (which includes your first drink) varies between 1,800-2,500 ptas. This makes for quite an expensive evening, but if you enjoy flamenco, or have never seen this unique Spanish spectacle, it's worth treating yourself.

Arco de Cuchilleros, Cuchilleros 7 (tel. 91-266-5867). A small, intimate club in the heart of old Madrid, just off Pza. Mayor. It is one of the cheapest and the show is quite good. It usually puts on two shows between 10:30 and 2:30.

Café de Chinitas, Torija 7 (tel. 91-248-5135). Chinitas is well known throughout Spain; shows are usually performed by famous *cuadros* (flamenco troupes). Open 9:30 (for dinner) till 3.

Corral de la Morería, Morería 17 (tel. 91-265-8446). Owned by the famous Lucero Tena, this is one of the best *tablaos* for serious flamenco. Open 9 (for dinner) till 3.

Corral de la Pacheca, Juan Ramón Jiménez 26 (tel. 91-458-1113). Right up in the north of town, this one puts on folk dancing and *sevillanas* as well as flamenco, and often encourages audience participation. Touristy but fun. Open 9:30 (for dinner) till 2.

◆

S P L U R G E S

A Glimpse Inside the Ritz Hotel, Pza. de la Lealtad 5 (tel. 91-521-2857). This aristocratic monument to the Belle Epoque came into being as the brainchild of King Alfonso XIII, who discovered his capital had no hotel worthy of accommodating his wedding guests when he married his English bride, Queen Ena, in 1906. Designed by the architect of the Paris Ritz and supervised by Charles Ritz himself, the Madrid Ritz opened its doors in October 1910, and has since been the choice of royalty, presidents, leading diplomats, and the exceedingly rich for over 80 years. In 1982 the Ritz, showing its age, was bought by the British Trust House Forte group and underwent a meticulous refurbishment program. The 158 rooms, regal restaurant, luxurious salons, antique furnishings, and famous handwoven carpets from the Royal Tapestry Factory were all restored to their former splendor.

The Ritz offers several affordable delights. You can go for a drink in the sumptuous bar—wise drinkers will limit themselves to a glass of wine or a sherry. Take afternoon tea in the lounge, or, in summer, sample a light lunch in the garden restaurant, whose *à la carte* menu is more modestly priced than that in the main dining room. In 1987 the delightful tradition of chamber concerts, which goes back to 1916, was revived with considerable success, and, though attending one of these may prove a rather dizzy extravagance, such an occasion may appeal as a special treat. These concerts are held one weekend a month in spring and fall, and, though the Saturday night concerts accompanied by a gourmet dinner are way beyond the limits of any acceptable splurge, the Sunday afternoon tea concerts, when sandwiches, cakes, and wine are served to the accompaniment of a string quartet *à la mode de 1916,* may just prove a permissible treat at around 5,000 ptas. a ticket. Tickets should be booked in advance from the Ritz concierge (tel. 91-521-2857, ext. 6). A further plus is that reduced-rate tickets are normally available at the beginning of the concert season. To enter the Ritz, men need a jacket and tie at all times.

A Drink at the Palace Hotel, Pza. de las Cortes 7 (tel. 91-429-7551). Across the Paseo del Prado lies the Palace, a slightly down-market stepsister of the nearby Ritz but a dignified turn-of-the-century hotel in its own right for all that. Like the Ritz it was built on the bidding of Alfonso XIII, opening in 1912. Lying right across the street from the Spanish Parliament, the Palace has played its own part in the course of the nation's history: It was favored by foreign spies in World War I—Mata Hari is rumored to have stayed here. Politicians of the right plotted in its salons in July 1936, and turned it into a hospital and operating theater during the Civil War. More recently, it was hastily set up as an operations center for loyal military commanders and news reporters during Colonel Tejero's seizure of the Cortes in February 1981. As you enter the splendid marble columned hall, you'll be struck by one of the hotel's best-loved features: the enormous stained-glass dome. The Palace's beautiful bar is a popular Madrid venue, lively throughout the day and evening and often busy into the morning. Here, over an only moderately extravagant drink, you can savor the atmosphere of Madrid society and the delights of this great hotel.

◆

ENVIRONS OF MADRID

Madrid, standing in the very center of the Iberian peninsula, is excellently located for easy excursions to places famed both for their beauty and their historic importance. The Monastery of El Escorial, the great showpiece of Philip II, lies conveniently in the foothills of the Guadarrama mountains, right on Madrid's doorstep. Only an hour or so to the south stands Toledo, the former capital, immortalized in the paintings of El Greco. To the northwest lie Avila, behind its splendid medieval walls, and romantic Segovia, with its dramatic alcázar and ancient aqueduct. Toledo is perhaps the most famous—and most commercialized—of these cities, Segovia the most picturesque, and Avila the most intriguingly medieval.

All these places are easily visited on day trips from Madrid. You can opt for one of the regular day trips organized by tour companies, or even a half-day tour in the case of Toledo or El Escorial. Alternatively, visit them on your own; inexpensive buses and trains run frequently from Madrid to all the places covered in this chapter. Several possibilities are open to you: You can continue your trip to Segovia with a visit to the beautiful palace and gardens of La Granja; spend, say, a morning in Segovia and an afternoon in Avila; or stop off and visit the Escorial en route to Avila. Another combination is a morning in Toledo and an afternoon in El Escorial.

You may of course decide to spend a day or two in any or all of these fascinating places to escape the hurly-burly of the capital for a while. Then you can enjoy the charm of Spain's smaller provincial towns and wander at leisure through their medieval streets long after the day-trippers have gone home. From Toledo you can easily move south into Andalusia, or westwards to the delights of Extremadura. Avila is only a short trip from Salamanca, and Segovia is a logical stepping-stone en route to Valladolid or Burgos.

Toledo, the closest to Madrid, lives largely off its huge tourist popularity and here you are likely to find prices as high as those in Madrid. Segovia and Avila, however, are far less sophisticated, and in these cities you could well experience a drop in your daily living expenses.

Avila

Avila, 112 km. (70 miles) northwest of Madrid, is Spain's highest provincial capital at a height of 1,127 meters (3,700 feet). Its winters are bitterly cold but its summers not oppressively hot. The reasons for visiting Avila are threefold: first, for the finest example of a walled city anywhere in Europe; second, for its distinctive unspoiled character and fine Romanesque churches; third, as a place of pilgrimage to the birthplace of Spain's most revered saint, Santa Teresa de Jesús (1515–82).

The presence of Santa Teresa, known here simply as "La Santa," is felt everywhere, from the convents and churches associated with her life to the restaurants and pastry shops selling the candied egg yolks known as *Yemas de Santa Teresa*. Roman Avila was converted to Christianity as early as the 1st century A.D. but was occupied by the Moors in 714 until reconquered in 1085 by Count Raimundo de Borgoña. From the 16th century onwards it assumed the air of saintliness which it still wears today.

Avila can easily be visited on a day trip from Madrid, or en route to Segovia or Salamanca. Its accommodations are reasonably priced, and there are several inexpensive places to eat. Start your visit with a tour of the walls, then make for the pleasant Plaza de Santa Teresa with its outdoor cafés and statue of the saint, erected for Pope John Paul II's visit in 1982. This is one of the focal points of the city, another being the Plaza de la Victoria inside the walls, near the central market. But don't assume that all the places of interest lie within the walls; the Old Town, to the east of the ramparts, and Calle San Segundo are just as fascinating.

Should you opt to stay overnight you will be well rewarded by the city's illuminations, when the walls, cathedral, and monastery of Santo Tomás are floodlit every night in high summer (July and August), and weekends the rest of the year.

GETTING THERE. By Train. Trains from Madrid (Chamartín or Atocha Apeadero) run at least every two hours. Trains also run regularly from Salamanca and Valladolid. Avila Station (tel. 918-22-01-88) is located at the bottom of Avda. José Antonio to the east of the city. From the station it is a 15-min. walk or short bus ride to the Pza. Santa Teresa or Pza. de la Victoria.

By Bus. Avila Bus Station (tel. 918-22-01-54) is on the Avda. de Madrid, northeast of the center. A 10-min. walk via Calle Duque de Alba will bring you to the Pza. Santa Teresa. There are daily buses from Madrid (La Sepúlvedana, Paseo de la Florida), Segovia, and Salamanca.

By Car. The quickest route from Madrid is to take NVI northwest, then A6 Guadarrama toll tunnel as far as Villacastín, then N501 to Avila. The shortest route is to leave Madrid on NVI, then branch off along C505. From Toledo, take N403 northwest; from Segovia, N110 as far as NVI, then N501; and from Salamanca, N501 southeast.

TOURIST OFFICES. Pza. de la Catedral 4 (tel. 918-21-13-87), opposite the cathedral. Open Mon. to Fri. 9-2 and 5-7; 4-6 in winter; Sat. 9-2; closed Sun. Here they will provide you with free detailed maps of the Old Town with the main monuments, churches, and convents clearly illustrated.

USEFUL ADDRESSES. Police. Avda. José Antonio (tel. 918-22-02-33), out near the station.

Post Office. Pza. de la Catedral 2.

Telephone Exchange. Pza. de la Catedral.

WHERE TO STAY. Many of the most moderately priced hotels and hostels are in the rather uninteresting part of town near the station. Most of our selections, however, are in the center of town, within the walls.

Reina Isabel (M), Avda. José Antonio 17 (tel. 918-22-02-00). 44 rooms. Although not in the center of things, this 1-star hotel is handy for the station. It has rooms with and without bathrooms—the latter are (I)—and serves both breakfast and dinner.

●**Rey Niño** (M), Pza. José Tomé 1 (tel. 918-21-14-04). 24 rooms. Long a favorite place to stay because of its location just down from the cathedral square, the Rey Niño is pleasant and friendly. All its rooms have bathrooms, but no meals are served.

Casa Felipe (I), Pza. de la Victoria 12 (tel. 918-21-39-24). 11 rooms. Located right on the central arcaded square, within the walls, the Casa Felipe is above its own bar and budget restaurant which serves good *platos combinados*. Some rooms have their own bathrooms.

Continental (I), Pza. de la Catedral 6 (tel. 918-21-15-02). 54 rooms. Once a genteel, old-style hotel, this establishment has come down a bit in the world and is now a 2-star hostel. But it is clean and friendly, if a little bare, and its location right next to the tourist office and opposite the cathedral is a virtue.

El Rastro (I), Pza. del Rastro 1 (tel. 918-21-12-18). 16 rooms. This is the hostel of the popular restaurant (see below) and is built right into the southern section of the city walls. Some rooms have bathrooms.

WHERE TO EAT. Avila is well endowed with very inexpensive eating places, many of them located around the Pza. de la Victoria and close by on the square around the central market. Most expensive establishments are to be found on Calle Estrada, between the Pzas. Italia and Santa Teresa.

●**Mesón El Rastro** (M), Pza. del Rastro 4 (tel. 918-21-31-43). Good Castilian fare in atmospheric surroundings—it is built into the city walls—have made this a very popular restaurant.

El Torreón (M), Tostado 1 (tel. 918-21-31-71). A little more upmarket than our other choices, El Torreón is located just off the cathedral square in the historic Velada mansion. Both its setting and menu are typically Castilian.

Las Cancelas (I), Cruz Vieja 6 (tel. 918-21-22-49). Very affordable *platos combinados* and *menus del día* are on offer in this inexpensive restaurant located in an alleyway between the cathedral and the Pza. Calvo Sotelo.

José Luis (I), Vallespíri 8 (tel. 918-21-15-48). Just to the west of the Pza. de la Victoria, this first-floor restaurant has a very good value *menu del día*.

●**El Rincón** (I), Pza. de Zurraquíri 6 (tel. 918-21-31-52). Sit down to a real value-for-money three-course *menu del día* at El Rincón, close to the market in the direction of the parador. Its *à la carte* menu specializes in regional Castilian dishes, such as *cochinillo* (suckling pig), and is well worth the extra money.

El Ruedo (I), Enrique Larreta 7 (tel. 918-21-31-98). A very modestly priced *menu del día* and typical Castilian fare are served in this restaurant next to the market.

MAJOR ATTRACTIONS. Basílica de San Vicente, *northeast of the walls, just outside the San Vicente gate. Open 10–1 and 4–6; Sun. 10:30–2.* San Vicente is Avila's finest Romanesque church and was built between the 12th and 14th centuries on the spot where San Vicente and his sisters Sabrina and Cristeta were martyred in A.D. 306 Its **west door** has beautifully carved figures of Christ and the Apostles, and in the **south transept** there is a splendid 12th-century sepulcher. The **crypt** holds the slats where the martyrs were executed, and a much venerated statue of the Virgin. It was while praying to this image that Santa Teresa is said to have received the vision which bade her reform the Carmelite Order.

Catedral. *Open 10–1:30 and 3–6; 3–5 in winter; Sun. 11–5.* Though of Romanesque origin, Avila Cathedral is usually claimed as Spain's first Gothic cathedral. It was built between the 12th and 15th centuries and the Romanesque parts are easily recognizable by their red and white brick. Worthy of note are the 16th-century **altarpiece,** whose *Scenes from the Life of Christ* are the work of Pedro Berruguete and Juan de Borgoña, and the ornate alabaster **tomb** of Cardinal Alonso de Madrigal, a 15th-century bishop of Avila, whose swarthy complexion gained him the nickname of "El Tostado" (Toasted One). This finely carved tomb is thought to be the work of Domenico Fancelli, who also sculpted the tomb of Prince Juan in Santo Tomás, and the sepulchers of the Catholic kings in Granada's Royal Chapel.

Monasterio de Santo Tomás, *Pza. de Granada. Open 10:30–1 and 4–7.* The monastery was founded in 1482 by the Dominicans, and its building was completed in 1493 by Ferdinand and Isabella, who used it as a summer palace. It also served as a base for the Inquisition for six years, and Torquemada, that most infamous inquisitor general, is buried in the sacristy. The **chapel** has a fine reredos and is decorated throughout with the yolk and arrows and pomegranate motif, symbol of the Catholic kings and their conquest of Granada. A moving monument is Domenico Fancelli's alabaster **tomb** of their only son, Prince Juan, who died at the age of 19 while still a student at Salamanca. The splendid **cloisters** of the monastery house a **Museum of Oriental Art** whose collection of works from China, Japan, and Vietnam has been built up by Dominican missionaries working in the east.

The Walls. Avila's impressive walls were begun in 1020 by Count

Raimundo de Borgoña on the orders of his father-in-law, King Alfonso IV, who wanted to strengthen its position against the Moors. Measuring more than 2½ km. (1½ mi.) and completed in only nine years, they were the most complete military installation in Spain during the Middle Ages. They contain 88 towers, nine gateways, and several posterns. The most impressive gates are the northeastern **Puerta de San Vicente** and the nearby **Puerta del Alcázar.**

Restoration and numerous untidy storks' nests have done nothing to lessen their grandeur, and the best overall view of these amazing fortifications is to be had from the Cuatro Postes, half a mile out on the Salamanca road. If you want to climb up on top of the walls, the only access point is from the garden of the parador.

OTHER ATTRACTIONS. The Avila of Santa Teresa. Santa Teresa was born in 1515 to a family of Jewish origin. Virgin and mystic, she set about reforming the Carmelite Order and established 18 religious institutions from Soria to Seville, Burgos to Granada. Of her many works, her autobiography *Mi Vida* and her letters to her spiritual director and fellow poet and mystic, St. John of the Cross, are the most moving.

The devoted citizens of her native town have turned her shrines into a veritable pilgrim trail, and each has its Teresian museum displaying countless of her possessions and one or another parts of her anatomy.

Casa de los Deanes, *Pza. Nalvillos 3. Open Tues. to Sat. 10–2 and 5–7:30, Sun. 10–2; closed Mon.* This 16th-century deanery houses the **Museo Provincial,** an excellent Archeological and Folk Museum, with sections on Avila's Celtic and Roman past, paintings, ceramics, folk crafts, costumes, and bullfighting.

Church of San Pedro. *Standing on the far side of the Pza. Santa Teresa, across from the Puerta del Alcázar,* this lovely Romanesque church with its beautiful rose window is one of Avila's finest small churches.

Convento de San José (Las Madres), *on Padre Sáveno, off Duque de Alba.* This was the first Carmelite convent (1562) Santa Teresa founded. *The convent itself is not open to visitors,* but you can visit its **Museo Teresiamo** *(open 10–1 and 4–7)* which houses some of the saint's memorabilia.

Convento de Santa Teresa, *Pza. de la Santa, just inside the southern gate. Open 9–1:30 and 3:30–7.* The convent was built in 1631–6 on the site of her parents' home, and an uninspired, ornate baroque **chapel** now stands over the bedroom where the saint was born. In the adjoining gift shop and small museum are some of her relics: her rosary, books, walking stick, and sole of her sandal, and, most amazing of all, her finger clad with a wedding ring.

Monasterio de la Encarnación, *Paseo de la Encarnación to the north of the walls across the Avda. de Madrid. Open 10–1:30 and 3:30–7 for guided tours (in Spanish) only.* Santa Teresa joined the Carmelite Order here in 1537 and lived in this convent for 27 years before setting off to found her new orders. There is a reconstruction of the cell in whose ascetic surroundings she planned her Carmelite reforms, and yet another **Teresian museum.**

SHOPPING. Boxes of the *Yemas de Santa Teresa* are on sale all over town if you like very sweet candy. On Friday from 9–2 there is a **craft market** in the Pza. de la Victoria.

El Escorial

The village of San Lorenzo de El Escorial, dominated by the imposing monastery-palace-mausoleum of Philip II, lies 50 km. (30 mi.) northwest of Madrid in the foothills of the Guadarrama mountains. Philip erected the monastery as a memorial to his father, Charles V, and as a thanksgiving for the Spanish victory over the French at the Battle of St. Quentin in Flanders in 1557.

Its architects were Juan Bautista de Toledo, a pupil of Michelangelo, and Juan de Herrera, who was to become Spain's greatest Renaissance architect. Between the two of them they established a new architectural trend, abandoning the cluttered ornamentation of Charles V's reign and creating instead a purity of line and an aspect of severity which endures to this day in many Spanish public buildings.

Philip chose the site in 1561 and construction began in 1563. It was completed just 21 years later in 1584 (employing 1,000 workers at any one time, and often as many as 1,500) and this explains the absolute unity of style. Reflecting Philip's somber religious fervor, the vast gray granite building is austere and fortresslike in appearance. The inside is an extraordinary combination of royal grandeur and monastic austerity, ranging from lavish tapestries, carpets, and porcelain to the contrastingly bare cell in which Philip died.

San Lorenzo is easily accessible from Madrid, and is becoming something of a dormitory town for the capital's commuters. Its cooler climate, pleasant setting, and wealth of (often expensive) restaurants make it packed on weekends with diners from the capital. In July and August the village is converted into a summer resort for those fleeing the capital's heat, and accommodations will be hard to come by. The monastery is one of the great showpieces of Spain, and is always crowded, no matter what the time of year.

GETTING THERE. By Train. The station (tel. 91-890-0413) is down below the village and quite a walk from the monastery, but a shuttle bus meets all trains. There are frequent trains from Madrid (Atocha Apeadero or Chamartín) and Avila.

By Bus. There are frequent buses from Madrid (Paseo Moret 7, near the Moncloa subway station) and Avila to the bus station not far from the monastery (tel. 91-890-4122).

By Car. From Madrid there are two routes: Either take NVI as far as Guadarrama, then turn left onto the road to the Valley of the Fallen and El Escorial; or leave NVI at Las Rocas and take C505 direct to San Lorenzo de El Escorial.

TOURIST OFFICES. Floridablanca 10 (tel. 91-890-1554). Open Mon. to Fri. 9:45–2:15 and 3–6, Sat. 9:45–1:15.

WHERE TO STAY. For such a small place, El Escorial has several inexpensive hostels. If you are planning an overnight stay in July or August, be sure to book ahead as rooms are hard to come by.

Miranda Suizo (M), Floridablanca 20 (tel. 91-890-4711). 47 rooms. You'll be just a stone's throw away from the monastery in this pleasant, old-fashioned hotel right on the main street. It is well run, all its rooms have bathrooms, and there is full restaurant service. Its old-world café is a very popular gathering place.

Cristina (I), Juan de Toledo 6 (tel. 91-890-1961). 16 rooms. The Cristina is a very popular and friendly hostel, set in pretty gardens just around the corner from the monastery. All the rooms have bathrooms. Breakfast only is served.

Parrilla Príncipe (I), Floridablanca 6 (tel. 91-890-1611). 14 rooms. The advantage of this pleasant hotel, located in an old house, is that it adjoins the restaurant of the same name. All rooms have bathrooms, breakfast is served in the hotel, and you can of course dine next door.

WHERE TO EAT. El Escorial has a disproportionate number of restaurants for its size due to its popularity with diners who come up here from Madrid. They are frequently crowded, especially at Saturday and Sunday lunchtimes, and prices are consequently high.

Alaska (M), Pza. San Lorenzo (tel. 91-890-4365). Standard Castilian fare is served in this popular restaurant in the center of town, next to the entrance to the Galería Martín. You can dine outside in the summer.

El Candil (M), Reina Victoria 6 (tel. 91-896-0111). Located on the corner of Pza. San Lorenzo, El Candil has tables outdoors in the summer, in addition to an attractive upstairs restaurant.

Castilla (M), Pza. Constitución 2 (tel. 91-890-5219). Of the several restaurants around this square, just off Calle Floridablanca, the Castilla is one of the most reasonable. It offers a good Castilian menu, and you can dine outside in the square in summer.

Hostal Vasco (I), Pza. Santiago (tel. 91-890-1619). This is one of the few places in El Escorial where you can really dine at very affordable prices. Its *menu del día* is very economical, and there are good Basque specialties for just a little more.

Madrid-Sevilla (I), Benavente 4, off the Pza. de Animas. With a certain style to its decor and a very reasonably priced menu, this pleasant, central restaurant is popular with the locals. Its *menu del día* is extremely good value.

MAJOR ATTRACTIONS. Monastery. *Open 10–1 and 3:30–6:30; 3–6 in winter; closed Mon.* Allow at least half a day to visit the monastery, better still a whole day. The entrance ticket is divided into different sections for the various parts of the complex, and there is an extra, nominal charge if you wish to use your camera. The Royal Apartments can only be visited on a guided tour; these are mostly in Spanish, though a couple of the guides speak English. Entry to the church and patios is free.

Begin with the **Royal Apartments,** the lavish apartments of the Bourbon kings, Charles III and Charles IV, who, though they preferred the royal residences of La Granja, Aranjuez, and Madrid to Philip's somber Escorial, nonetheless embellished their living quarters with all the finery of their age. From the Bourbon apartments you pass into the **Sala de Batalles,** a vast hall decorated with a vivid fresco depicting the defeat of the Moors at the Battle of Higueruela (1431). Another fresco shows scenes from the Battle of St. Quentin.

In contrast to the excesses of the Bourbon residence, the **Apartments of Philip II,** at the southern end of the complex, are indeed stark and somber, although the sweeping views of the countryside towards Madrid are stunning. Philip's apartments are entered through a suite of rooms belonging to his daughter the Infanta Isabel Clara Eugenia, and a small oratory used by the king for private prayer. The bedroom where Philip died in 1598 of gangrene, aged 71, is little more than a spartan cell. His bed was so positioned that he could view the high altar of the church through a peephole and so take part in mass as he lay dying. The outer rooms are decorated in simple blue and white tiles from Talavera, and the last room contains the sedan chair which bore the gout-stricken Philip on his final, week-long journey from Madrid to his place of death.

In the **Nuevos Museos** is a picture gallery housing the Escorial's famous collection of paintings by Titian—court painter to Charles V—Tintoretto and Veronese, Dürer and Bosch, and of the Spanish school, Ribera, El Greco, and Velázquez. The Escorial's Venetian collection, along with those works now in the Prado, gives Spain one of the finest collections of the Venetian School outside Venice.

The church (or Templo), in the shape of a Greek cross, owes much to the designs of St. Peter's in Rome, and contains a white marble Christ by Benvenuto Cellini and a tabernacle by Herrera. To the left of the altar are statues of Charles V with his wife Isabel of Portugal, their daughter Doña María, and Charles' two sisters, while to the right is Philip II with three of his four wives. The church is dark and gloomy, and it is worth putting a coin in the slot to light up the altar.

The **Royal Pantheon,** entered down a flight of stairs from the Patio de los Evangelistas, lies directly beneath the high altar of the church. The brainchild of Charles V, it houses the tombs of all Spanish monarchs from Charles V to Alfonso XIII, with the exceptions of Philip V and Ferdinand VI. On the one side lie all the kings plus Isabel II, and on the other, all the queen consorts who gave birth to kings, plus Francisco de Asís, husband of Isabel II. The adjacent **Pudredero** (literally "rotting house") is where the bodies of the monarchs were left to rid themselves of flesh before their skeletons were placed in their black marble sepulchers. The Panteón de los Infantes is the final resting place of those queens who did not bear heirs to the thrones, and of the 60 or so royal children who died in infancy.

The **sacristía** and **Salas Capitulares** around the **Patio de los Evangelistas** house further paintings and temporary art exhibitions, and are really of only minor interest.

The magnificent **library** (biblioteca), one floor up above the monastery, houses Philip II's invaluable collection of 40,000 rare volumes and 2,700 illuminated manuscripts, among them the diary and autograph of Santa Teresa, a 5th-century text of St. Augustine, a poem of Alfonso El Sabio ("the wise"), rare Arab manuscripts and a beautiful copy of the Koran, and the prayer books of the Catholic kings. The ceiling frescoes by the Italian Tibaldi (1590–2) depict the seven liberal arts, and the shelves of exotic woods were designed by Herrera.

OTHER ATTRACTIONS. Casita de Abajo (del Príncipe), *in the*

Jardines del Príncipe below the monastery. You can visit the Prince's House on the same ticket as the Escorial. This royal lodge, built by Juan de Villanueva in 1772 for the Prince of Asturias, heir to the throne and future Charles IV, is full of splendid furniture, tapestries, and objets d'art.

Casita de Arriba, *3 km. (2 mi.) out on the road to Avila.* This simpler lodge can also be visited on the same ticket as the Escorial, and was again designed by Villanueva, this time for Gabriel de Borbón, the younger brother of Charles IV. It commands wonderful views of the surrounding countryside, and was converted for use by Prince Juan Carlos, the present king, when he was a student at Madrid University. A little before the Casita, a track winds up the mountainside to the **Silla de Felipe II,** one of four boulders shaped like seats. It is said that Philip II would sit here and admire the view and work going on in his palace, while at the same time making constant changes to the building plans.

Valle de los Caídos. *Open 10–7, 10–6 in winter.* Buses run here from the monastery twice daily to make the 8 km. (5 mi.) journey from El Escorial. The Valley of the Fallen lies just off the C600 to Guadarrama. It is a grandiose monument built by General Franco between 1940–59 as a memorial to the dead, ostensibly of both sides, of the Civil War. However, the fact remains that it was built mainly by Republican prisoners, and that Franco chose the site as a setting for his own tomb. The monument comprises a vast tunnel of a basilica hewn out of 260 m. (854 ft.) of rock, surmounted by a granite cross 150 m. (500 ft.) high which dominates the landscape for miles around. The base of the cross is surrounded by black marble statues of the four evangelists and four cardinal virtues.

The first victim to be buried here was José Antonio Primo de Rivera, founder of the Falangist party, whose tombstone lies right in front of the altar; in a corresponding position behind the altar is General Franco's slab. Some 43,000 war dead are believed to rest in the crypt. Though far from beautiful, this somber Fascist architecture is undoubtedly impressive, and the setting is superb, commanding magnificent views of the foothills of the Guadarrama mountains.

Segovia

The ancient, golden-stoned city of Segovia, 88 km. (55 miles) from Madrid across the Guadarrama mountains, stands perched on a rock between two streams—the Eresma and Clamores—at a height of 1,000 meters (3,280 feet). Famed for its magnificent 2,000-year-old Roman aqueduct and its fairy-tale *Alcázar* castle, Segovia's strikingly beautiful setting and small-town charm, free from the overcommercialization of Toledo, make it eminently worth visiting either on a day trip or, better still, for an overnight stay.

Segovia was conquered by the Romans in 80 B.C. and the aqueduct is proof enough of the city's past. The city declined under the Visigoths and the Moors, but rose again under the Trastámara dynasty when John II (1406–54) and Henry IV (1454–74) set up court here. In 1474, supported by local nobles, Isabella (Henry's half sister) was proclaimed queen of Castile here. This historic event paved the way for the unification of Spain under the Catholic kings, for Isabella was already married to Ferdinand of Aragón.

In the 1520s the city was badly destroyed during the War of the Comuneros when it rebelled against Charles V, and did not regain its splendor until the mid-18th century when Philip V established himself at nearby La Granja.

Though the aqueduct, *Alcázar,* and cathedral are likely to be your prime targets, do visit at least a couple of the superb Romanesque churches for which Segovia is famous. Segovia is also a city that repays countless wanderings, and you could begin with the Calle Real which leads up past the Plaza San Martín to the delightful arcaded Plaza Mayor, where, in the shadow of the very beautiful cathedral, you can take your bearings over a drink in one of the sidewalk cafés.

GETTING THERE. By Train. Segovia Station (tel. 911-42-15-3) is way out to the east of town on Paseo Obispo Quesada, but bus no. 3 will take you to the Plaza Mayor. There are frequent trains from Madrid (Atocha and Chamartín). The ride takes two hours and you can make connections at Villalba for El Escorial and Avila. Trains also run from Valladolid and Medina del Campo, a major rail junction where there are connections to Salamanca, Zamora, Galicia, Santander, Valladolid, and Burgos.

By Bus. The bus depot is down in the new town on Paseo Ezequiel González (tel. 911-42-77-25), about a 10-min. walk from the aqueduct. Buses run from Madrid (La Sepulvedana, Paseo de la Florida 11), Avila, Aranda del Duero, Valladolid, and La Granja.

By Car. If approaching from Madrid, there are several routes you can take. Probably the most spectacular is to leave via the Pza. de Castillo, taking C607 to Colmenar Viejo and Navacerrada, then N601 over the Navacerrada pass via San Ildefonso de la Granja to Segovia. The quickest but least spectacular route is to take NVI/A6 and the toll tunnel under the Guadarrama, and exit at San Rafael onto N603. Tolls, however, are quite expensive.

From Avila, take N501 to Villa Castín, then N110. From Valladolid or Galicia the most striking approach to Segovia is from C605 from Santa María de Nieva.

TOURIST OFFICES. Pza. Mayor 10 (tel. 911-43-03-28). Open Mon. to Fri. 9–2 and 4–6, Sat. 9–2; closed Sun. The staff here is very helpful and will provide you with a free map, essential for exploring Segovia.

USEFUL ADDRESSES. Police. Perucho 2 (tel. 911-42-51-61).
Post Office. Pza. Dr. Laguna 5.
Telephone Exchange. Pza. de los Huertos. Open 9–2, closed Sat.

WHERE TO STAY. Segovia is surprisingly short of budget hotels, but don't let this deter you from staying overnight or even longer. The city, at its best once the tour buses have departed, is especially lovely for nighttime strolls, and when illuminated (usually on summer weekends) makes a memorable impression.

Acueducto (M), Padre Claret 10 (tel. 911-42-48-00). 73 rooms. If you stay on the edge of town in this older, but well-modernized hotel, you will have great views of the aqueduct. It has full restaurant service, but is much more expensive than our usual selection. We have recommended it because of the shortage of affordable hotels in Segovia.

☛Las Sirenas (M), Juan Bravo 30 (tel. 911-43-40-11). 39 rooms. You won't be able to get meals in this deluxe hostel, but it is the best cost-conscious accommodation in town. In addition, its location is a virtue—right on the main street overlooking the Church of San Martín, and only a 5-min. walk from the Pza. Mayor. All rooms have bathrooms.

Plaza (I), Cronista Lecea II (tel. 911-43-12-28). 28 rooms. The location of this simple but well-modernized hostel is ideal for it is just off the Pza. Mayor and above a good restaurant. Its rooms are spotlessly clean and some have bathrooms.

Sol Cristina (I), Obispo Quesada 40–42 (tel. 911-42-75-13). 22 rooms. Although right out of town close to the train station, a regular bus service connects this very inexpensive hostel to the Pza. Mayor. It has clean, modern facilities, although none of its rooms has private bathrooms.

WHERE TO EAT. What Segovia lacks in reasonably priced hotels it more than makes up for in good restaurants. The Calle Luganta Isabel, just off the Pza. Mayor, is one long line of easily affordable restaurants. Segovia is famous for its hearty Castilian fare; specialties are *cochinillo* (suckling pig) and *cordero asado* (roast lamb), and to start with there's *sopa castellana,* and for dessert *ponche segoviano.*

● Mesón El Cordero (M), El Carmen 4 (tel. 911-43-41-80). You'll find good service and excellent food in this imaginatively converted noble mansion, located just 5 min. from the aqueduct. All the usual Castilian dishes are on offer, but lamb *(cordero)* is the house specialty.

Mesón Don José María (M), Cronista Lecea 11 (tel. 911-43-44-84). Good food at very reasonable prices is served at this modern but traditionally Castilian-style restaurant. It is centrally located, just off the Pza. Mayor.

La Oficina (M), Cronista Lecea 10 (tel. 911-43-16-43). Step back into the past in this typical Castilian restaurant just off the Pza. Mayor. It dates back to 1893 and is brimming with paintings, knickknacks, and memorabilia.

La Taurina (M), Pza. Mayor 8 (tel. 911-43-05-77). Enjoy a bullfighting ambience and standard Castilian fare in this friendly, colorful restaurant right on the central square.

El Abuelo (I), Alhondiga 1 (tel. 911-43-06-49). You will have a wide choice from the several inexpensive set menus at this colorful tavern. It is located just off the Calle Real and Pza. Juan Bravo.

● La Cocina de San. Millán (I), San Millán 3 (tel. 911-43-62-26). It's quite hard to find this restaurant—it's on the corner of Arturo Merino, in the vicinity of El Cordero (see above)— but it's well worth the effort. Located in an old Segovian house just below the city walls, it serves delicious home cooking, and its Mon.-to-Fri. lunch menu is amazing value.

La Criolla (I), Ruiz de Alda 4 (tel. 911-42-80-21). Dine in this simple taverna located alongside the aqueduct and the famous Mesón de Cándido. It offers a choice of inexpensive menus which are clearly displayed in its windows.

Tasca La Posada (I), Judería Vieja 5 (tel. 911-43-56-32). An ideal place for budgeteers, this rock-bottom, colorful tavern offers some real shoestring menus. You'll find it just off the Calle Isabel la Católica.

MAJOR ATTRACTIONS. Alcázar. *Open 10–6 in winter; 10–7 in summer.* The *alcázar* rises majestically on the crest of a rock 80 m. (262 ft.) above the meeting of the Eresma and Clamores. Begun in the reign of Alfonso El Sabio in the 13th century, it was considerably enlarged 200 years later when the Trastámaras set up court in Segovia. The Alcázar was largely destroyed by fire in 1862, and what you see today is very much a fanciful restoration of the 1880s, but its imposing fairy-tale silhouette and dramatic position beat any Rhineland castle, and the views from its terraces, chambers, and tower are quite breathtaking. The decoration of the facade, embellished with small pieces of coke, is an architectural peculiarity of Segovia known as *esgrafiado,* and can be seen elsewhere in the city.

The inexpensive entrance ticket includes a useful leaflet with a plan and explanations of each room. Of particular note are the beautiful Mudéjar-style ceilings, the fresco of Isabella's proclamation as queen in the **Sala de Galera,** and the polychrome wooden figures of all the kings of Asturias, León, and Castile, from Don Pelayo (716) to Juana la Loca (1555), in the **Sala de los Reyes.** Beside Queen Isabella's bed a 15th-century tapestry depicts the Conquest of Granada, and in the adjoining **chapel** Philip II married his fourth wife, Anne of Austria. A collection of armor, weapons, and swords, and an early coin-making machine (Segovia once boasted a mint) complete the visit.

Aqueduct. Segovia's monumental Roman aqueduct towers 28 m. (92 ft.) at its highest point over the Plaza del Azoguejo. It is thought to date from the 1st or early 2nd centuries, and was most probably built during the reign of the Emperor Trajan (98–117). Its great granite blocks, hewn from the Guadarrama mountains, hold together without the aid of mortar, and 118 arches span the 728 m. (2,393 ft.) between two rather distant hills. The aqueduct used to bring water into the city from Riofrío, 12 km. (7 mi.) away.

In 1071, during a siege by the Moors, 35 of its arches were destroyed, and it was not until 1483 that Queen Isabella commissioned its restoration. The original statue of Hercules was replaced by one of the Virgin Mary, who now stands demurely, and somewhat incongruously, high in her niche overlooking the Plaza del Azoguejo. On the opposite side the small bronze statue of Romulus and the wolf was presented to Segovia in 1974 by the city of Rome as an acknowledgment of the 2,000 years of existence of the most complete Roman monument in Spain.

Cathedral. *Open 9–7 in summer; Mon. to Fri. 9:30–1 and 3–6, Sat. and Sun. 9:30–6 in winter.* Segovia Cathedral was the last Gothic cathedral to be built in Spain (nearby Avila was the first). It was begun in 1525 by order of Charles V, and designed by the architect of Salamanca Cathedral, Juan Gil de Hontañón. With its golden pinnacles and flying buttresses the cathedral from the outside is one of the loveliest in Spain, but its interior is a sad disappointment, being spoiled by an ugly *coro,* and is generally rather bare, as many of its furnishings were carried off by Napoleon's troops during the Peninsular Wars.

Nevertheless, among the cathedral's works of art are a *Pietà* by Juan de Juni (1571) and a collection of valuable 17th-century Gobelin tapestries in the **chapter house,** under a fine coffered ceiling. In the **Capilla Mayor** stands a neo-Classical marble reredos by Sabatini, and in the **Capilla del Sagrario** a *Christ in Agony* by Churriguera. The museum has paintings by Berruguete, Luis de Morales, and Van Eyck, a reliquary by Cellini, and the first book ever to be printed in Spain (1472). If they are open, don't miss the beautiful 15th-century Isabelline-style cloisters by Juan Guas, a Flemish architect. They were transferred here, stone by stone, between 1524–5 from the old cathedral which stood on the terrace in front of the Alénzar before it was destroyed by the Comuneros.

OTHER ATTRACTIONS. Outside the Walls. Even if you do not visit the monuments below, don't leave Segovia without taking a walk down below the ramparts. There is no better place than the esplanade in front of the Convento de Carmelitas for a magical picture of the *alcázar,* and from the Carretera de los Hoyos, south of the city, the silhouette of the cathedral towering above the ramparts and ancient houses is equally memorable.

Church of Vera Cruz. *Open 10:30–1:30 and 3:30–7; 3:30–6 in winter.* This 12-sided church was built by the Knights Templar in 1208 and was probably modeled on the Church of the Holy Sepulcher in Jerusalem. Its name, "True Cross," comes from the fact that it once housed a sliver of wood from the cross of Christ. Inside, a circular ambulatory surrounds an inner two-story chamber, also 12-sided, in which the knights performed their secret rites. Climb the tower for tremendous views of the city.

Convento de Carmelitas Descalzas. *Open 10–1:30 and 4–7.* San Juan de la Cruz (1542–91), friend of Santa Teresa of Avila, great mystic and lyrical poet, famed for his use of sexual analogy to describe mystical experience, was once prior of this Carmelite monastery. He is buried here in a chapel founded in 1618, and you can see the grandiose marble urn to which his devoted followers removed his remains in 1927 from their previous resting place in a simple tomb beneath the floor. The museum has a collection of his personal belongings, including the original manuscript of his work *Cántico Espiritual*.

Monastery of El Parral, *open Mon. to Sat. 9–1 and 3–6:30; Sun. 9–12.* This Hieronymite monastery was founded in 1459 by Henry IV, and is largely the work of Juan Guas, architect of the cathedral cloisters. The church boasts a splendid five-tiered **altarpiece** by Juan Rodríguez (1528).

Romanesque Churches. These churches, built between the 12th and 13th centuries, are one of the great glories of Segovia. They are characterized by their rounded apses, tall, square bell towers, and porticoed outer galleries which served as meeting places for the city council and medieval trade guilds. Unfortunately, they are only *open during services, and San Esteban and San Justo are now closed permanently.*

San Esteban, *just northwest of the Pza. Mayor,* is one of the latest (largely 13th century) and most beautiful of the Romanesque churches. It is famous for its five-story **tower** surmounted by a spire.

San Juan de los Caballeros, *Pza. Colmenares,* is the oldest, dating from the end of the 11th century. The capitals of its porticoes are beautifully carved with human heads, plants, and animals. The church was bought by the ceramic artist Daniel Zuloaga (1852–1921) around the turn of the century and used as a studio. The Zuloaga Museum, now housed in the church, is temporarily closed for restoration.

San Martín, *in the Pza. San Martín on the Calle Real,* is beautiful from the outside, with an arcaded porch on three sides and finely carved capitals depicting sirens, birds, and human figures, but the interior has been messed around by later baroque additions.

San Millán, *out of the center off Fernández Ladreda,* is one of the oldest and most beautiful of Segovia's churches, built by Alfonso I in 1111–24. It has an 11th-century **Mozarabic tower** and arcades on both its north and south sides, and its sculpted capitals show scenes from the Bible, including the *Adoration of the Magi* and the *Flight into Egypt.*

La Trinidad, *Pza. Dr. Laguna, near San Esteban,* is worth a visit as its interior has been restored to its original Romanesque purity.

EXCURSIONS. La Granja. *The palace is open Tues. to Sat. 10–1:30 and 3–5:30, Sun. 10–2:30; closed Mon.* Buses leave Segovia for San Ildefonso de la Granja, 11 km. (7 mi.) away, every two hours or so, and the ride takes 20 min. The palace, which was built between 1719–39 by the homesick Philip V, first Bourbon king of Spain and grandson of Louis XIV, to remind him of his beloved Versailles, has become one of the showpieces of Spain.

In magnificent country at the foot of the Guadarrama mountains, the palace, with its marble floors and elegant chandeliers crafted in the local glass factory, stands amid statues, fountains, chateaus, retreats, trimmed hedges, and formal gardens—an exquisite bit of France in a Spanish wood. The splendid gardens are open daily until dusk, and you can stroll around them free except on Thurs., Sat., and Sun. afternoons (but check), when the fountains are turned on and the cascades and great water jets transform the palace and grounds into a magical fantasy land.

Riofrío. *The palace, located 8 km. (5 mi.) south of Segovia off the road to San Rafael,* can only be reached by car or tour bus (Mon. only) from Madrid. It was originally a hunting lodge and was purchased by Isabel Farnese, widow of Philip V, who intended to turn it into a neo-Classical palace along the lines of the Royal Palace in Madrid. Her project was never completed and the palace, of minor importance, now houses a Hunting Museum. It is in fact less attractive than its surrounding parkland, a huge cork-oak forest where roaming deer will come right up to your car. The palace is *open 10–1:30 and 3–5:30, Sun. 10–2:30; closed Tues.*

SHOPPING. There is a weekly market on Thursdays in the **Plaza de los Huertos** which sells mostly food produce, but you may find some handicrafts. Ceramics are much in evidence around the Plaza Mayor and the prices here are generally cheaper than in Madrid or Toledo. The main shopping street is the Calle Real with some charming, quaint shops. Typical sweet candies, *dulces, yemas,* and *ponche segoviano,* are on sale in the pastry shops of **Calle Real** and the **Plaza Mayor.** At all costs, steer well clear of the pestering vendors near the aqueduct: Their "handmade wares" are mass-produced, machine-made frauds.

Toledo

Toledo stands on a rocky promontory surrounded on three sides by the Tagus River and presents one of the most dramatic skylines in all of Spain. A former capital and the city of El Greco, Toledo is the very essence of a Castilian city, yet at the same time it blends together the cultures of Arab, Jew, and Christian. A walk through its narrow cobbled alleyways reveals a rich past when mosque, synagogue, and church flourished side by side, and Toledo was one of the greatest centers of learning in the Western world.

Toledo was occupied by the Romans and then by the Visigoths, whose capital it became in 567. From 712 until 1085 it was held by the Moors until its reconquest by El Cid and Alfonso VI, who made Toledo the capital of Christian Spain. Alfonso El Sabio ("the Wise") founded the famous medieval School of Translations here, and for nearly four centuries scholars of all creeds lived in harmony, promoting the learning of all three cultures: Jewish, Muslim, and Christian.

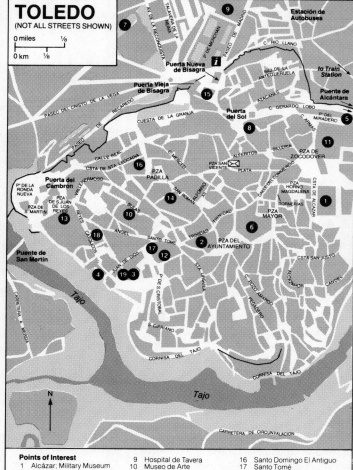

TOLEDO
(NOT ALL STREETS SHOWN)

0 miles	⅛
0 km	⅛

Estación de Autobuses

Puerta Nueva de Bisagra

Puerta Vieja de Bisagra

to Train Station

Puente de Alcántara

Puerta del Sol

PZA DE ZOCODOVER

Puerta del Cambrón

P° DE LA RONDA NUEVA

PZA DE S. MARTIN

Puente de San Martín

PZA PADILLA

PZA MAYOR

PZA DEL AYUNTAMIENTO

Tajo

CARRETERA A MERIDA

CORNISA DEL TAJO

CORNISA DEL TAJO

Tajo

CARRETERA DE CIRCUNVALACION

N

Points of Interest

1 Alcázar; Military Museum
2 Ayuntamiento
3 Casa Museo de El Greco
4 Casa Museo de Vitorio Macho
5 Castillo de San Servando
6 Catedral
7 Circo Romano
8 El Cristo de la Luz

9 Hospital de Tavera
10 Museo de Arte Contemporáneo
11 Museo de Santa Cruz
12 Palacio de Fuensalida; Taller del Moro
13 San Juan de los Reyes
14 San Román (Museo Visigótico)
15 Santiago del Arrabal

16 Santo Domingo El Antiguo
17 Santo Tomé
18 Sinagoga de Santa Maria la Blanca
19 Sinagoga del Tránsito

 Tourist Information
✉ Post Office
— City Walls

But with the Catholic kings came the Inquisition, leading eventually to the expulsion of all Moors and Jews from Spanish soil. After Philip II moved his court and capital to Madrid in 1561 Toledo retained its supremacy only in church matters—its cardinal archbishop is primate of Spain. Today the city lives largely off tourism. For this reason there are few bargains to be found in Toledo, which has become very commercialized. But if you do stay overnight you will find that the city assumes an altogether different character at dusk, when the floodlights are turned on, and it is then that its medieval atmosphere can best be appreciated.

GETTING THERE. By Train. Toledo Station is on Paseo de la Rosa (tel. 925-22-30-99) to the east of town. It is at least a 20-min. walk into town, but buses no. 1, no. 3, and no. 5 all connect the station with the central Pza. Zocodover. The RENFE office in town is on Sillería 7 (tel. 925-22-12-72) and is open 10–2 and 4–7, Sat. 10–1; closed Sun. Trains from Madrid (Atocha) are frequent. From Andalusia, make connections at Aranjuez.

By Bus. The new bus station is to the north of town on La Vega, between the Ctra. de Madrid and the river. Buses run from Madrid's Estación Sur de Autobuses on Calle Canarias, from Ciudad Real, Talavera de la Reina, and from the surrounding towns and villages of La Mancha.

By Car. From Madrid, take N401 south to Toledo. From Avila, N403 runs southeast directly to Toledo.

TOURIST OFFICES. Puerta Nueva de Bisagra (tel. 925-22-08-43). Open Mon. to Fri. 9–2 and 4–6, Sat. 9:30–1:30; closed Sun. The office is on the corner of Paseo de Merchári, at the end of the Ctra. de Madrid. Visit it when you arrive, as it's a long walk back down a steep hill from the center. It has excellent free maps of Toledo. Local guides, many of them English-speaking, operate from here, but they are mostly waiting to pounce on tour buses and will be expensive for private hire.

USEFUL ADDRESSES. Police. Plata 25, opposite the Lino Hotel.
  Post Office. Calle de la Plata 1, on the corner of Pza. San Vicente.
  Telephone Exchange. Plata 18.

GETTING AROUND. No other city in Spain is quite as difficult to negotiate as Toledo with its warren of medieval alleyways, so arm yourself with a good map, and wear sturdy walking shoes for the steep cobbled streets. If you want a taxi for the bus or train stations, or the

Hospital de Tavera outside the walls, you can hail one anywhere, but the main rank is on Plaza Zocodover. Otherwise the best way to find Toledo's monuments is on foot.

Whatever you do, do not miss the magnificent view of the city from the Carretera de Circunvalación to the south of town. If you're not up to a 2-mi. walk and haven't a car, it is well worth paying a cab fare because this is one of the most dramatic views in Spain.

WHERE TO STAY. Good-value hotels are few and far between in Toledo, and the rates are generally rather high, but don't let that put you off spending a night here. Rooms are often full, and you may have to hunt around a bit, especially at Corpus Christi time.

Los Cigarrales (M), Ctra. Circunvalación 32 (tel. 925-22-00-53). 29 rooms. You will need a car to reach this hotel. Make your way over the San Martín bridge and you will find a pleasant country house whose terrace affords marvelous views over Toledo. The hotel has a good restaurant, and all the rooms have bathrooms.

Los Gavilanes II (M), Marqués de Mendigorría 14 (tel. 925-21-16-28). 15 rooms. It's a 15-min. (uphill) walk into town from this clean modern hostel on the Ctra. de Madrid. It is located right opposite the bullring.

☻Maravilla (M), Barrio Rey 7 (tel. 925-22-33-04). 18 rooms. An excellent good-value restaurant is the added attraction of this old-world hotel. It is located right in the center of town, just off the Pza. Zocodover. All rooms have bathrooms.

Imperio (I), Cadenas 7 (tel. 925-22-76-50). 21 rooms. The Imperio is a clean but simple, modern hotel in the Old Town, just down from the Pza. Zocodover. Its rooms are a little bare, but very adequate, and the location is convenient. Rooms all have bathrooms, and breakfast, but not dinner, is served.

Madrid I (I), Marqués de Mendigorría 6. 10 rooms. If you can't find this street on your map it's because it is also called Ctra. de Madrid. This is a clean, modern hotel in the same building as Los Gavilanes II (see above). If it is full you could try the annex, Madrid II (I), just across the street on Covarrubias 4 (tel. 925-22-11-11).

☻Sol (I), Azacanes 15 (tel. 925-21-36-50). 14 rooms. No meals are served in this small, new hotel, but cafés and restaurants are close at hand as it is only a 5 min. walk from the central Pza. Zocodover. The Sol is in a modern building on an old street and has the advantage of its own garage.

WHERE TO EAT. Toledo is bursting with restaurants of all price ranges. The local specialties are partridge (*perdiz*) and quail (*codorniz*), and rabbit *(conejo)* is another popular dish. A common feature of Toledo's restaurants is that few of them seem to include the IVA tax in their menu prices, so be prepared for a further 6% to be added to your bill. If you're looking for very inexpensive eating places which offer basic *menus del día*, then the best place to hunt is in the Barrio Rey leading into the Pza. Magdalena, just off the Pza. Zocodover. There are some more of these *económicos* in Real del Arrabal, down near the Bisagra Gate.

Casa Aurelio (M), Sinagoga 6 (tel. 925-22-20-97). The prices here may be a little high, but this is one of the best-known and longest established restaurants in town. It has typical decor and specializes in local fare such as partridge, quail, and other game dishes.

Los Cuatro Tiempos (M), Sixto Ramón Parro 7 (tel. 925-22-37-82). There is a good *tapas* bar with splendid ceramic decor here on the ground floor, and upstairs a more traditional restaurant in rather somber Toledo style offering typical fare at reasonable prices.

⬤**Maravilla** (M), Barrio Rey 7. The restaurant of this modest hotel is an excellent choice for the cost-conscious traveler as it offers a selection of menus at graded prices. A four-course meal here will only cost around 1,000 ptas. The decor is old-fashioned, and the standards reliable.

⬤**Venta de Cervantes** (M), Circo Romano 15 (tel. 925-21-28-62). If you feel like a walk on a summer evening, why not stroll out to this very pleasant and typically Toledan *venta?* You can dine outdoors in the garden, or inside in the tastefully decorated dining room. Offering a good choice of inexpensive *menus del día*, as well as a slightly more expensive *à la carte* selection, this restaurant is extremely good value for money.

El Aljibe (I), Pza. Padre Mariana 9. A good choice of budget tourist menus is on offer here. The restaurant is located in some ancient vaults in a small square near San Román church and there are some tables outdoors.

⬤**Los Arcos** (I), Cordonerías 11 (tel. 925-21-00-51). Good-value menus and inexpensive main courses has meant that this modern restaurant is fast gaining in popularity. It is located in a street parallel to Calle Comercio and just off Toledo de Ohio.

Casa Paco (I), Pozo Amargo 1. Typical and popular, this ideal budget restaurant is to be found just below the Pza. Ayuntamiento.

El Casino de los Monteros (I), Pza. Magdalena 11 (tel. 925-22-12-56). The surroundings here are quite smart, with some nice art nouveau touches, but the *menus del día* are still really low cost.

El Patio (I), Calle de la Plata 2, opposite the post office on the corner of San Vicente. Though rather touristy with rather high prices, this restaurant is pleasantly typical and has a pretty patio.

MAJOR ATTRACTIONS. Cathedral. *Open 10:30–1 and 3:30–7; 3:30–6 in winter. Entrance to the cathedral is by the Puerta de Mollete, just above the Pza. Ayuntamiento, and tickets for its various sections—chapels, sacristy, treasury, etc.—are on sale in the cloisters to your left.* Toledo Cathedral, one of the great glories of Spain, was begun in 1226 and completed in 1493. It is the second largest cathedral in Spain, after Seville, although its Gothic magnificence is somewhat dwarfed by the surrounding houses which leave little space for an overall view of the remarkable exterior, with its 90-m. (300-ft.) tower, flying buttresses, rose windows, and impressive doors. It stands on the site of both a Visigoth basilica and a Moorish mosque.

Proceeding clockwise from the **Puerta de la Presentación** around the circumference of the interior, the following are some of the most outstanding features:

The **sacristía** is, in effect, the art gallery of the cathedral. Its magnificent collection includes works by El Greco, Bellini, Titian, and Goya.

In the southeast corner the **Sala Capitular** (Chapter House), with a fine ornate doorway and magnificent ceiling, houses a series of pictures of Toledo's archbishops and cardinals.

Just beyond the **Puerta de los Leones,** the *Cristobalón,* a huge mural of St. Christopher painted by Gabriel Rueda in 1638, towers over 9 m. (30 ft.) towards the roof. The **Capilla Mozárabe** in the southwest corner was begun by Cardinal Cisneros in 1504, and on *Sunday mornings (the only time the chapel is open)* mass is still celebrated according to the ancient Mozarabic rite handed down from the days of the Visigoths. The three frescoes by Juan de Borgoña are the only surviving decoration from the days of Cardinal Cisneros.

The outstanding piece in the small **tesoro** is Enrique de Arfe's spectacular 16th-century **monstrance** in which the host is paraded through the town on Corpus Christi. It is made of gold and silver and was supposedly brought back from the New World by Christopher Columbus.

The central **coro** is famous for its carvings, notably its choir stalls which depict the Fall of Granada in 1492. They were carved by Rodrigo Alemán just three years after the great conquest.

The **Capilla Mayor** (sanctuary) is dominated by an enormous carved altarpiece telling the story of the life of Christ (1502–4). It houses the **tombs** of Alfonso VIII and Sancho III (on the left) and

Sancho II and Cardinal Mendoza (on the right). Finally, in the nave behind the **Capilla Mayor,** look up and you will see the 18th-century **Transparente,** a wildly baroque roof opening which seems to give a theatrical glimpse into heaven as the sunlight pours down through a mass of figures and clouds. Created in 1732 by Narciso Tomé and his four sons, it is one of the most important baroque conceits in Europe.

Museo de Santa Cruz, *Calle Cervantes, through the Arco de Sangre off the Pza. Zocodover. Open Tues. to Sat. 10–6:30, Sun. 10–2; closed Mon.* This fine Plateresque charity hospital, built between 1504 and 1544 for Cardinal Mendoza, is worth a visit for the beauty of its early Renaissance architecture alone. But it also houses Toledo's archeological collection, magnificent paintings—including 22 El Grecos and works by his pupil Luis Tristán, Ribera, and Goya—outstanding tapestries, and, among its prize possessions, the standard from Don Juan's flagship at the Battle of Lepanto.

Santo Tomé, *Travesía de Santo Tomé, in the Judería, open 10–1:45 and 3:30–6:45; 3:30–5:45 in winter.* The chapel houses El Greco's greatest masterpiece, *The Burial of the Count of Orgaz.* Domenico Theotocópulos, otherwise known as El Greco (the Greek), was born in Crete in 1541, and came to Spain from Italy, hoping for work on the Escorial. He came to Toledo around 1572 after his painting failed to find favor with Philip II, and settled in the city which for the next 40 years was to feature so prominently in his works.

The various spectators in this great painting are all portraits of El Greco's contemporaries, and rumors abound that Lope de Vega and Cervantes figure amongst the earthly contingent, and Philip II (though not yet dead) among those in heaven. It is certain, however, that the sixth figure from the left, on earth, is a self portrait of the artist, and that the boy in the left-hand corner is El Greco's son. Note how only El Greco and his son stare straight out of the picture directly at the viewer.

Sinagoga Del Tránsito, *corner of Samuel Levi and Reyes Católicos. Open 10–2 and 4–7; 3:30–6 in winter; closed Sun. afternoon and Mon.* The Tránsito was commissioned in 1336 and is one of the two remaining synagogues in Toledo. Though it later became a Christian church after the expulsion of the Jews in 1492, the Mudéjar influence is very apparent in the ornate ceiling and stucco decorations on the walls. The Tránsito also houses the Sephardic Museum which chronicles the life of Toledo's former Jewish community.

OTHER ATTRACTIONS. Alcázar. *Open Apr. through Aug. 9:30–7;*

Sept., Oct., and Mar. 9:30–6; Nov. through Feb. 9:30–6. The Romans, Visigoths, and Moors all built a fortress on this, the highest point in Toledo, and after the Reconquest of 1085 Alfonso VI turned the *alcázar* into a royal residence. The palace-fortress was built in its present form by Charles V, and later Philip II, with Corarrubies and then Herrera as its architects. It has twice been destroyed, first by Napoleon's troops and again in 1936 during the Civil War, since when it has been rebuilt as a faithful reconstruction of Charles' original.

The two-month siege of the *alcázar,* then a military academy, during the opening days of the Civil War turned into one of the biggest propaganda exercises of the Nationalist forces, and the **Military Museum** it now houses is very much a museum of the Fascist cause. Inside you can see the office of Colonel Moscardó, leader of the besieged Nationalist defenders, and plaques in 19 languages record the telephone conversation between the colonel and his son, held for ransom by the Republicans. Moscardó's farewell bidding and his son's subsequent shooting have passed into Spanish legend. The dungeons which served as a shelter for women and children, and a hospital for the wounded, further recall life under the siege.

Casa y Museo del Greco, *Calle de los Alamillos. Open 10–2 and 4–7; 3:30–6 in winter; closed Sun. afternoon* P.M. *and Mon.* This 1910 reconstruction of El Greco's house is a faithful copy of a typical 16th-century house such as the artist might have lived in. The most that can be said is that El Greco lived close by. The house is nevertheless interesting for its period furnishings, and the museum contains yet more of his works.

Hospital de Tavera, *Paseo de Madrid, outside the walls beyond the·tourist office. Open 10:30–1:30 and 3:30–6.* Founded in 1541, this fine Renaissance building is now owned by the duchess of Lerma. Its rooms, furnished in early 17th-century style, house some great works of art, including paintings by Titian, Ribera, and El Greco. The fine **library** and a reconstructed 16th-century **pharmacy** are also open to visitors.

San Juan de los Reyes, *Reyes Católicos, above the Cambrón Gate. Open 10–2 and 3:30–7; 3:30–6 in winter.* Ferdinand and Isabella founded this beautiful Gothic church in 1476 to celebrate their victory over the Portuguese in the Battle of Toro. The architect was Juan Guas (who designed the cloisters of Segovia Cathedral) and the church is a perfect example of the Isabelline style.

Sinagoga de Santa María la Blanca, *Reyes Católicos. Open 10–2 and 3:30–7; 3:30–6 in winter.* Begun in 1180, this was once Toledo's main synagogue. Its unlikely name comes from the fact that it later became a Christian church after it was given to the Knights of Calatrava in 1405. Its history may have been Jewish and Christian, but its architecture is definitely Mudéjar: The interior resembles a mosque, with its five naves divided by white columns supporting Moorish horseshoe arches. The capitals and pedestals are decorated with texts from the Koran.

SHOPPING. The streets around the Santo Tomé Chapel and El Greco's house are a souvenir hunter's paradise. The two principal crafts of the province are pottery from Talavera de la Reina and the traditional Toledo Damascene ware, a legacy of the Moors, which consists of intricate patterns of filigree gold inlaid on blackened steel. Most Damascene ware and Talavera pottery is now simply mass-produced for the tourist market; hand-produced crafts are hard to come by and would be very expensive, so hunt around and compare prices before you buy.

Other specialties are embroidery and needlework, especially the handworked linens from the village of Lagartera—look for places selling *bordados de Lagartera*. Finally, you should not leave Toledo without sampling some of its wonderful marzipan *(mazapán),* candies, and small pastries, a specialty made originally by the nuns of the city. The main shopping street is the **Calle Comercio** leading from the Plaza Zocodover down towards the cathedral.

◆

S P L U R G E S

Lunch or Dinner at the Mesón de Cándido, Segovia, Pza. del Azoguejo 5 (tel. 911-42 81 02). Cándido's *mesón,* located at the foot of the aqueduct, has been going strong for 60 years and is the most famous restaurant in Segovia, if not all Spain. Its rustic dining rooms pulsate with atmosphere and the walls are hung with bullfighting memorabilia and photos of all the dignitaries, from many countries, who have dined here during its long history. Don Cándido, who has traveled the world promoting his cookbooks and spreading the fame of his restaurant far and wide, glories in the title of Master Innkeeper of Castile, an honor authenticated by no less a person than King Juan Carlos himself.

The ambience and wholesome, hearty fare on offer are the very essence of Castile, and no trip to Segovia would really be complete without a visit to this most famous of Segovian inns. The prices are far from outrageous—if you have just come from Madrid you will find they compare very favorably—and the menu ranges from game specialties, partridge or hare, to local river trout with ham, roast lamb or pork, and the most succulent of suckling pigs. It is wise, though not always essential, to book, and if you so choose, there are tables actually overlooking the famous aqueduct.

◆

OLD CASTILE

In the Middle Ages, long before Madrid became the seat of power, it was the inhabitants of the ancient kingdoms of Castile and León who led the conquest against the Moors, and ultimately united and dominated the whole of Spain. Blazing hot in summer and bitterly cold in winter, this often monotonous landscape is dominated by vast wheat fields stretching to the distant horizon: green in spring, endlessly yellow in summer. The land is dotted with castles and fortifications which bear witness to its stormy past. The very name of Castile comes from the hundreds of castles built as fortresses against the Moors, and the language which we, as foreigners, call Spanish is known to Spaniards as *castellano*, or Castilian.

The kingdom of Castile arose in Christian Spain around 957 through a rebellion initiated by Count Fernán González of Burgos. United with León in 1037, Castile went on to absorb the medieval powers of Aragón and Catalonia through the marriage in 1469 of Isabella of Castile with Ferdinand of Aragón. Within 20 years, this joint enterprise succeeded in expelling the Moors from Spain's southern regions. Castile then turned its attention to financing the voyages of discovery which were to lead to Spain's domination of the New World for the next four centuries. Castile was long recognized as the dominant kingdom in Spain. In this century one of the mainstays of General Franco's recipe for power was the supremacy and championing of Castile to the detriment of Spain's other regions. These days, however, with the end of dictatorship and the establishment of regional autonomies throughout the country, Castile's influence is much diminished.

Its land is harsh and its villages for the most part underpopulated, their inhabitants having long ago moved to the three major centers: Burgos, Salamanca, and Valladolid. All three are lavishly endowed with artistic treasures created by the greatest Spanish artists, architects, and sculptors. Burgos and Valladolid both served as capitals of Spain and royal residences, and were generously rewarded by successive Castilian monarchs. Burgos is blessed with one of Spain's greatest cathedrals; Valladolid has Spain's leading display of that uniquely Spanish art form, the polychrome image (highly colored wooden figures), while Salamanca's fame and beauty is centered around its ancient university.

Few regions of Spain can be easier to get around. There are numerous direct and inexpensive trains and plenty of good bus services. Salamanca and Burgos, though both landmarks on any visitor's itinerary, are far less swamped by tourists than Madrid, Barcelona, or the ever-popular cities of Andalusia. Salamanca is probably the most popular Castilian center, due to its academic associations and popularity with foreign students; it also offers the best range of good-value hotels. Burgos and Valladolid are adequately if not overly endowed with affordable accommodations, and rarely present problems in finding a room.

An easy journey from one another, and not too far from Madrid, the capital, all three cities offer an excellent chance to become acquainted with and further appreciate the rich and varied history of Castile, for long the focal point of Spanish civilization.

Burgos

Burgos, city of El Cid and cradle of Castile, straddles the Arlanzón River, halfway between Madrid and the French border. It was founded in 884 by Diego Rodríguez, who erected a castle here on the frontier against the Moors. In 950 Fernán González set himself up as an independent count, declaring Burgos' independence from the kingdom of León; thus was Castile born. The citizens of Burgos pride themselves on speaking the purest Castilian and revel in their city's associations with that greatest Castilian hero, Rodrigo Díaz—known as El Cid Campeador (Lord Champion)—who was born in the nearby village of Vivar. Burgos was for long a favored royal residence and capital of Castile. It joined the War of the Comuneros against Charles V, and was held by the French (who wrought much destruction) during the Peninsular War. Franco set up his headquarters in Burgos during the Civil War, formed his first Nationalist government here, and from here, too, on April 1, 1939 declared the ceasefire that ended the conflict. Throughout his dictatorship, the name of Burgos was synonymous with the precepts of Francoism: the military, the church, and deep conservatism.

Today, many of the city's 156,000 inhabitants are engaged in industrial projects that have created dreary suburbs, but the Gothic character of the inner core has been well preserved. Characterized by its light gray stone and red-roofed houses, the monumental district on the north bank is dominated by the magnificent Gothic cathedral. The exquisite carvings adorning the facades and interiors of Burgos' many churches and monasteries are largely the work of two famous families of sculptors, the Siloés and the Colonias, whose genius and mastery of the Isabelline Gothic style supplies the icing on the cake of this eminently visitable city.

GETTING THERE. By Train.

There are frequent trains from Madrid Chamartín, a journey of three to four hours; the most direct route goes via Aranda de Duero, a slightly longer route is via Avila and Valladolid. Burgos lies on the line between the French border at Irún and both Madrid and Portugal; there are good direct connections with intermediate stations such as San Sebastián, Vitoria, Valladolid, and Salamanca. There are also through trains to Burgos from Bilbao, Santander, La Coruña, Santiago, León, Palencia, Oviedo, Logroño, Pamplona, Zaragoza, Lérida, and Barcelona.

Burgos Station is at the end of Avda. Conde de Guadalhorce (tel. 947-20-35-60) in the south of the city across the river from the center. The central RENFE office is at La Moneda 21 (tel. 947-20-91-31).

By Bus. The central bus station is at Miranda 4 (tel. 947-20-55-75), across the river just off Pza. de Vega. There are regular connections with Madrid, Barcelona, Soria, Logroño, San Sebastián, Bilbao, Santander, León, Valladolid, and Palencia.

By Car. Coming from the French frontier at Irún and San Sebastián, Burgos lies at the point where the main highway forks; N1 continues south for 240 km. (150 mi.) to Madrid, and the N620 heads southwest towards Portugal via Valladolid for 121 km. (75 mi.) and

Salamanca for 234 km. (146 mi.). North from Burgos, N623 heads through the Cantabrian mountains to Santander on the coast, and, due east, N120 leads to Logroño where it joins the Bilbao–Zaragoza–Barcelona tollway, A68.

TOURIST OFFICES. Pza. Alonso Martinez 7 (tel. 947-20-31-25).

WHERE TO STAY. Asubio (M), Carmen 6 (tel. 947-20-34-45). 30 rooms. A clean, comfortable, 3-star hostel in a somewhat faceless modern apartment building on the south side of the river, serving breakfast (quite expensive) only.

    España (M), Paseo del Espolón 32 (tel. 947-20-63-40). 69 rooms. This friendly, if slightly faded, hotel is pleasantly set on the central promenade alongside the river, surrounded by sidewalk cafés in summer.

    Norte y Londres (M), Pza. Alonso Martínez 10 (tel. 947-26-41-25). 55 rooms. Close to the tourist office and oozing old-world charm and decor, the cheery Norte y Londres lies close to major sights and the inexpensive *mesones* area.

    Avila (I), Almirante Bonifaz 13 (tel. 947-20-55-43). 57 rooms. This simple, squeaky-clean, family-run hostel provides ideal accommodations for those seeking good value for money. Centrally located.

WHERE TO EAT. For tasty bargain meals, canvass the area around the Pza. Alonso Martínez and along Fernán González, where there are several good-value *mesones*. You may also fare well snacking on *tapas* in the numerous *mesones*, especially around Huerta del Rey, a popular evening gathering spot.

    Arriaga (M), Laín Calvo 4 (tel. 947-20-20-21). Dining at this charming, old-fashioned restaurant has long been a tradition with food-conscious locals. Both food and service are good, and you will enjoy its aura of a bygone era.

    Gaona (M), Paloma 41 (tel. 947-20-61-91). Excellent fish and seafood specialties and a colorful *mesón*-type atmosphere are what you'll find in this long-established restaurant close to the cathedral.

    Papamoscas (M), Llana de Afuera (tel. 947-20-45-65). Named after the famous "flycatcher" clock in the cathedral, the Papamoscas is a typically atmospheric *mesón* and bar with a good upstairs dining room. In summer the tables outdoors in the square provide a magnificent view of the cathedral's sculptured east facade.

    Mesón Astorga (I), Avellanos 8. Numerous hams and strings of garlic hanging from the ceiling set a colorful tone at this relaxed *mesón*, which also has a very inexpensive restaurant. If it's too crowded, try **La Riojana** (I), next door at no. 10.

Villaluenga (I), Laín Calvo 20 (tel. 947-20-61-54). This very simple, friendly, family-run *económico* is extremely popular, and great value for a quick, informal lunch or supper at rock-bottom prices.

MAJOR ATTRACTIONS. Cathedral. *Open 9–1:30, 4–6:30. Tickets required for the choir and cloisters.* Burgos Cathedral, one of the great Gothic treasures of Spain, and its third largest cathedral after those of Seville and Toledo, was begun by Fernando El Santo III in 1221. A masterpiece of Flamboyant Gothic, its twin spires tower against the sky, and its imposing yet exquisitely delicate silhouette dominates the historic core of Burgos. Before entering the cathedral, take a few minutes to admire the building's beautiful spires and innumerable pinnacles, the flying buttresses, and the superb ornamentation of the three main doors.

The interior is no less imposing. The **Escalera Dorada** (1523), a diamond-shaped flight of steps with heavy gilt balustrades leading up to the **Puerta de la Coronerá** (end of north transept), is a masterpiece of the great 16th-century sculptor, Diego de Siloé. In the transept crossing, a simple stone marks the tomb of El Cid and his wife Doña Jimena, whose mortal remains were interred here in 1921. The original, and much more lavish, tombs can still be seen at the **Monasterio de San Pedro de Cardeña,** 10 km. (7 mi.) from Burgos. Here the remains of El Cid and his wife rested for over 700 years, before being stolen by the French during the Napoleonic Wars. The magnificent **choir stalls** of the enclosed *coro* were carved between 1507–12 by Felipe Bigarny, and the **tomb,** topped by a copper effigy, belongs to Bishop Mauricio, one of the cathedral's founders. Of the many lovely chapels, the octagonal **Capilla del Condestable** (east end behind the high altar) is the most outstanding, designed by Simón de Colonia in 1482 to house the tombs of Pedro Hernández de Velasco, high constable of Castile, and his wife Doña Mencía. Two of the cathedral's more intriguing features are the bizarre image of Christ covered with a buffalo hide to resemble human skin in the **Capilla del Santo Cristo,** and the famous **Papamoscas** (fly-catcher) clock just inside the west door. It has a face with a gaping mouth to strike each hour.

Cartuja de Miraflores, *3 km. (2 mi.) out in the eastern suburbs. In summer, buses from El Cid's statue to San Pedro de Cardeña pass close by. Open Mon. to Sat. 10:15–3 and 4–6, Sun. 11:15–12:30,*

1–3, and 4–7. This Carthusian monastery, founded by King Juan II in 1441, is still inhabited by the silent monks. *Only the church,* built by Simón de Colonia in the late 15th century, *is open to visitors.* Juan II is buried here alongside his second wife, Isabel of Portugal. Their beautiful alabaster **tombs** were carved by Gil de Siloé—one of the greatest itinerant artists of the late Middle Ages—by order of Juan's daughter, Queen Isabella la Católica. Isabella's brother, the Infante Don Alfonso who died in 1468 when only 16, is also buried here. The elaborate wooden **retable** with its biblical scenes in unusual circular panels is another work by Gil de Siloé, and is said to be gilded with some of the first gold brought back from the New World by Columbus.

Monasterio de las Huelgas, *about half a mile southwest of the city. Reached by bus no. 5 from El Cid. Open Tues. to Fri. 11–2 and 4–6, Sat. and Sun. 11–2; closed Mon.* Las Huelgas began life as a summer villa of the kings of Castile, but in 1187 was converted into a convent for noble ladies by Alfonso VIII. The Gothic church is flanked by Romanesque **cloisters** and Mudéjar **chapels.** Fernando el Santo instituted the ordination of the Knights of the Order of Santiago here, and the church once served as the pantheon of Castilian kings and queens. Most of its tombs were destroyed by Napoleon's armies in 1809, however. The **Sala Capitular** houses a unique, if tattered, collection of ancient medieval fabrics, costumes, and flags. A highlight is the banner captured from the Moors in the Battle of Las Navas de Tolosa in 1212. It was in this chamber in 1936 that General Franco proclaimed his first revolutionary National government, and here, too, that the Falange swore allegiance to the new regime.

OTHER ATTRACTIONS. Arco de Santa María, *overlooking the river on Avda. Gen. Franco.* This is the city's most famous gateway, through which El Cid departed for exile. The present gate was built in the 14th century, though the facade facing the river was added 200 years later. The statues, starting from the top, are of the Virgin and Child, the guardian angel of Spain, Charles V, with Fernán González, count of Castile, on his right, and El Cid on his left. Below them, Diego Rodríguez, the city's founder, is flanked by Laín Calvos and Nuño Rasuro, both 10th-century magistrates.

Casa del Cordón, *Pza. Calvo Sotelo.* The House of Ropes, a lovely example of 15th-century civil architecture, takes its name from the Franciscan girdle *(cordón)* which frames the doorway. It was built in 1485 by Pedro Hernández de Velasco, constable of Castile, for his wife Doña Mencía de Mendoza (whose tombs are in the cathedral's Condestable Chapel). Here the Catholic kings received Columbus in

1497 on his return from his second visit to the New World, and here, too, their son-in-law, Philip the Fair, husband of Juana la Loca, died of a sudden chill after a game of *pelota*.

Museo Marceliano de Santa María, *Pza. de San Juan. Open in summer 10–2; in winter 11–2 and 5–8; closed Sun. evening and Mon.* This charming art gallery occupies the cloisters of the ruined San Juan Monastery. On exhibition are over 150 paintings by the Burgos artist Marceliano de Santa María (1866–1952), whose style was much influenced by the painters Sorolla and Zuloaga.

San Nicolás. This beautiful small church just off the Pza. Santa María has an outstandingly lovely stone altarpiece with over 450 figures carved by Simón de Colonia and Gil de Siloé towards the end of the 15th century. Other fine Gothic churches include **San Estebran, San Gil, San Lesmes,** and **Santa Agueda.**

SHOPPING. The main shopping area lies in and around **Plaza Mayor José Antonio** and the streets leading north towards **Calle San Juan.** Antique shops are dotted along **Laín Calvo, Paloma, the Plaza Mayor,** and the **Plaza Santa María** in front of the cathedral. Religious carvings and statues are found in abundance around the Plaza Mayor and cathedral area.

Salamanca

Should you approach Salamanca from Madrid or Cáceres, your first glimpse of this ancient city will be unforgettable. In front of you flows the Tormes River, spanned by an impressive Roman bridge, while beyond rise the old houses of the city, topped by the golden walls, turrets, and domes of the cathedral. Salamanca's history goes back to the time of Hannibal, but it suffered almost total destruction in the ebb and flow of the centuries-long struggle to eject the Moors. Its truly great days began when Alfonso IX of León founded the university in the early years of the 13th century, which became one of the greatest centers of medieval learning in Europe. Through its halls have passed some of Spain's greatest scholars: Antonio Nebrija, compiler of the first Spanish grammar in 1492; the great Golden Age poets, Fray Luis de León and his pupil San Juan de la Cruz; and, in this century, the respected Basque philosopher, Miguel de Unamuno. Though Barcelona and Madrid Universities are today far more prestigious institutes of learning, the university is still the *raison d'etre* of this small city, and it endows Salamanca with a unique student atmosphere year round.

Along with the country's oldest university, Salamanca also houses

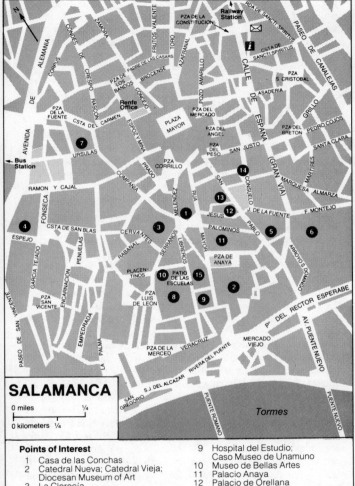

SALAMANCA

0 miles ¼

0 kilometers ¼

Points of Interest

1 Casa de las Conchas
2 Catedral Nueva; Catedral Vieja; Diocesan Museum of Art
3 La Clerecía
4 Colegio del Arzobispo Fonseca
5 Convento de las Dueñas
6 Convento de San Esteban
7 Convento de las Ursulas
8 Escuelas Menores

9 Hospital del Estudio; Caso Museo de Unamuno
10 Museo de Bellas Artes
11 Palacio Anaya
12 Palacio de Orellana
13 Palacio de la Salina
14 Torre de Clavero
15 University
ℹ️ Tourist Information
✉️ Post Office

two cathedrals and the most beautiful Plaza Mayor in Spain. The city's network of narrow streets and small squares, and its multitude of churches and convents, together form a treasure trove of architectural styles, from Romanesque to Gothic, Plateresque—an ornate ornamental style sometimes incorporating Moorish motifs—to baroque. Few other baroque monuments can equal the beauty and harmony of Salamanca's Plaza Mayor, the surprisingly restrained architectural masterpiece of the prolific Churriguera family known for their overly ornate altarpieces. And there can be no better introduction to the intricacies of Spanish Plateresque than Salamanca's exquisite facades, delicately chiseled from the soft golden sandstone that is the hallmark of this attractive university city.

GETTING THERE. By Train. From Madrid there are three trains a day from the Estación del Norte via Avila; journey time is about four hours from Madrid, and two hours from Avila. Salamanca also lies on the Paris–Lisbon and Paris–Oporto lines; there are direct connections on this route from Irún, San Sebastián, Burgos, and Valladolid. From Burgos to Salamanca it takes approximately three and a half hours; and from Valladolid about two hours. Salamanca can also be reached directly from Bilbao via Valladolid. From other destinations in northern Spain, including Galicia, connections can be made at Medina del Campo.

Salamanca Station lies at the far end of Paseo de la Estación (tel. 923-22-57-42) in the northeast of town. The central RENFE office is on Pza. de la Libertad 11 (tel. 923-21-24-54), just north of the Pza. Mayor.

By Bus. Most bus companies use the modern bus station on Filiberto Villalobos 73 (tel. 923-23-67- 7), which can be reached by bus from the Pza. Mercado. *Auto Res* runs a fairly frequent service from Madrid, and other companies serve Avila, Valladolid, León, Zamora, Ciudad Rodrigo, Cáceres, Mérida, and Seville.

By Car. From Madrid, head for Avila, then take N501 to Salamanca, a total distance of 210 km. (130 mi.) N620 connects Burgos, Valladolid, Salamanca, and Ciudad Rodrigo, and forms the main highway across northern Spain and into Portugal. On a north-south route, Salamanca lies just north of the midpoint on N630 (Oviedo–Seville) by way of León, Zamora, Plasencia, Cáceres, and Mérida.

TOURIST OFFICES. Gran Via (Calle de España) 39–41 (tel. 923-24-37-30). The Municipal Tourist Office functions from a booth on the east side of the Pza. Mayor.

WHERE TO STAY. Pasaje (M), Espoz y Mina 23 (tel. 923-21-20-03). 62 rooms. Its central location is the chief virtue of this 2-star hotel, which is connected to the west side of the Pza. Mayor via a passageway. Lunch and dinner are served, and several good restaurants are nearby.

Ceylan (I), San Teodoro 7 (tel. 923-21-26-03). 32 rooms. This elderly but renovated hotel provides good low-cost accommodations in a central location close to the market and Pza. Mayor. Dinner is available.

Clavero (I), Consuelo 21 (tel. 923-21-81-08). 26 rooms. Excellent value-for-money accommodations and meals are offered at this simple but friendly hotel, well renovated in the early '80s.

Emperatriz (I), Compañía 44 (tel. 923-21-92-00). 37 rooms. The old-world Emperatriz abounds with atmosphere and charm, in a historic building to the west of the Pza. Mayor near La Clerecía and the university area. It serves meals.

Milán (I), Pza. del Angel 5 (tel. 923-21-77-79). 25 rooms. Adjacent to the Ceylan (above), this old hotel overlooking the market offers rooms and meals at very reasonable prices.

Las Torres (I), Pza. Mayor 26 (tel. 923-21-21-00). 33 rooms, most with bathrooms. A very simple hotel in one of the old houses around the Pza. Mayor; some rooms overlook the magnificent square. Dinner is served.

WHERE TO EAT. Several of Salamanca's restaurants close for a month in summer, often July or August. There is no shortage of cheap places to eat in the student area, especially along Calle Meléndez and around the Pza. del Mercado and Pozo Amarillo.

El Candil (M), Ruiz Aguilera 10 (tel. 923-21-72-39). The two Candil restaurants have good long-standing reputations in Salamanca. This one has a colorful *tapas* bar, on a lively street dedicated to good eating.

El Mesón (M), Pza. Poeta Iglesias 10 (tel. 923-21-72-22). Traditional Castilian dishes are the specialty of this cozy *mesón* beside the Gran Hotel.

Río Plata (M), Pza. del Peso 1 (tel. 923-21-90-05). Closed Mon. and July. Another restaurant near the Gran Hotel, the Río Plata serves superb food in an intimate setting: a real find.

El Bardo (I), Compañía 8 (tel. 923-21-90-89). This very affordable restaurant near La Clerecía offers a good-value *menu del día*. It's always packed to the gills with students and teachers.

King Long (I), Pza. Libertad 7 (tel. 923-21-34-56). A simple but extremely successful Chinese restaurant providing a pleasant change from Spanish fare, and at very reasonable prices, too.

Roma (I), Ruiz Aguilera 8 (tel. 923-21-72-67). Locals and visitors alike have long known about this old-fashioned Salamancan haunt. The decor is nothing special, but service is friendly and the menu supplies a wide choice of dishes at unbelievably affordable prices.

MAJOR ATTRACTIONS. Cathedrals—Old and New. *Open 10–1 and 3:30–6 in summer; 9:30–1:15 and 3:30–5:45 in winter.* Salamanca boasts not one, but two, cathedrals standing side by side. From the outside the Gothic pinnacles and Renaissance domes of the **New Cathedral** dominate the skyline, but behind its impressive late Gothic exterior lies a rather barren early Renaissance interior. Begun in 1513 and finished in 1733, the New Cathedral is, outside at least, one of Spain's last great Gothic edifices. Inside, the oldest **chapels** are the first two on the left, both by Gil de Hontañón, and the three on the right by Juan de Alava. Of these, the **Capilla Dorada,** with its lavish sculptures, is the most outstanding. The **choir stall** is by Alberto Churriguera, and the **Capilla del Sagrario** near the main altar contains the statue of Cristo de las Batallas, believed to have been carried into battle by El Cid.

Dating from the early 12th century, the **Old Cathedral** far outshines its younger sister. The great Romanesque **shrine** is dominated by Nicolás Florentino's beautiful **altarpiece,** whose 53 painted wooden panels depict the lives of Christ and the Virgin Mary. In the center of this stunning reredos sits the *Virgen de la Vega,* patroness of Salamanca, a 13th-century copper statue adorned with Limoges enamel. Overhead the blessed and damned are dispatched to their respective fates in Florentino's vivid *Last Judgment.* Note the rich carvings on the capitals of the five naves, and the frescoes dated 1232 in the **Capilla de San Martín,** at the back of the cathedral beneath the tower.

The Romanesque cloisters house the **Diocesan Museum of Art.** Of the many notable works of art, the paneled ceiling and superb **triptych** by Salamanca's most famous painter, Fernando Gallego (1466–1507), are worthy of special attention. So, too, are Juan de Flandes' triptych of *St. Michael* and the painted 16th-century Salinas organ named for the blind musician who once played it. The **Capilla de Santa Catalina** now holds the famous cock (*gallo*), a weathervane which once adorned the Torre de Gallo (Cock Tower), the lantern-shaped dome of the Old Cathedral decorated with pinnacles and fish-scale tiles.

Plaza Mayor. The pride and joy of Salamanca is its magnificent 18th-century Plaza Mayor, whose three-tiered, golden-stone houses were designed by Alberto Churriguera, one of the great masters of Spanish baroque. The landmark square was completed by Andrés García de Quiñones, who designed the Ayuntamiento in the center of the square's northern flank, surmounted by its easily recognizable bells and clock. The medallions on the pillars between the arches serve as a portrait gallery of Spain's great and famous—El Cid, Cervantes, even Franco, are all depicted. Those on the front of the Ayuntamiento are still blank, awaiting future bigwigs. As with Madrid's 17th-century Plaza Mayor, the trapezium-shaped square was used for bullfights up till the middle of the last century, but today the plaza is given over to open-air cafés, and traffic has been banned since the early 1970s.

University. *Entrance on Patio de las Escuelas, off Calle Libreros. Open Mon. to Fri. 9–1:30 and 4–6, Sat. 9:30–1:30, Sun. 11–1.* Founded by Alfonso IX of León in 1218, this is Spain's oldest university. In its heyday in the late Middle Ages, over 10,000 students were enrolled in its colleges, and it ranked as one of the great European centers of learning. Begin your visit in the **Patio de las Escuelas,** where a statue of Fray Luis de León, eminent 16th-century scholar and poet, faces the magnificent carved **portal** of the main university. A wonderful example of early Plateresque, the doorway was sculpted by unknown craftsmen but gold- and silversmiths are thought to have outnumbered the stonecutters. In its center, a medallion of Ferdinand and Isabella sits beneath the coat of arms of Charles V, assorted popes and cardinals, and even Hercules and Venus, the whole surrounded by a profusion of heraldic emblems and floral motifs. A frog on a skull sits passively among all the ornamentation, said to bring good luck to students in their examinations.

Inside, the two levels of Gothic cloisters are connected by a splendid Renaissance stairway. On the lower level, the **University Chapel** contains the ashes of Fray Luis de León, while the friar's lecture room, the **Aula de Fray Luis,** remains much as it was in the great man's day. The wooden benches are intact, as is the lectern from which after five years of imprisonment by the Inquisition, the scholar spoke the legendary words: "As I was saying yesterday . . ."

On the upper level is the **library,** containing over 50,000 parchment and leather-bound volumes.

OTHER ATTRACTIONS. Casa de las Conchas, *Rua Antigua opposite La Clerecía.* An outstanding example of civil architecture in the time of the Catholic kings, the house was built in 1483 for Dr. Talavera

Maldonada, a knight of the Order of Santiago. Its **facade** is decorated with 400 scallop shells, the symbol of pilgrims to the shrine of St. James at Santiago de Compostela. The elaborate window grilles and the beautiful double-galleried patio are fine examples of Isabelline style.

La Clerecía, *corner of Serranos and Compaña.* This splendid baroque church was begun in 1617 during the reign of Philip III, and now belongs to the Jesuit order; its patio forms part of the Pontifical University. Inside are some notable works of art, including Luis Salvador Carmona's figure of *Christ Flagellated.*

Convento de las Duenas, *Pza. Concilio de Trento. Open 10–1 and 4–7 in summer; 10:30–1 and 4–5:30 in winter.* Originally a noble residence, this Mudéjar palace was given to Dominican nuns in the early 15th century. Its unusual five-sided **cloisters**—adorned with Dante-like medallions and grotesque capitals on the upper gallery— form one of the city's most striking patios.

Convento de San Esteban, *Pza. Concilio de Trento. Open 9–1 and 4–7.* Juan de Alva built the Dominican Monastery of St. Stephen in the 16th century, its magnificent ornate **facade** a remarkable example of pure Plateresque. The **high altar** is the work of José de Churriguera, with sculptures by Carmona and a painting by Claudio Coello. The 16th-century **Cloister of the Kings** is by Sardiña.

Museo de Bellas Artes, *Patio de las Escuelas. Open Tues. to Sat. 10–2 and 4–7, Sun. 10–2; closed Mon.* This fine Isabelline-style house was once the home of Dr. Alvarez Abarca, physician to Queen Isabella. It now houses Salamanca's Museum of Fine Arts, which includes a good art collection, polychrome statues, stone carvings, and archeological finds.

SHOPPING. Salamanca's main shopping streets are **Azafranal** and **Toro,** leading north out of the Pza. Mayor. Good buys are the moderately priced silver-and-black *charro* jewelry, a local handicraft which is a specialty of this region. *Charro* is characterized by a silver-and-black flowerhead, with petals picked out in silver against a black (charred silver) background. Most of the shops around the **Plaza Mayor** sell *charro,* or try the **Calle Tostado,** just below the Palacio de Anaya, in a small store and craft room where you can order them to your own design.

Valladolid

Valladolid was founded in 1084 during the reign of Alfonso VI. Count Pedro Ansúrez, its founder and the city's first governor and benefactor, bestowed upon it the Arabic name of *Belad Walid*, meaning "the town of the governor." Valladolid first served as Spain's capital in 1282, and again during the reigns of Philip II and Philip III. The court often resided here and the city saw the coronation of Fernando El Santo, as well as the marriages of both Pedro the Cruel and, in 1469, Ferdinand and Isabella, the Catholic kings. It was the birthplace of Henry IV of Castile and of Philip II, who was born in Los Pimenteles across from the Church of San Pablo (where he was baptized). Philip IV and his sister, Anne of Austria, mother of Louis XIV of France, were also born here. Cervantes lived and wrote for some years in Valladolid—his house is now a museum—and in 1506 Christopher Columbus died here in poverty and disillusionment. Napoleon set up headquarters in Valladolid in 1809, and reviewed his troops on the Campo Grande.

Despite its role in history, Valladolid is a fairly unattractive place. If this is your first visit to Spain, and time is short, you could well pass it up. But for those already acquainted with the major tourist centers of Castile, Valladolid does reward a day or two's exploration. Dotted around this rather dilapidated city are a number of old churches, museums, and palaces which bear witness to the greatness of Valladolid's past. Lovers of the art of polychrome carving will be well rewarded by a visit to the National Museum of Sculpture, and the Museum of Oriental Art promises a treat for enthusiasts of Chinese art and antiquities.

Valladolid is the industrial giant of Old Castile; engineering, car manufacturing, and food production are chief employers. The population has risen fast to 325,000, though the city's expansion has been achieved with little thought to aesthetics or conservation. The historic center is a mix of decaying old houses and ugly modern buildings, many of them faceless and anemic. Hidden among the sadly neglected ancient arcades you will come across some genuine treasures, however. Further factors in its favor are that its citizens are friendly, you can eat well, and above all, rest assured you will not be swamped by the excesses of mass tourism.

GETTING THERE. By Air. Villanubla Airport (tel. 983-56 -01-62) is 13 km. (8 mi.) to the northwest of the city on N601 to León. It has one flight daily, Mon. to Fri., to and from Barcelona. The *Iberia* office in town is at Gamazo 17 (tel. 983-30-06-66).

By Train. There are over a dozen trains a day from Madrid Chamartín via Avila, and several good connections from Palencia, León, Oviedo, Santander, and Burgos. Trains also call at Valladolid twice daily from Madrid Norte en route to León and El Ferrol in Galicia. It also lies on the main line from Paris to Portugal, which calls at Irún, San Sebastián, Burgos, Valladolid, and Salamanca.

Valladolid Station is in the south of town at the far end of the Paseo del Campo Grande (tel. 983-30 35 18). The central RENFE office is at Atrio de Santiago 3.

By Bus. The central bus station at Puente Colgante 2 (not far from the train station) has regular services to Madrid, Barcelona, Bilbao, San Sebastián, Burgos, Palencia, León, Salamanca, Zamora, Toro, Tordesillas, Segovia, and Seville.

By Car. Halfway between Madrid and León, Valladolid is best reached from the capital by way of NV1/A6 to Adanero, then by N403, a distance of 191 km. (120 mi.) It also lies midway on N620 between Burgos and Salamanca, and there are easy main road connections from Zamora and Palencia.

TOURIST OFFICES. The Valladolid Tourist Office is on Pza. de Zorrilla 3 (tel. 983-35-18-01) on the far side of Campo Grande Park from the train station.

WHERE TO STAY. Imperial (M), Peso 4 (tel. 983-33-03-00). 80 rooms. An old-style hotel in an ideal central location just off the Pza. Major. It offers full dining-room service, and rooms are both functional and comfortable.

Roma (M), Héroes del Alcázar de Toledo 8 (tel. 983-35-46-66). 38 rooms. Another older hotel with full dining facilities, the Roma lies in a good central location just off the main shopping street, the Calle Santiago. It's close to the Pza. Mayor; parking can be difficult.

Campo Grande (I), Acera Recoletos 12 (tel. 983-30-15-60). 7 rooms, a few with bathrooms. This small, family-run hostel is spanking clean, on the first floor of a house overlooking the Campo Grande Park. It's just a short walk from the train station.

Colón (I), Acera Recoletos 22 (tel. 983-30-40-44). 20 rooms, 8 with bathrooms. An ideal economical hostel close to the station, overlooking the Pza. de Colón and the Campo Grande Park. Clean, comfortable, and cheery.

WHERE TO EAT. Valladolid has many restaurants specializing in both traditional Castilian roasts and excellent seafood. Two of the busiest restaurant areas are the Calle Marina Escobar and the Calle-Correos at the back of the Pza. Mayor. The latter is packed with *económicos,* a budgeteer's culinary paradise.

Machaquito (M), Calixto Fernández de la Torre 5 (tel. 98335-13-51). Sandwiched between the Pza. Mayor and the Calle María de Molina, the Machaquito has an unpretentious setting but has long been popular with locals for serving top-quality dishes at reasonable prices.

Mesón de Cervantes (M), Rastro 6 (tel. 983-30-61-38). Closed Mon. and Nov. Prices can run a bit high at this excellent Castilian restaurant close to Cervantes' house. One of its specialties is river crabs, and the menu includes all kinds of unusual dishes as well as more traditional fare.

Mesón Combarros (I), Correos 3. This is far and away the most popular of the low-priced restaurants on this street. There is a small downstairs dining room and another tiny room upstairs with pleasant ceramic tile decor. It is *always* crowded, so go early or ask the head-waiter to hold a table for you.

Santy (I), Manzana 4 (tel. 983-35-00-31). The menu might be limited at this small tavern beside the City Hall, but Santy's fare is the best of good home cooking and the prices are right. Just off the Pza. Mayor.

Zamora (I), òn the corner of Correos and José Antonio (tel. 983-33-00-71). A simple restaurant with good old-fashioned service. It's less crowded and easier to negotiate than many others on this bustling street, too.

MAJOR ATTRACTIONS. Colegio de San Gregorio, *Calle San Pablo. Open Tues. to Sat. 9–2 and 4:30–7, Sun. 10–2; closed Mon.* This beautiful Plateresque building was built between 1488–96 for Bishop Alonso de Burgos, confessor of Ferdinand and Isabella; his coat of arms appears in the center of the splendid **facade.** Inside is a **patio** of exquisite design, its lower spiralling pillars supporting a lavishly carved **upper gallery.** Today, the building houses the **Museo Nacional de Escultura** (National Museum of Polychrome Sculpture), and on view within its numerous galleries are the finest carved wooden figures from all Castile. The sculptors carved the figures from wood—usually pine, oak, or cedar—which was then polished, and the polychrome applied by painters who specialized in this art form. The process was highly technical and the results have never been equaled elsewhere. Of the many priceless carvings, statues, and fragments on display, look especially for Alfonso de Berruguete's magnificent **altarpiece** (1526–32) from the Church of San Benito, mounted on blue velvet-clad walls in Rooms 1–111; Diego de Siloé's elaborately carved **pews** in Room XI; Juan de Juni's *Entierro de Cristo* (1541–44) in Room XV; and Gregorio Fernández's *Cristo Yacente* in Room IV. In Room XXVIII note the *Head of St. Paul* (San Pablo) by Villabrille y Ron; hold a mirror to the mouth to see the details of the finely carved tongue and teeth.

Museo de Arte Oriental, *Paseo Filipinos 7, overlooking Campo Grande Park. Open Mon. to Sat. 4–7, Sun. 10–2.* This museum, containing the country's best collection of Oriental art, is housed in the 18th-century College of the Augustinian Fathers, designed by the neo-Classical architect Ventura Rodríguez. The splendid Chinese collection includes porcelain figurines dating from the 7th century B.C. to the 18th century; some 1,300 coins from 2,500 years of Chinese history; ornaments of jade, marble, and mother-of-pearl; lacquer work; precious silks; exquisite hand-embroidered dragon costumes from the Imperial Court of 18th-century Peking; and over six centuries worth of Chinese paintings and calligraphy. The Philippine section has a collection of religious paintings and imagery from the Spanish colonial years of the 17th and 18th centuries, plus popular Filipino folk art from the last century.

OTHER ATTRACTIONS. Casa de Cervantes, *Rastro 7. Open Tues. to Sat. 10–6, Sun. 10–2; closed Mon.* Cervantes spent some of the last years of his life here, and you can visit the **study** where he wrote two of his novels. One of his manuscripts is displayed there, alongside contemporary maps, tapestries, furniture, and a painting of the *Battle of Lepanto*.

Casa de Colón, *Calle Colón. Open Mon. to Sat. 11–2 and 4–7, Sun. 11–1.* History buffs will enjoy this delightful small museum, built on the site of the house in which Columbus died in 1506. The original house was demolished in 1965; a stone in the garden marks the site of the explorer's deathbed. The museum chronicles Columbus' journeys to the New World, the conquest of America, and the history of Latin American nations from the Spanish conquest to independence.

Cathedral. *Open Mon. to Sat. 10–2 and 5–8, Sun. and fiestas 9:30–2.* This sombre Renaissance cathedral was begun by Juan de Herrera, architect of the Escorial. Construction was continued in the 18th century by Churriguera, in his own special style of baroque, but the Cathedral remains unfinished. The **reredos** behind the high altar, carved by Juan de Juni in 1572 for the Church of Santa María la

Antigua, is notable, and the adjacent Diocesan Museum contains an enormous **silver monstrance** by Juan de Arfe.

San Pablo, *Calle San Pablo, beside the Museum of Sculpture.* Originally a Dominican monastery, the Church of St. Paul was built in the 15th century. The **lower facade** by Simón de Colonia is pure Isabelline Gothic, while the **upper facade** is a frothy profusion of ornate Plateresque. Inside, the lack of furniture is more than compensated for by the ornate doors of the north and south transepts, and the beautiful gold-and-blue roof beams, studded with fascinating bosses.

SHOPPING. The **Calle Santiago,** leading between Zorilla and the **Plaza Mayor,** is Valladolid's main shopping street, though small stores are dotted throughout the rambling city center.

———————————◆———————————

S P L U R G E S

Lunch or Dinner at La Fragua, Valladolid, Paseo de Zorilla 10 (tel. 983-33-71-02). Open for lunch 1:30–4 and for dinner 9 till midnight; closed Sun. evening. One of the epithets bestowed upon Valladolid is "Gastronomic Capital of Castile," as the numerous excellent restaurants dotted around the city well testify. Culinary specialties include not only the region's traditional roasts and suckling pig, but also an excellent repertoire of seafood and fish fresh from the shores and *rías* of Galicia. In this city of fine restaurants, La Fragua is a clear standout. Its gourmet menu is nothing less than first class, featuring roast lamb, suckling pig, seasonal game, and superb fish dishes along with many original creations dreamed up by an ever-imaginative chef. The desserts are guaranteed to delight. The price tag for this bit of indulgence will not be low, but the food is excellent and the high standards of service, along with La Fragua's atmospheric yet intimate decor and welcoming ambience, contribute to the particular style and charm which makes La Fragua worthy of that extra-special treat.

Lunch or Dinner at the Landa Palace, Burgos (tel. 947-20-63-43). Lunch is served from 1–3 and dinner from 9–11. Just a short cab ride to the south of Burgos lies the Landa Palace, one of Spain's most opulent hotels. Opened in 1962 by Jesús Landa in a 14th-century castle (transported stone by stone from a nearby village), a night in this magnificent setting would set you back 12,000 ptas. While we don't suggest throwing caution to the wind and booking a room for the week, if you can allow yourself a substantial splurge just once, why not treat yourself to lunch or dinner in the Landa's famous restaurant? The menu, a glorious mix of regional specialties and international favorites, does more than ample justice to the romantic setting, and the service and ambience will not make you regret your choice. The bad news comes at around 4,000 ptas. a head.

A Meal at the Mesón del Cid, Burgos, Pza. Santa María 8 (tel. 947-20-59-71). Open for lunch 1–4 and for dinner 8 till midnight; closed Sun. evening. If a fling at the Landa Palace is beyond your means, lower your sights a little and dine instead at this restaurant right opposite the main facade of Burgos Cathedral. With its 15th-century palace setting, this cozy tavern has lashings of atmosphere (very reasonable prices, too!) and is well known for excellent food. There are traditional Castilian specialties as well as more innovative dishes, and the restaurant's already high reputation is on the rise. From the dining room you'll have unbeatable views of the west door of the cathedral, further enhanced when the Gothic facade is floodlit.

◆

LEÓN, GALICIA, AND ASTURIAS

In the northwestern corner of Spain lie three regions all with their own distinctive character and identity. The province of León, on the northwestern fringes of Castile, bridges the gap between the arid *meseta* of central Spain and the lush green mountains of Asturias, and shares the characteristics of both, with rolling yellow wheat fields to the south, and soaring mountain peaks in the north. The principality of Asturias—heirs to the Spanish throne are traditionally princes of Asturias—with its waterfalls and reservoirs, its green pastures and majestic Picos de Europa mountains, is more reminiscent of Switzerland than most people's conception of Spain. Here mountain peaks soar to 1,500 to 2,500 meters (5,000 to 8,000 feet) and the fat contented cattle on the grassy slopes provide most of Spain's dairy produce. Here, too, are the country's major coalfields, and orchards of small bitter apples that go to make the local drink of cider. Galicia, with its green misty hills and peaceful *rías* (estuaries), is a land apart. Its rolling Celtic landscape, with its gray stone villages, tiny farms, traditional grain stores (*hórreos*), and peasant women toiling in the fields or gathering seaweed from the beaches, is more often than not enveloped in mist and drizzle. It is far more akin to Ireland than to the traditional image of a sun-drenched Spain.

This northwest corner has its own particular brand of history, too. In Galicia and Asturias you'll see little Moorish influence: Galicia was overrun only briefly and Asturias never at all. Asturias, secure in its mountain fastnesses, was the cradle of the Reconquest and it was from these rugged mountains that the early Christian warriors under Pelayo launched their first attack on the Infidel invader. At the Battle of Covadonga in eastern Asturias in 718 they won their first victory. In the early 11th century León took over from Oviedo as capital of Christian Spain and became the base for the Reconquista of the Middle Ages, until its power was in turn eclipsed by Castile.

León and Galicia also grew rich and famous in another direction, for they both lay on one of medieval Europe's principal pilgrimage routes, the Camino de Santiago, or Way of St. James. Their wealth of monasteries and Romanesque churches owes its origin to the hospices and chapels which sprang up to cater to the needs of pilgrims traveling this route. Two of the region's greatest treasures are splendid luxury hotels which both began life as hospices for pilgrims to the Shrine of St. James in Santiago de Compostela.

Sights apart, there is another very good reason for visiting this region—it's the gourmet corner of Spain. Galicia, with its

Atlantic shoreline and well-stocked *rías,* supplies most of Spain's shellfish, and there is no better place to sample this superb seafood than when it's at its freshest on its home base. You'll see restaurant windows piled high with *pulpo* (octopus), *vieiras* (scallops), *centollas* (crabs), and much more. Galician *empanadas,* a kind of pasty filled with meat, fish, and vegetables, make a tasty inexpensive snack at any time of day, and to wash them down try Ribeiro wine and a *queimada* or two, a local firewater set aflame (its name means "burning") to complete your meal. *Lacón con grelos* (ham and turnip tops) and *queso de cabrales* (a breast-shaped cheese) are two other specialties that might take your fancy.

Asturias, too, has wonderful fish and a famous bean and sausage casserole called *fabada asturiana,* as well as excellent dairy produce—try *cuajada,* a thick-set yoghurt, or *queso de cabrales,* a pungent blue cheese made in the mountains from ewes' and goats' milk. Be sure also to sample the cider—watch how they pour it—drunk only in this region of Spain. León's reliable wholesome fare offers a good balance of meat and fish dishes, and here you should try the trout and salmon from local rivers and the *cocido,* a rich meat and bean stew.

Communications are generally good in northern Spain, with especially good roads and train services between Madrid and León and Oviedo. Galicia too is easily reached from Madrid and most major cities of Castilla-León, and you can often journey overnight in a train *couchette,* saving yourself the expense of a hotel room. Be prepared for high prices in Oviedo, although as the city is small you won't need to tarry long. León is more reasonable, and Santiago's students ensure plenty of good-value eating places and an abundance of inexpensive hostels, surprising for such a major tourist destination.

León

Founded by the Roman Seventh Legion in the first century A.D., León became capital of Spain when King Ordoño II moved his court here from Asturias in 913. For the next 100 years León led the Reconquest and was Christian Spain's most powerful city. However, the 11th and 12th centuries saw the rise to preeminence of an independent Castile, and by the 13th century León was forced to cede its power for good to Castile.

Today, united once more for administrative purposes in the autonomous region of Castilla-León, León is a delightful city for a short visit. You can enjoy strolling round the well-laid-out modern section of town, with its gardens and wide avenues radiating from the main plazas of Guzmán el Bueno, Santo Domingo, and Calvo Sotelo, or explore the narrow streets and squares of the Old Town clustered around the cathedral and now rather dilapidated Plaza Mayor. The old Barrio Húmedo round Plaza San Martín is a warren of colorful taverns and restaurants where you can drink, spear *tapas,* and sample the wholesome Leonese fare at fairly modest prices. Romanesque churches and Renaissance palaces line the streets, and there is even a Gaudí mansion—though not one of his best—on one of the prime central sites.

But the real highlights of León are its lovely Gothic cathedral, justly renowned for its superb stained glass, the Basílica San Isidoro, whose vaults boast some of Spain's earliest and best preserved Romanesque art, and the magnificent San Marcos Hotel, once a hostel for medieval pilgrims and now a splendid 5-star hotel—an eternal monument to León's important position on the ancient Camino de Santiago.

GETTING THERE. By Train. León is well served by trains, lying on two major routes from Madrid to the north coast, and on through routes from Galicia to Bilbao, San Sebastián, and Barcelona. From Madrid Chamartín trains leave for Oviedo several times a day, calling at León en route. The service from Madrid Norte to El Ferrol also calls at León. In addition to the RENFE trains León is also served by a branch of the north coast FEVE line linking it with Bilbao. Eurail and InterRail passes are not valid on FEVE routes, and RENFE and FEVE trains operate out of different stations. León's RENFE station is on Avda. de Astorga (tel. 987-22-37-04/08) across the river from the city center. The central RENFE ticket office is at Travesía Roa de la Vega 26 (tel. 987-22-26-25). The Feve station is the Estación de Matallana (tel. 987-22-59-19) on Avda. del Padre Isla to the north of the city center.

By Bus. León's main bus terminal is on Cardenal Lorenzana 2 (tel. 987-22-62-00) near the bottom of Avda. de Roma. Buses run from Madrid, Valladolid, Salamanca, Burgos, Oviedo, and Santander.

By Car. León is 327 km. (204 mi.) northwest of Madrid via Tordesillas and Benavente, or Valladolid. Salamanca to León via N630 is 196 km. (122 mi.). León lies 120 km. (75 mi.) due south of Oviedo via either the N630 route crossing the Picos de Europa mountains at the Pajares Pass, or by the quicker A66 toll road.

TOURIST OFFICES. Pza. de Regla 3 (tel. 987-23-70-82) right in front of the cathedral.

USEFUL ADDRESSES. Police. Villa Benavente (tel. 987-25-26-08).

Post Office and Telephone Exchange. Located between Avda. Independencia and Calle Santa Nonia.

WHERE TO STAY. Quindos (M), Avda. José Antonia 24 (tel. 987-23-62-00). 96 rooms. If you can't afford León's showpiece, the fabulous San Marcos, then the Quindos is the next best bet. It is a comfortable hotel in the modern part of the city, only a short walk from the historic center. It is well known for giving good value.

Ríosol (M), Avda. de Palencia 3 (tel. 987-22-36-50). 141 rooms. Located just across the river from the Glorieta Guzmán el Bueno, this comfortable but functional hotel is very convenient for the main train station.

Don Suero (I), Suero de Quiñones 15 (tel. 987-23-06- 00). 106 rooms. Not far from the famous San Marcos hotel lies this 2-star hotel. It offers inexpensive rooms, with and without bathrooms, and serves breakfast.

París (I), Generalísimo Franco 20 (tel. 987-23-86-00). 77 rooms. Be right at the center of things, very close to the cathedral, in this simple 1-star hotel. It occupies part of an old mansion and the rooms, some with bathrooms, have been modernized.

WHERE TO EAT. Bodega Regia (M), Pza. San Martín 8 (tel. 987-25-41-51). The Bodega Regia is located in a 12th-century house with beamed roof and three floors of atmospheric dining rooms. It specializes in traditional Leonese dishes like *cocido* (a stew of beans, meat, and vegetables). Service can be a little slow.

Casa Paza (M), Arco de Animas 15 (tel. 987-22-30-39). A real León tradition, this restaurant has been run by the same family for over a century. The menu concentrates on typical Leonese fare but is especially good on fish, particularly trout and salmon dishes.

Fornos (M), Calle del Cid 8 (tel. 987-23-69-21). Generous portions and excellent trout are served in this large family-run restaurant. It is located in the heart of the Old Town between the Basílica San Isidoro and the Guzmán Palace.

Mesón San Martín (I), Pza. San Martín 8 (tel. 987-25-60-55). One of the most popular of the inexpensive restaurants which line the streets of the Barrio Húmedo, this cozy *mesón* is always crowded with locals, but its good home cooking and regional specialties are worth a short wait.

MAJOR ATTRACTIONS. Basilica de San Isidoro, *Pza. San Isidoro 4. Open 9–2 and 4–6.* Ferdinand I, who united the kingdoms of León and Castile, commissioned this Romanesque basilica to house the remains of San Isidoro of Seville, rescued from the Moors in 1063. The church was completed in 1067 and the bones of the 6th-century saint, who reputedly cured the lame and the blind and exuded divine odors 500 years after his death, were placed in a silver urn on the high altar.

Adjoining the church, Ferdinand built the **Panteón de los Reyes,** *open 9–2 and 3:30–8 in summer, 10–1:30 and 4–6:30 in winter,* as a resting place for his own tomb and those of his successors. It constitutes one of the earliest and most magnificent examples of Romanesque art in Spain. The columns with their lavishly carved capitals—the first in Spain to be decorated with scenes from the Gospels—support a vaulted roof decorated with beautifully preserved frescoes from the late 12th century. The tombs were damaged by the French during the Peninsular War, but the museum contains some of the treasures they failed to destroy: the chalice of Doña Urraca, medieval banners, and a beautifully illustrated early Bible.

Cathedral, *Pza. de Regia. Open 8:30–1:30 and 4–7; closed Sun. evening.* The cathedral was begun in 1205, just as León was ceding its supremacy to Castile, is a jewel of pure Gothic, and is famous throughout Spain for the beauty of its superb stained-glass windows. Inside, the cathedral may seem dark at first until the sun floods in (late afternoon is a good time to visit), lighting up the rich reds and yellows of over 130 massive windows and three magnificent roses. The vast areas of glass are simply incredible, and the stone seems only to serve as a frame for these glowing panels. In fact the walls have had to be strengthened to maintain the weight of this priceless 13th-century glass. It is worth buying a guidebook to explain the biblical events recounted in the windows and, before you leave, pause for a while on the Plaza de Regia and study the west front of the cathedral with its beautiful towers, splendid rose windows, and triple archways boasting superb carvings. Pay special attention to the amusing Day of Judgment scene over the center door.

San Marcos Hotel, *Pza. San Marcos.* The luxurious San Marcos Hotel was once a hospice for pilgrims on the road to Santiago de Compostela. It was built originally for the Knights of the Order of Santiago whose duty it was to protect the pilgrims on this long and arduous route. By the 16th century, when the number of pilgrims had dwindled and the Order was more concerned with the pursuit of pleasure and privilege than protective duties, the monastery was rebuilt in its present form. (See *Splurges.*)

Adjoining the hotel is the Gothic **Church of San Marcos** decorated with the cockleshell, symbol of Santiago pilgrims. Its **choir stalls** were carved by Juan de Juni, a pupil of Michelangelo, and its **sacristy** houses the **Museo Arqueológico,** *open 10–2 and 4–6; closed Mon. and Sun. afternoon.* Its valuable treasures include Limoges enamels and portraits of the knights of Santiago, but the highlight of the museum is a 12th-century ivory crucifix, *El Cristo del Carrizo,* whose true value was only realized when an American museum offered $450,000 for it.

OTHER ATTRACTIONS. Casa de Botines, *Pza. Santa Domingo.* This mansion, with its roof pinnacles and St. George and the Dragon over the door, was built by the Barcelona architect Antoní Gandí in 1891–4. Rather more solid and restrained than his usual flamboyant excesses, it is now used as a bank.

Nuestra Señora del Mercado, *Pza. Sta. María del Camino. Open 8:30–12 and 5:30–8:30.* This Romanesque church with its superb wrought iron grilles dates from the 12th century.

Palacio de los Condes de Luna, *Pza. Condes de Luna.* The Quiñones family owned this 14th-century palace and their coat of arms, alongside that of the Bazán family, can be seen over the doorway. The tower was a 16th-century addition.

Palacio de los Guzmanes, *Pza. Santo Domingo.* Facing the Gaudí mansion, this palace was built in 1559–66 by Gil de Hontañón for Bishop Quiñones y Guzmán on the site of the birthplace of Guzmán el Bueno, the 14th-century hero and defender of Tarifa against the Moors.

Oviedo

Oviedo, capital of the Principality of Asturias, is a small gray-stoned city lying at the foot of the imposing Mount Naranco. Built around a pleasant central park, Oviedo has both a modern section, arising from the damage wrought during the Asturian Miners' Revolt of 1934 and the Civil War, and an Old Quarter clustered around the cathedral where traces of the old city wall can be seen among ancient palaces. In the early years of the Reconquest, during the 9th century, Oviedo was capital of Christian Spain and was busy leading the battle against the Moors, and bequeathing to posterity fine buildings which still stand today. Alfonso II (792–842), known as Alfonso El Casto (the Chaste King), set up his court here in 810 and built the Church of Santullans, as well as the city's most treasured monument, the Cámara Santa. His successor, Ramiro I (842–50), built himself a summer palace on the slopes of Mount Naranco and in so doing not only gave his name to Ramiresque, a style of pre-Romanesque architecture which is unique to this part of Spain, but also endowed Oviedo with two of its finest buildings, the churches of San Miguel de Lillo and Santa María Naranco, which are the highlights of any visit to the Asturian capital.

Its cathedral and Ramiresque heritage apart, the rest of Oviedo is rather industrial—iron and coal mines lie nearby—and the city's main monuments can easily be seen in a day's sightseeing. This is perhaps just as well as, though you may be tempted to tarry in Oviedo's colorful cider bars, hotels and restaurants here are expensive and can easily run away with a good part of your travel budget. But if you do decide to stay a little longer, Oviedo is a good base for a trip to one of Asturias' picturesque coastal towns or eastwards to the magnificent mountains of the Picos de Europa and the famous shrine of Covadonga.

GETTING THERE. By Air. Asturias Airport (tel. 985-56- 34-03) is 47 km. (29 mi.) north of Oviedo and has daily flights from Madrid and Barcelona, as well as three or four flights a week from Bilbao and Santiago de Compostela. The *Iberia* ticket office in town is on Uría 21 (tel. 985-23-24-00/04/08).

By Train. Three daytime trains run to Oviedo from Madrid Chamartín, and one overnight train on which sleeping cars and *couchettes* are available. Oviedo is also a stop on the Gijón-Barcelona line. The RENFE station is the Estación del Norte (tel. 985-24- 33-64) at the far end of Calle Uría.

Oviedo also lies on the independent narrow-gauge FEVE line which runs from San Sebastián to El Ferrol. Eurail and InterRail passes are not valid on this line. Oviedo has two FEVE stations depending on direction of travel. One is at Jovellanos 19 (tel. 985-21-43-97) and the other at Calle Económicos (tel. 985-28-01-50).

By Bus. The main long-distance bus station is the ALSA depot on Pza. Primo de Rivera 2 (tel. 985-28-12-00) with services from Madrid, Barcelona, Valencia, Seville, La Coruña, and Vigo. For buses to the Picos de Europa and elsewhere in Asturias, inquire at the tourist office.

By Car. Oviedo lies at the junction of the main N634 coastal highway and N630 leading south from Gijón to Salamanca. Oviedo is 30 km. (20 mi.) from Gijón, 118 km. (74 mi.) from León, and 446 km. (278 mi.) from Madrid.

TOURIST OFFICES. Pza. de la Catedral 6 (tel. 985-21-33-85).

USEFUL ADDRESSES. Police Exchange. General Yague 5 (tel. 985-21-19-20).

Post Office. Alonso Quintanilla 1.

Telephone Exchange. Pza. de Porlier.

WHERE TO STAY. Hotel rates in Oviedo are high and you may have to lower your sights a little. With the exception of the Barbón, the places listed below are all fairly modest.

Barbón (M), Covadonga 7 (tel. 985-22-52-93). 40 rooms. You may well find the price of this 2-star hotel a little more expensive than usual, but it is located in the center and is undoubtedly the best moderate bet. It serves breakfast only.

Tropical (M), 19 de Julio 6 (tel. 985-21-87-79). 44 rooms. Just one block from the Barbón (above), this 1-star motel offers rooms with and without bathrooms at more modest rates. No meals are served.

Fruela (I), Fruela 2 (tel. 985-21-82-78). 21 rooms. Very central, and just a block or so from the Plaza Mayor, this simple boarding-house offers rooms with and without bathrooms. Its meals are very moderately priced, which makes a welcome change from most of Oviedo's restaurants.

Mexico (I), Uría 25 (tel. 985-24-04-04). 24 rooms. Rooms in this 2-star boardinghouse are just a little more expensive than those in the Fruela (see above) and it is located on Oviedo's main thoroughfare. You can have breakfast here, but no other meals.

WHERE TO EAT. Oviedo has plenty of *tapas* bars and colorful cider houses (*sidrerías* or *chigres*), but finding modestly priced restaurants can be something of a problem. There is no shortage of excellent restaurants offering plenty of opportunities for a splurge, but finding somewhere where you can stay within the limits of your budget is not so easy.

Marchica (M), Dr. Casal 8 and 10 (tel. 985-21-30-27). There are two dining rooms in this well-established restaurant; the one at no. 8 is slightly simpler and has more modest prices than the one at no. 10, though the food in both is excellent. The fish is superb and the meat dishes are also of high quality, and there is a colorful cider bar at the entrance serving a good array of *tapas*.

Principado (M), San Francisco 6 (tel. 985-21-77-92). Located right in the center of town, opposite the old university building, this classic Oviedo hotel has long been held in high regard for its out-standing restaurant. You can opt for the reasonably priced set menu, or make your selection from the slightly more expensive *à la carte* offerings.

La Campana (I), San Bernabé 7 (tel. 985-22-49-31). La Campana is a sound, reliable bet which features good home cooking. Its soups and casseroles are especially good. Closed Sun. and Aug.

Casa Muñiz (I), Calle de la Lila 16 (tel. 985-21-64-54). The prices here will allow you to make up for any extravagant splurges. Part cider bar and part budget diner, the decor is far from special, but it is always crowded with locals who appreciate its cheap meals.

MAJOR ATTRACTIONS. Cámera Santa, *within the cathedral enclosure. Open 10–1 and 4–8; 4–6 in winter*. Oviedo's greatest treasure, the Holy Chamber, was built by Alfonso II in 802 to house precious Christian relics rescued from Visigoth Toledo when it fell to the Moors. The Cámera Santa consists of two chambers: the **outer chapel** is Romanesque from the early 1100s, and the **inner chamber** is what remains of Alfonso's original shrine. The whole building was badly damaged in an explosion in 1934 and has since been rebuilt in keeping with the original. Its most precious relics are a beautiful reliquary chest dating from 1073, and two gold crosses encrusted with jewels. The **Cruz de Los Angeles** dates from 808 and marks the beginning of the Court in Asturias; the **Cruz de la Victoria** dates from 908 and is in fact a jeweled sheath made to cover the oak cross borne by the Valiant Pelayo at the Battle of Covadonga.

Cathedral. *Open 8–1 and 4–6*. This flamboyant Gothic cathedral was built in the 14th and 15th centuries around the shrine of Alfonso II's Cámera Santa. Only one of its two projected towers was ever completed, but this graceful spire, now one of the symbols of Oviedo, is well worth climbing for a fine view of the city. Inside, in the north transept, the **Chapel of the Chaste King** was built by Alfonso II as a royal pantheon for Asturian kings, and the elaborately carved wooden retable above the high altar, with its gold pinnacles and intricately painted figures, is very striking.

Santa María del Naranco, *just below San Miguel de Lillo. Open the same hours as San Miguel*. Built by Ramiro I in the 9th century in soft golden stone, this is one of the great jewels of Ramiresque architecture. It was probably built not as a church but as part of a hunting lodge, the lower section most likely serving as a bathhouse. Note the open porticoes of the upper section with their rough-and-ready altar, and the medallions decorating the top of the arches. One of Spain's most unusual churches, built in a style that is unique to Spain as it predates the spread of Romanesque influence from France, Santa María is one of the true gems of Asturian architecture.

San Miguel de Lillo. *Open 10–1 and 3–7 in summer; 10–1 and*

3–5 in winter; closed Sun. afternoon. but do check times with the tourist office. Situated about 5 km. (3 mi.) out on the slopes of Mount Naranco, you can walk here in around 45 min. Make for the RENFE station, then cross the bridge over the tracks and continue on up. Alternatively, catch bus no. 6 or splash out on a taxi for the outward journey and walk back down. This ancient pre-Romanesque church was built by Alfonso's successor, King Ramiro I, and was probably the chapel of a much larger palace. Notice the fascinating carvings on the door jambs and the squat form of the church built in the shape of a Byzantine cross. Over 1,100 years of history and magnificent views are well worth the climb up here: Don't miss it.

OTHER ATTRACTIONS. Museo Arqueológico, *in the old San Vicente Convent behind the cathedral. Open Tues. to Sun. 11:30–1:30 and 4–6; closed Mon. and Sun. afternoon.* The most interesting part of this archeological collection is the pre-Romanesque room with its treasures from the interiors of Oviedo's notable Ramiresque churches.

Museo de Bellas Artes, *Santa Ana 1. Open 11:30–1:30 and 5–8; closed Mon. in winter, Sun. in summer.* The old Velarde Palace makes a pleasant setting for this collection of 16th 20th-century art and contemporary Asturian painting and sculpture.

Santullano, *a 10-min. walk northeast of the center out along the road to Gijón.* Also known as San Julián de los Prados, this church is the third of Oviedo's pre-Romanesque heritage. Larger, but somewhat less appealing than its sister churches on Mount Naranco, it was built in the reign of Alfonso II around 830 by Tiodo, architect of the Cámera Santa. It has some interesting wall paintings and a strange **secret chamber** in one of its walls. *If closed, the priest next door has the key.*

Santiago de Compostela

The small town of Santiago de Compostela is the uncontested showpiece of Galicia, and indeed of all northwestern Spain. It boasts a famous university and an even more famous cathedral, believed to be the last earthly resting place of Spain's patron saint, St. James the Apostle. Legend has it that in 813 a star led to the discovery of St. James' tomb in this far-flung corner of Spain, and on this Field of the Star (Compostela), where the long-lost relics were found, Alfonso El Casto (the Chaste) built a church and monastery which grew into the city and shrine of Santiago. In need of a champion for the war against the Infidel, Christian Spaniards adopted St. James as the great hero of the Reconquest, and over the next few hundred years Santiago Matamoros (Moor-slayer) was seen to slay thousands of Moors in no fewer than 40 battles.

Medieval pilgrims flocked to the shrine in the thousands; as many as half a million a year in the 12th century donned the cape and broad-brimmed hat with the cockleshell emblem and set out to trudge the roads of medieval Europe along what came to be known as the Camino de Santiago. The poor and the humble, the rich and famous—among them such luminaries as the Wife of Bath, St. Francis of Assisi, Ferdinand and Isabella, Charles V, and, in later times, General Franco and Pope John Paul II—came to pay their respects, Santiago ranking with Rome and Jerusalem as one of the Christian world's leading pilgrimage centers.

St. James continues to attract pilgrims—now known as tourists—especially in July when the town celebrates his feast day on the 25th with a week of great pomp and splendor, fireworks and festivities. Yet for all its centuries-long appeal Santiago has lost none of its charm and this small golden-stoned city, with its narrow flagstoned streets and pretty squares, remains a delight to visit. Linger in the magnificent Plaza del Obradoiro, wander under the arcades of the ancient Rua del Villar and Rua Nueva, and stroll down the lively Calle del Franco with its street vendors, bars, and colorful restaurants. At nighttime you can expect to be serenaded by the *tuna,* traditional university minstrel groups dressed in black cloaks and ribbons, who roam the city's oldest squares. And finally, for the best view of the city, go down to the park on the Paseo de Herradura, and though the charm of this lovely town surrounded by the gentle green hills of Galicia is never likely to fade, remember that Santiago is also an excellent base for exploring the picturesque rías (estuaries) of Galicia, and that both Pontevedra and La Coruña lie only a short bus or train ride away.

GETTING THERE. By Air.

Santiago Airport (tel. 981-59-74-00) is 12 km. (7 mi.) out at Labacolla. There are daily direct flights from Madrid and Barcelona, and flights from Bilbao, Málaga, Seville, and Vitoria. Regular international flights run from London and Paris and, in summer only, from Zurich. The *Iberia* office in town is at Gen. Pardinas 24 (tel. 981-59-41-00) in the New Town.

By Train. Daytime and nighttime trains with sleeping accommodations run from Madrid, and trains on the Bilbao–La Coruña line stop at Santiago. Santiago Station (tel. 981-59-60-50) is at the far end of Calle Gen. Franco (sometimes called Hórreo).

By Bus. The San Cayetano Bus Depot (tel. 981-58-77-00) is on the northern edge of town, some way from the center, but bus no. 10 runs regularly between Pza. Galicia (sometimes called Pza. de Vigo) and the bus station. There are services from Madrid, Barcelona,

Pontevedra, Vigo, Orense, Lugo, and La Coruña. There is also a direct bus service from London to Santiago run by Spanish Express.

By Car. Santiago has good road connections from all the main towns of Galicia. From La Coruña it is a 65-km. (40-mi.) drive along N550 or toll road A9. Pontevedra is 57 km. (36 mi.) along N550, and Vigo 80 km. (50 mi.) León to Santiago is 384 km. (240 mi.) and Madrid to Santiago is a long drive of 638 km. (400 mi.) by way of NV1 to Lugo, then C547.

TOURIST OFFICES. The main tourist office is at Rua del Villar 43 (tel. 981-58-40-81) in the heart of the Old Town. It has an English-speaking staff and will provide a good free map of the city and help with accommodations. It also organizes afternoon walking tours of the city for a fee, but these are usually in Spanish only. There is also a Municipal Tourist Office in the Palacio de Rajoy on the Pza. del Obradoiro in front of the cathedral (tel. 981-58-29-00, ext. 125).

USEFUL ADDRESSES. Police. Avda. Rodrigo del Padrón (tel. 981-58-11-10).

Post Office. Travesía de Fonseca.

Telephone Exchange. Alfredo Brañas in the New Town, 5 min. from Pza. Galicia.

WHERE TO STAY. Santiago is a major tourist destination and there is a wide choice of places to stay, especially in the lower end of the price range where hostels (often called *hospedajes* here) abound. Rooms are hardest to find around July 25, Santiago's major feast day, but here, as at other times of the year, impromptu landladies often greet you at the train or bus station with offers of rooms in their homes. If you take up these offers, be sure to check how far out of town they live, and don't be afraid to bargain over the room rate.

Rey Fernando (M), Fernando III El Santo 30 (tel. 981-59-35-50). 24 rooms. You'll find yourself rather far away from the historic center in this 2-star hotel in the New Town, but it is reasonably priced and you can walk to the Old Town in 20 min. or so.

Universal (M), Pza. Galicia 2 (tel. 981-58-58-00). 54 rooms. If you arrive at the bus depot, a bus no. 10 will drop you right outside this simple but comfortable hotel located right on the edge of the Old Town.

Windsor (M), República de El Salvador 16 (tel. 981-59-29-39). 50 rooms. The Windsor is a deluxe 3-star hostel right in the heart of the New Town but not too far from the main sights. Its rooms are very comfortable and are the most expensive in this category.

Fornos (I), Gen. Franco 7 (tel. 981-58-51-30). 14 rooms. The location of this hostel, right on the Pza. Galicia opposite the Universal Hotel, is very convenient. It is simple, but very clean and friendly and family-run. There are rooms with and without bathrooms.

Maycar (I), Dr. Teijeiro 15 (tel. 981-56-34-44). 40 rooms. The Maycar is just one of the many good-value hostels that line the streets of the New Town. Only a couple of minutes from the Fornos (see above), its rooms are a little more modern and all have bathrooms or showers.

Suso (I), Rua del Villar 65 (tel. 981-58-66-11). 9 rooms. One of the very few hostels actually in the Old Town, this charming, but very simple, old house is located on one of Santiago's prettiest streets. Don't expect luxury, but it is clean and friendly and there's plenty of old world atmosphere; one or two of the rooms have a bathroom.

WHERE TO EAT. Few other places in Spain can rival Santiago's Calle del Franco (not to be confused with Calle Gen. Franco) when it comes to treats for the lover of good food. It is packed from end to end with moderate and inexpensive eating places displaying all the usual Galician specialties: fresh fish, octopus, and *empanadas*. Most of the restaurants have colorful *tapas* bars where you can sample scallops and the local Ribeiro wine served in china bowls while you check out the menu. Strolling along here and making your pick from the hundreds of places on offer is one of Santiago's most enjoyable pastimes.

Alameda (M), Puerta Fajara 15 (tel. 981-58-47-96). The Alameda café with its tables spilling over the sidewalk and its ever-crowded bar is one of Santiago's favorite haunts. Its upstairs restaurant has long been famous for good food, traditional old-fashioned service, and one of the best views of what's going on in town.

El Franco (M), Calle del Franco 28 (tel. 981-58-12-34). One of the best of the many colorful restaurants on this street, El Franco offers a superb choice of fresh seafood and friendly service. There is also a moderately priced *menu del día*.

La Tacita de Oro (M), Gen. Franco 31 (tel. 981-56-32-55). Just a couple of minutes south of the Pza. Galicia, this is another long-standing favorite with locals who come here for all the traditional Galician classics—superb seafood, a great choice of *empanadas* (Galician pastries), *lacón con grelos* (boiled ham and turnip tops), and even game in season. Prices may be a little high, but its consistently good standards are worth the little extra money.

El Asesino (I), Pza. de la Universidad 16 (tel. 981-58-15-68). This modest tavern, so well known that there is no sign outside, has been catering to students, writers, and connoisseurs of gourmet food alike since 1870. Steeped in history, and a veritable Santiago institution, you can still obtain a generous meal here for as little as 700 ptas. Closed Sun.

Camilo (I), Raiña 24 (tel. 981-58-11-66). Located in the heart of Santiago's restaurant quarter, this is one of the many traditional, inexpensive eating places that are the town's hallmark. Good home-cooked food and local Ribeiro wine are the staples of this genuine Galician bistro.

San Jaime (I), Raiñe 4 (tel. 981-58-31-34). Drink your Ribeiro wine from traditional china bowls while enjoying the delightful views from this charming first-floor restaurant. Songs from the *tuna* minstrels playing in the Pza. Fonseca below may well accompany your dining.

MAJOR ATTRACTIONS. Cathedral. *Open 10–1:30 and 3:30–7.* **Interior:** Spain's greatest shrine was begun in 1075 to house the body of Spain's patron, St. James the Apostle, and building continued into the 13th century. The interior is one of the supreme masterpieces of Romanesque architecture, with three broad aisles leading to the sumptuous high altar where a lavish baroque fantasy of gold and silver serves as a truly monumental throne for the seated figure of St. James. In a silver coffer in the **crypt** below the high altar rest the mortal remains of the saint. The ropes and pulleys alongside the high altar are used to swing the famous **Botafumeiro,** the world's largest censer, over the heads of the congregation on special holy days. This huge silver incense burner, weighing 54 kilos (118 lbs.) and dating from 1602, is usually displayed in the library of the Sala Capitular; it takes six to eight men to keep it in motion. But the cathedral's greatest glory is the exquisite **Pórtico de la Gloria,** the work of the famed Maestro Mateo, and one of the crowning achievements of 12th-century sculpture. Concealed from the outside by the baroque additions of the 18th century, the Pórtico de la Gloria now serves as an inner doorway to the original Romanesque temple. From 1168–88 Maestro Mateo adorned the doorway with over 200 figures. In places, the stone has worn away where it has been caressed by the hands of millions of thankful pilgrims at the end of their long and arduous trek across Europe.

The cathedral is the only one in Spain which can be viewed from squares on all four sides, and a tour of the outside is just as rewarding as a visit inside. Start on the south side and make an anticlockwise circle, ending up in the Pza. del Obradoiro.

Platerías Facade (*south side*). This is the oldest and, many think, the loveliest of the cathedral's facades. The **Puerta de Platerías**

(1104), the only remaining Romanesque doorway, opens onto a delightful square once surrounded by silversmiths (platerías) and overlooked by the **Casa del Cabildo** and the 17th century clock tower.

Quintana Facade *(southeast corner and east end)*. The eastern facade is dominated by the cathedral's highest tower, **La Berenguela,** designed by the 17th-century baroque architect Domingo Andrade. The east door, the **Puerta Santa** (Holy Door), was designed by Fernández Lechuga in 1611 and incorporates figures carved by Maestro Mateo for the original choir. *It is opened only in holy years when St. James's Day falls on a Sunday (the next one is 1993).* The square is bordered at the lower end by the **Casa de los Canónigos,** a former canon's residence, and at the top of the steps at the upper end, by the **Casa de la Parra** (House of Grapes), a 17th-century baroque mansion.

Azabachería Facade *(north side)*. The Azabachería (jet carvers') facade is the least impressive, being a rather confused jumble of styles added in the 18th century. Overlooking the Pza. Inmaculada, where jet carvers once sold figures of St. James to souvenir-seeking pilgrims, is the **Monasterio de San Martín** Pinario finished in 1738. The monastery church, entered from the Pza. San Miguel and *open 10–1 and 4–7,* has an ornate **retable** by Casas y Novoa who designed the main (Obradoiro) facade.

Obradoiro Facade *(west side)*. The elaborate gray granite facade with which Fernando Casas y Novoa reclothed the front of the cathedral in 1750 is a monumental flight of baroque fantasy. A quadruple flight of steps leads up to the massive studded doorway, crowned by a profusion of carvings and flanked by two soaring towers. Casas y Novoa's masterly interpretation of baroque creates an overall effect that is ornate, yet still very elegant.

Plaza del Obradoiro. This monumental square in front of the cathedral is the perfect place to savor the atmosphere of Santiago. Always humming with activity, packed with street vendors, tourists, and Gallegos out strolling, it is overlooked from the east by the cathedral and adjoining 12th-century **Bishops' Palace,** the Palacio de Gelmirez; from the south by the 17th-century **San Jerónimo College;** from the west by the classical 18th-century **Palacio de Rajoy,** founded as a seminary and choir school and now the City Hall; and from the north by the magnificent **Hostal de los Reyes Católicos.** This imposing hotel, with its lovely Plateresque doorway, was founded by Ferdinand and Isabella as a hospice for poor pilgrims. Now a luxury 5-star hotel, *tours of the building can be made between 10–1 and 4–7.*

OTHER ATTRACTIONS. Casa de Troya, *on Calle Azabachería,* is home to one of Santiago's *tunas,* groups of university minstrels who serenade nightly on the nearby Pza. Inmaculada.

Convento de Santo Domingo de Bonaval, *at the end of Sto. Domingo, beyond Puerta del Camino. Open 10–1 and 4–7; closed Sun. afternoon.* Legend has it that St. Dominic founded this convent whose church now houses the Pabellón de Gallegos Ilustres, the pantheon of tombs of famous Galicians, among them that the poetess Rosalín de Castro. In an adjoining building the **Museo do Pobo Galego** has a good display of Galician folklore and rural life.

Monasterio de San Pelayo de Antes-Altares, *Pza. Quintana. Open Mon. to Sat. 10–1 and 4–7, Sun. 10–2.* The highlight of this fine collection of religious art is an amusing statue of the Virgin holding the Christ Child in one hand, whilst busy spanking the Devil with the other.

Santa María del Sar, *Calle Castron d'Ouro, about one mile from the center, off Calle Sotelo. Open Mon. to Sat. 10–1 and 4–6 (later in summer).* This, the loveliest of Santiago's churches, is 12th-century Romanesque, with beautiful cloisters and carved capitals, and amazing leaning walls and columns whose precarious incline may just be due to a fault in the foundations, but was possibly an intentional joke on the part of the architects. Whatever the reason, Santiago's answer to the Leaning Tower of Pisa is well worth the walk out here.

◆

S P L U R G E S

A Drink or a Meal at the San Marcos Hotel, León, Plaza San Marcos 7 (tel. 987-23-73-00). Built originally in 1168 as a hospice for pilgrims to Santiago, and completely rebuilt between 1513–49, the magnificent Plateresque building had deteriorated to being used as a barracks and stud farm for army horses before it was converted by the Spanish government into a luxury hotel in 1963–5. Today, the beautiful facade shelters not only one of Spain's top five hotels, but also a museum, a church, historic cloisters, fine formal gardens, stone passageways, vast elegant public salons, 258 rooms (all individually furnished with antiques), a reception area adorned with sculptures, and a TV room with a hand-carved sandalwood ceiling and three-foot-thick walls. Furthermore, the whole interior is lavishly decorated with antique clocks, some 800 handmade tapestries and rugs from the Royal

Tapestry Factory in Madrid, and over 1,027 original Spanish paintings by old masters and contemporary artists.

The set lunch or dinner menu is priced at 2,300 ptas. (1987 price). In the Rey Sancho restaurant, the *à la carte* menu offers a wide choice of regional specialties: roast quail, partridge, rabbit, and woodcock are just some of the roasts and game sizzling away in the huge floor-to-ceiling ovens, and trout and bream from nearby mountain streams are further San Marcos specialties. The restaurant's hand-embroidered tablecloths, napkins, and gold-edged china are just some of the specially crafted features commissioned exclusively. Should such a potentially sumptuous meal make too great an inroad into your vacation budget, a cocktail or pre-lunch *fino* in the San Marcos bar will afford you equally memorable glimpses of the unique historic atmosphere of one of Spain's most outstanding hotels.

Casa Fermín, Oviedo, San Francisco 8 (tel. 985-21-64-52). Close to the central park and located beside the Principado hotel, this fine restaurant with its elegant, stylish dining rooms has been run by the same family since the '20s. Its menu offers a combination of classic Asturian dishes and international favorites: Its game is excellent in season, and fish specialties include *reo, salmón,* or *lubina a la asturiana;* or you can choose *pimientos rellenos de chipirones* (peppers stuffed with baby squid), or, for steak-lovers, *entrecot al queso de cabrales.* For dessert try the *frixuelos de manzana,* a local apple fritter. Good service and an extensive wine list back up this quality menu. Casa Fermín closes Sunday evenings.

La Goleta, Oviedo, Covadonga 32 (tel. 985-21-38-47). This small restaurant with seafaring decor opened 10 years ago with the aim of providing Oviedo with some of its best fish and seafood, and has steadily gained in popularity. Downstairs is a lively *tapas* and *mariscos* bar, upstairs, in the cozy restaurant, *fabes con almejas* (beans and clams) and *pimientos rellenos de centolla* (peppers stuffed with crab) feature among the Asturian seafood specialties. Local meat dishes are on offer, too, and there is a good wine list and an excellent choice of liqueurs *(aguardientes).*

Trascorrales, Oviedo, Pza. Trascorrales 19 (tel. 985-22-24-41). Closed Sun., Holy Week, and end of Aug. Considered one of the finest restaurants in Asturias and winner of the Premio del Principado de Asturias (Principality of Asturias gastronomic prize), Trascorrales is located behind the Ayuntamiento in a lovely old stone building which formerly served as a fruit store. The most expensive of our three splurge suggestions (it takes credit cards) but worth it, its menu combines traditional Asturian dishes with innovative creations. Reservations are advisable, and menu suggestions include *anguilas con patatas* (eels and potatoes) and *entrecot al queso de cabrales*.

A Drink in the Hostal de los Reyes Católicos, Santiago, Plaza Obradoiro 1 (tel. 981-58-22-00). A comparatively minor extravagance will enable you to savor the atmosphere of this truly historic building, one of Spain's, and the world's, greatest hotels. Commissioned by Ferdinand and Isabella and built between 1501–11, it began life as a welcome shelter for pilgrims, rich and poor, at the end of their trek along the route of St. James. In 1953, in a bad state of deterioration, the decision was taken to convert it into a luxury hotel: 2,000 men labored night and day for nine months and at a cost of over $10 million. The hotel opened its doors amid triumphant celebrations in the Plaza Obradoiro on St. James's Day 1954. King Juan Carlos, General Franco, ex-president Giscard d'Estaing of France, guitarist Andrés Segovia, and barman Pedro Chicote have all slept in its four-poster canopied beds, sat in its hand-carved wooden chairs, wandered the graceful patios, and admired numerous original paintings, ceramic urns from Talavera, gilded Phoenix doorpulls, hand-forged chandeliers, and wall hangings and handmade rugs from the Royal Tapestry Factory in Madrid, all specially commissioned for the hotel. Though you may be tempted to dine here, reports of the hotel's cuisine have been mixed, and for that extra-special meal you would probably be better advised to try the **Vilas** or **Don Gaiferos** restaurants in town.

BARCELONA

Barcelona, capital of Catalonia and Spain's second city, with a population of just over three million, has long rivaled, even surpassed, Madrid in commercial muscle, business acumen, and as a leading cultural center. Though Madrid has now finally well and truly taken up the mantle of capital city, Barcelona has relinquished none of its former prowess, and is currently celebrating its latest cause for rejoicing: the 1992 Olympics nomination. It is also justly proud of its cultural heritage. For long Spain's most liberal and progressive city, this home of Gaudí, Picasso, and Miró can claim Spain's only opera house, and acknowledges with pride the contribution to the arts of native Catalans like cellist Pau Cassals, surrealist Salvador Dalí, actress and director Nuria Espert, and opera singers Montserrat Caballe and Josep Carrers. Barcelona also boasts one of the world's most glamorous soccer clubs, and a fashion industry that is fast rivaling those of Paris and Milan.

Founded by the Phoenicians and first called Barcino by the Carthaginians in 237 B.C., the Romans made the city the capital of their province of Layetana. After a spell of occupation by Visigoths, Moors (713), and Franks, the city attained its independence, starting in 874 under the counts of Barcelona. But in 1137 Catalonia became part of Aragón. During the 14th and 15th centuries the city prospered immensely thanks to its maritime trade. Finally, in 1474, Barcelona became part of a united Spain and ceased to be a capital. Furthermore, with the discovery of America, maritime emphasis shifted away from the Mediterranean to the Atlantic, and it was not until the Catalan *Renaixença* (Renaissance) of the late 19th century that Barcelona once more came into its own.

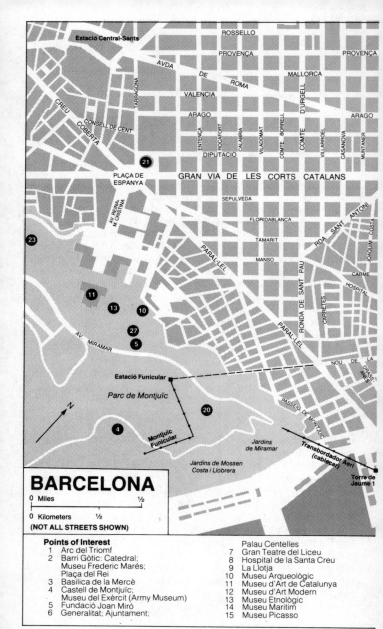

BARCELONA

0 Miles ½

0 Kilometers ½

(NOT ALL STREETS SHOWN)

Points of Interest

1. Arc del Triomf
2. Barri Gòtic: Catedral;
   Museu Frederic Marés;
   Plaça del Rei
3. Basílica de la Mercè
4. Castell de Montjuïc;
   Museu del Exèrcit (Army Museum)
5. Fundació Joan Miró
6. Generalitat; Ajuntament;

Palau Centelles
7. Gran Teatre del Liceu
8. Hospital de la Santa Creu
9. La Llotja
10. Museu Arqueològic
11. Museu d'Art de Catalunya
12. Museu d'Art Modern
13. Museu Etnològic
14. Museu Marítim
15. Museu Picasso

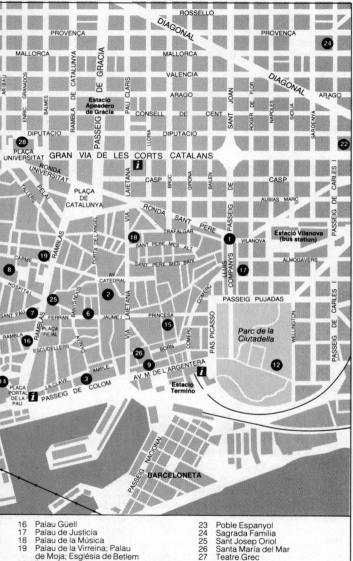

16	Palau Güell
17	Palau de Justicia
18	Palau de la Música
19	Palau de la Virreina; Palau de Moja; Església de Betlem
20	Parc d'Atraccions (Amusement Park)
21	Plaça de Toros Les Arenes (Les Arenes Bullring)
22	Plaça de Toros Monumental (Monumental Bullring)

23	Poble Espanyol
24	Sagrada Familia
25	Sant Josep Oriol
26	Santa María del Mar
27	Teatre Grec
28	Universitat

i   Tourist Information

Nevertheless, the tradition of independence has always remained, and on numerous occasions the region has revolted against the central authority of Madrid. During the Civil War, Barcelona was a Republican stronghold and a base for many anarchists and communists. As a result it suffered a rigorous suppression of both Catalan identity and language during the Franco dictatorship. But this repression had little lasting effect, for the Catalans have jealously guarded their language and culture and still only reluctantly think of themselves as Spaniards.

Regional autonomy was granted not long after Franco's death, and in 1980 the ancient Generalitat, Catalonia's home-rule parliament, was reinstated. The Catalan language is now heard on every street, street names are now in Catalan, and newspapers, radio stations, and a TV channel publish and broadcast in Catalan. The City Hall actively promotes free Catalan language classes, and the sardana, the great symbol of Catalan pride, is danced regularly all over town. The triumphant culmination of this relentless pursuit of Catalan pride and independence has been Barcelona's long-coveted Olympic nomination. Stadiums and pools are being renovated, new harborside promenades created, roads built, beaches are undergoing a cleanup, and an entire railroad station is to be moved to make way for the Olympic Village.

On a sightseeing front Barcelona is indeed rich, with its superbly contrasting medieval Gothic Quarter and elegant Modernista Eixampla, its colorful Ramblas, bustling port, and surrounding sea and mountains. Barcelona offers its visitors everything, from luxury to a wide range of moderate accommodations, restaurants, and entertainments. Its wealth of museums ranks among the best in Spain, and its parks and mountains will cost you no more than the transport to them. You are certain to leave Barcelona with a memorable impression of this vibrant and dynamic Catalan capital.

A word of warning on safety. Pickpockets and muggers are unfortunately common in Barcelona. It is best never to carry purses in the street. Put your money, one credit card, and just one or two travelers' checks in an inside pocket and lock the rest away in the hotel safe. Generally speaking it is your money the "delinquentes" are after, and not your personal safety. If you bear this warning in mind, your vacation should not be marred.

PRACTICAL INFORMATION
How to Get There

FROM THE AIRPORT. The least expensive means of getting from the airport into town is to take the airport train to Sants-Central Station. Trains leave every 20 minutes between 6:30 A.M.–11 P.M. and the journey takes about 20 minutes. From the station taxis, buses, or the subway will quickly take you to your hotel. RENFE provides a nighttime bus service when the trains are not running. There is also a day- and nighttime-bus service which will take you to the Plaça de Espanya.

A taxi into town will cost about 1,200 ptas. (1987 prices), and there is an airport supplement of about 150 ptas. for luggage.

BY TRAIN. Barcelona has three main railroad stations: Sants-Central at the end of Avda. de Roma; Estació Srança-Término on Avda. Marquès del Argentera near the port (trains to France leave from here); and the underground station Passeig de Gràcia, at the intersection of the Passeig de Gràcia and Arago. For destinations in Catalonia, local trains leave from the underground stations in the Plaça de Catalunya and from the Plaça de Espanya to Martorell, Igaualda, Montserrat, Manresa, and Berga. For the Costa Brava trains leave from the Rodalies Station near Término.

BY BUS. There is no central bus station in Barcelona though buses to most Spanish destinations leave from Estació Nord on Avda. Vilanova. For buses to Madrid, check with the tourist office.

Facts and Figures

USEFUL ADDRESSES. Tourist Offices. Tourist offices are located at Sants-Central Station (tel. 93-250-2594), open daily 7:30 A.M.–10:30 P.M.; Término Station (tel. 93-319-2791), open Mon. to Sat. 9 A.M.–9 P.M.; Gran Viá Corts Catalanes 658 (tel. 93-301-7443), open Mon. to Fri. 9–1:30 and 4–7; Plaça Sant Jaume in the City Hall *(Ajuntament)* (tel. 93-318-2525), open Mon. to Fri. 9 A.M.–9 P.M., Sat. 9–2; in the Columbus monument in Plaça Portal de la Pau, open 9:30–1:30 and 4:30–8:30; closed Mon.; and at the airport, open Mon. to Sat. 8 A.M.–8 P.M., Sun. 8–3.

Consulates. U.S.: Viá Laietana 33 (tel. 93-319-9550). **U.K.:** Diagonal 477 (tel. 93-322-2151).

Lost and Found. Go to Objetos Perdidos in the Ajuntament in Plaça Sant Jaume (tel. 93-301-3923).

Pharmacies. Farmacias de Guardia (open 24 hours) are listed in the daily newspaper *La Vanguardia*.

Police. Viá Laietana 43 (tel. 93-301-6666). In an emergency dial 091.

Main Post Office. Plaça Antoní López, at the bottom of Viá Laietana.

Main Telephone Exchange. Carrer Fontanella, on the corner of Plaça de Catalunya. Open 8 A.M.–9 P.M.

American Express. Rosselló 257, on the corner of Passeig de Gràcia (tel. 93-217-1750). Open Mon. to Fri. 9:30–6, Sat. 10–12. 24 hour service for lost cards.

Iberia Office. Passeig de Gràcia 30 (tel. 93-301-3993); Carrer Mallorca 277 (tel. 93-215-7636). Open Mon. to Fri. 9–1 and 4–7, Sat. 9–1. Reservations (tel. 93-301-6800). Flight information (tel. 93-325-4304).

Getting Around

There is a transport information booth on the Plaça de Catalunya (tel. 93-237-4545), open Mon. to Fri. 8–7, Sat. 8–1, which deals mainly with city bus transport. Get maps of the bus and subway system here.

BY SUBWAY. This is the cheapest form of public transport, and probably the easiest to use. You pay a flat fare (around 50 ptas.) no matter how far you travel; on Sundays and fiestas, fares are 5 ptas. higher. You can make moderate savings by buying a **tarjeta multiviaje,** good for 10 rides on the subway tramvia blau (for Tibidabo), and Montjüic funicular. These are available from main subway stations or from branches of the Caixa de Ahorros de Barcelona.

BY BUS. Again there is a flat-fare system, and a **tarjeta multiviaje** can be bought from the transport booth in Plaça de Catalunya. To go to the beach at Castelldejels, take the VC from outside the university, or the quicker, and slightly more expensive but less frequent, T11.

BY TAXI. Distances between places of interest in Barcelona are not especially great, so a taxi ride should not work out too expensive. When you begin your ride a standard charge of about 80 ptas. will be shown on the meter. Make sure your driver turns down the flag when you start. There are small supplements for luggage, night fares (10 P.M.–6 A.M.), Sunday and public holiday rides, rides from a train station and the port, and for going to or from the bullring or soccer game (about 50 ptas.)

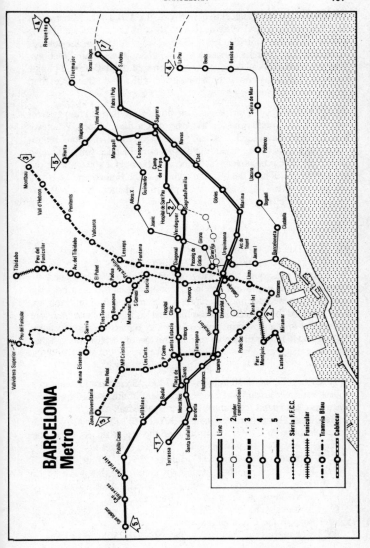

BARCELONA
Metro

ON FOOT. Modern Barcelona, north of the Plaça de Catalunya, is largely built on a grid system, though there is no helpful numbering system as in the United States. However, the old part of the town is quite different; here the narrow streets wind and twist in all directions. It is an area which can only be explored on foot, so, before you plunge into this fascinating labyrinth, arm yourself with a good free street map from one of the tourist offices.

STREET NAMES. Street names can pose a problem as most street maps on sale at press time still used the old Castilian names. Wherever possible, we have used Catalan street names and museum names throughout this chapter to tie in with the name plaques you will see in the streets. The problem can be further complicated if you come across a map which still uses the old street names of the Franco era. So if you see a street whose name is General something, chances are it will now be called something else.

Where to Stay

HOTELS. Barcelona's modestly priced accommodations tend to be elderly compared to those of other Spanish cities, but they are usually comfortable and good value. Most of our listings are in or around the Gothic Quarter, and a few are in the lower part of this area near the port. Though we have had several reports of muggings in this area, we have included these hotels because the location is central and therefore convenient for the cost-conscious traveler. If you are worried, then opt for the hotels in the Eixample or near the top of the Ramblas, rather than near the port.

Moderate

El Casal, Tapineriá 10 (tel. 93-319-7800). 36 rooms. Located in a pedestrian street just off Viá Laietana, a night in this 3-star hostel will place you just round the corner from the cathedral.

Cataluña, Santa Anna 22 (tel. 93-301-9150). 40 rooms. A prime central location in a lively street between the top of the Ramblas and Porta de l'Angel is the advantage of this good budget hotel.

☛**Continental,** Rambla de Carraletas 138 (tel. 93-301-2508). 32 rooms. Friendly service and a perfect location make this 3-star hostel one of the best budget bets. It is well maintained and located in a cozy old Barcelona house at the top of the Ramblas.

Cortés, Santa Anna 25 (tel. 93-317-9212). 46 rooms. The Cortés is a sister hotel to the Cataluña (above).

☛**Internacional,** Ramblas 78 (tel. 93-302-2566). 62 rooms. A recent face-lift has done wonders for this pleasant old hotel. It is located just across from the Liceo.

Lleo, Pelai 24 (tel. 93-318-1312). 42 rooms. The Lleo is conveniently situated between the Plaça de Catalunya and the university. It is a long-standing budget hotel, but rooms on the front can be noisy.

Mesón Castilla, Valldonzella 5 (tel. 93-318-2182). 56 rooms. You will find this reasonable 2-star hotel in the old part of town, just off Carrer Tallers. It is located in a street running parallel to Pelai and is quite handy for the Ramblas.

Moderno, Hospital 11 (tel. 93-301-4154). 57 rooms. Popular with Spaniards, and one of the most expensive in this category, this well-maintained hotel enjoys a colorful location just off the Ramblas, between the Liceo and the central market.

Nouvel, Santa Anna 18 (tel. 93-301-8274). 76 rooms. The Nouvel is a simple hotel located in a charming house with an old world air and touches of Modernista architecture.

Paseo de Gràcia, Passeig de Gràcia 102 (tel. 93-215-5824). 34 rooms. You can enjoy staying in the same block as Gaudí's famous La Pedrera apartment building if you sample this comfortable 3-star hostel.

Rubí, Viá Laietana 42 (tel. 93-319-9500). 15 rooms. Be sure to ask for a room at the back of this hostel. It is comfortable and central, but on a very noisy road.

San Agustín, Plaça Sant Agustín 3 (tel. 93-317-2882). 70 rooms. You'll be close to the Ramblas and the Boquería market in this adequate, oldish hotel located in a small square.

◓**Urbis,** Passeig de Gràcia 23 (tel. 93-317-2766). 61 rooms. The Urbis is an excellent, smart hostel near the junction with the Gran Viá. It is very popular with Spanish business people and is the most expensive in this category.

◓**Villa de Madrid,** Placa Villa de Madrid 3 (tel. 93-317-4916). 28 rooms. This elderly, but pleasant, 3-star hotel overlooks a small square off Carrer Caruda, between the Ramblas and Porta de l'Angel. It is a good budget bet.

Inexpensive

Antibes, Diputació 394 (tel. 93-232-6211). 65 rooms. The Antibes is a functional but adequate hotel. The nearest cross street is Carrer Sicilia.

◓**Condestable,** Ronda Universitat 1 (tel. 93-318-6268). 37 rooms. Long patronized by those seeking good-value accommodations, this is a reliable hotel with a pleasant breakfast room and lounge. It is located just south of the Eixample, close to the university and Alt Heidelberg beer hall.

Cosmos, Escudellers 19 (tel. 93-317-1816). 67 rooms. Although located close to several famous restaurants, the Cosmos is in the lower reaches of the Ramblas, nearer the port end. It does, however, offer good functional accommodations for the price.

Din, Valencia 191 (tel. 93-254-1200). 18 rooms. The advantage of this small hostel located between Ariban and Enric Granados is that it has a couple of cheerful budget restaurants close by.

Inglés, Boquería 17 (tel. 93-317-3770). 29 rooms, including 10 singles. Located in a colorful narrow street off the Ramblas, with its own good-value restaurant, the Inglés has long been a budgeteer's favorite.

Lider, Rambla de Catalunya 84 (tel. 93-215-5065). 29 rooms. The Lider is a simple budget hostel in the same house as the Windsor (see below).

Monegal, Pelai 62 (tel. 93-302-6566). 12 rooms. Overlook the top of the Ramblas and Plaça de Catalunya from this small third-floor hostel. The entrance is next to McDonald's on the corner of Pelai.

Neutral, Rambla de Catalunya 42 (tel. 93-318-7370). This may be an old-fashioned and basic hostel, but it is clean and very inexpensive.

Turin, Pintor Fortuny 9 (tel. 93-302-4812). 45 rooms. The Turin, formerly a hotel, has now been reclassed as a hostel. It is not a first choice, but possible if pressed.

Windsor, Rambla de Catalunya 84 (tel. 93-215-1198). 15 rooms. The Windsor is a 2-star hostel which is just a little more expensive than its neighbor the Lider (see above).

Where to Eat

RESTAURANTS. Many restaurants in Barcelona close on Saturday night and all day Sunday; some also close one other day during the week, and for a month in July or August. Be sure to check before making a special journey.

Moderate

El Bell Lloc, Legalitat 74 (tel. 93-219-7338). Located in the charming Gràcia area, this attractive, clean restaurant serves typical Catalan cuisine at most affordable prices.

● **Can Culleretes,** Quintana 5 (tel. 93-317-6485). It is well worth searching out this restaurant sandwiched in a narrow street between Boquería and Ferran, just off the Ramblas. There are three dining rooms hung with photos of visiting celebrities, and locals come here regularly for its typical Catalan dishes at very moderate prices. A good time for atmosphere is Sunday lunchtime as long as you don't mind waiting for a table.

Can Sole, Sant Carlos 4 (tel. 93-319-5012). You'll find lots of local color and old world charm at this famous seafood restaurant in Barceloneta.

Mesón Gallego, Avinyo 29. A very inexpensive *menu del día* is served at this bright and cheerful *mesón* in the heart of the Gothic Quarter.

Mesón de las Ramblas, Ramblas 92 (tel. 93-302-1180). Why not wander down the Ramblas to this cozy mesón located right on the main thoroughfares. It is popular with locals and visitors alike for its good choice of Catalan and Spanish dishes.

Raco d'en Jaume, Provença 98 (tel. 93-230-0029). Though a little off the beaten tourist track, this restaurant is justly famous for its traditional Catalan home cooking. It gives a good insight into the way Catalan families eat at home.

El Raim, in Pescatería, a narrow alleyway off Avda. Marquès de l'Argentera, not far from the Church of Santa Mariá del Mar. This tiny restaurant has been a famous Barcelona institution for over 50 years. There is no menu, so it is best negotiated by those with some Spanish and the adventurous.

●**Sopeta Una,** Verdaguer i Callis 6 (tel. 93-319-6131). Exclusively Catalan cuisine is served at this delightful restaurant. It has charming decor, and is located in a narrow street near the Palau de la Musíca.

●**El Tunel,** Ample 33 (tel. 93-315-2759). El Tunel is a real old Barcelona standby, with old-fashioned service and good reliable cooking. It is best at lunchtime.

Inexpensive

●**Agut,** Gignàs 16 (tel. 93-315-1709). The Agut has long been famous for its home cooking Catalan style, at very affordable prices.

Casa Amalia, Passatje Mercat 4 (tel. 93-258-9485). It's hard to find this family-run restaurant located in an alleyway just above Aragó, between Bruc and Girona, but it's well worth the effort. It serves real home cooking and is very popular with the locals of the area.

●**Del Teatre,** Montseny 47 (tel. 93-218-6738). Del Teatre is a charming and innovative restaurant located in the Teatre Lliure. Its daily menu is imaginative and always good value.

Egipte, Jerusalem 12 (tel. 93-317-7480). Hidden behind the

Bouqería market, this small, friendly restaurant is well known to locals for its good value, good home cooking, and huge desserts.

Elche, Vilá-Vilá 71 (tel. 93-241-3089). This is another old Barcelona favorite, serving hearty helpings you will have trouble finishing. It is located a little out of the Ramblas area in Poble Sec, across the far side of the Paral-lel.

La Pizza Nostra, Ave de Sant Viceno 2 (tel. 93-319-9058). If you've been to the Picasso Museum or Santa Mariá del Mar, then drop into this bright, friendly pizzeria and café on the corner of Carrer Montcada.

● **La Ponsa,** Enric Granados 89 (tel. 93-253-1037). Catalan food is served in this family-run restaurant at amazingly low prices.

El Rey de la Gamba, Passeig Nacíonal. There is nothing pretentious about this restaurant, to put it mildly, but this is where the locals eat. It serves a vast range of seafood and the typical Catalan *pan tomate* at very affordable prices. It is just one of many very inexpensive restaurants along the Barceloneta waterfront.

Sandoval, Comtal 28 (tel. 93-302-2187). Located between Porta de l'Angel and Viá Laietana, this popular budget restaurant is especially good for a quick lunch. Its *menu del día* is amazingly inexpensive.

Self Natrurista, Sta. Anna 13. Long lines form at lunchtime at this popular self-service, vegetarian whole-food restaurant. Prices are very cheap.

Viá Napoleone, Pelai 5. Although basically a pizzeria, this restaurant does serve other dishes too. It is hugely popular with the locals, very crowded, and incredible value.

Exploring Barcelona

The Ramblas and the Harbor

The Ramblas runs from the Plaça de Catalunya, the business nucleus and transport hub of the modern city, down through the ancient Gothic Quarter to the statue of Columbus overlooking the port. One of the liveliest promenades in Europe, traffic roars down either side of it, while in the center, a wide walkway flanked with plane trees is crammed full of newspaper stands, book stands, flower stalls, fish tanks, and bird cages. It is difficult to know where to begin, whether to plunge into the warren of narrow streets, or to head steadfastly on, concentrating on the many venerable old buildings that line your way. As you stroll, note such landmarks as the Church of Belen on the corner of Carrer Carme, and opposite, the lovely ocher baroque Palau de Moja, the swirling Modernista dragon that announces an old umbrella and fan shop, and the beautiful multilobed art nouveau street lamps.

MAJOR ATTRACTIONS. Gran Teatre del Liceu, *Ramblas and Sant Pau. Open for guided visits (some in English) Mon., Wed., and Fri. at 11:30 and 12:15.* The Liceu, built between 1845–47, is Spain's only, and the world's oldest, opera house. A fairly mundane facade hides a beautiful baroque interior where nothing has changed since its opening 140 years ago, save the installation of electricity. Anna Pavlova danced here in 1930 and Maria Callas sang in 1959. Today sees regular appearances of native Catalans Montserrat Caballe and Josep Carrers. (See *Splurges* at the end of the chapter.)

Museu Maritim, *Plaça Protal de la Pau 1. Open Tues. to Sat. 10–2 and 5–7, Sun. 10–1; closed Mon.* The museum stands in the Atarazanas Reales, the Royal Dockyards, which date from the 13th century and are some of the oldest shipyards in Europe. It houses a magnificent collection of ships and nautical paraphernalia, and several early charts, including one by Amerigo Vespucci.

Palau Güell, *Nou de la Rambla 3. Open Mon. to Sat. 11–1 and 5–8.* This palace was built by Gaudí between 1885–90 for his patron, the financier Count Eusebi de Güell, and is the only Gaudí building readily open to visitors. It offers a chance to see characteristic traits of Gaudí's eccentric style: swirling columns, decorative chimneys, parabolic arches, and fanciful cupolas. The palace makes an intriguing setting for the **Museu de les Arts de l'Espectacle** (Museum of Scenic Arts), a collection of memorabilia connected with the history of Barcelona's theater, cinema, opera, and dance.

Plaça Reial, *entrance opposite Nou de la Rambla.* The Plaça is a beautiful, if rather dilapidated, 19th-century square where harmonious arcaded houses look out onto palm trees, a wrought iron **fountain of the Three Graces,** and lampposts designed by Gaudí in 1879. Sadly, the Plaça has become a meeting place for dropouts and drug addicts, and you should steer clear of the chocolate (hash) pushers. The time to see it at its best (and safest, so long as you're wary of pickpockets) is on Sunday mornings, when crowds throng into the square to listen to orators and peruse the stalls of the weekly stamp and coin market.

OTHER ATTRACTIONS. Hospital de la Santa Creu, *between Carme and Hospital.* This ancient hospital, surrounded by a cluster of other 15th-century buildings, is the home of various cultural institutions and the **Biblioteca de Catalunya.** The lovely patio of the **Casa de Convalecencia** is the setting for summer evening concerts.

Església de Sant Josep d'Oriol, *on Plaça del Pi and Plaça Sant Josep Oriol, at the top of Casañas, off the Plaça de la B[a]Boquería. Open 8–1 and 6–9.* The church, named for Sant Josep, a 17th-century miracle worker and healer of the sick, was begun in 1322 and is a typical example of Catalan Gothic.

Mercat de la Boquería, *on the Rambla de las Flores (or Sant Josep).* This fruit and vegetable market in a 19th-century iron structure is one of the most colorful produce markets in the city. Drop in for a while and explore the narrow streets around the market building; they house some of the best bargain restaurants in town.

Plaça Portal de la Pau. *In the center of the square is the* **Monumento a Colom,** *open Mon. to Sat. 9:30–1:30 and 4:30–8:30, Sun. and fiestas 11:30–7:30.* A bronze statue of Columbus gazes out over the city and port from a vantage point 50 m. (165 ft.) on top of an iron column. The monument was begun in 1882 and opened in 1888. Inside the column is a small tourist information center and an elevator which will whisk you to the top for a magnificent view.

In the harbor in front of Columbus you can go aboard the **Carabela de Santa María,** *open 9–2 and 3 until sunset,* a replica of the flagship on which Columbus made his first voyage to the New World, or take one of the Golondrina harbor boats (9:30 A.M.–9:30 P.M.) on a half-hour ride to the lighthouse and breakwater in Barceloneta.

Barri Gotìc

No other city in Spain can boast an ancient quarter that rivals Barcelona's Barri Gotìc in either historic atmosphere or sheer wealth of monumental buildings. The Gothic Quarter is the name given to that area around the cathedral, packed with glorious Gothic buildings of the late Middle Ages, which marked the zenith of Barcelona's power in the 15th century. Traces of Barcelona's Roman past are also much in evidence. Begin your visit in the Plaça Nova, near the cathedral, where Picasso's frieze of naive figures adorns the facade of the College of Architects.

MAJOR ATTRACTIONS. Cathedral, *Plaça de la Seu. Open 7:30–1:30 and 4–7:30.* The present cathedral stands on the site of an earlier church dating from A.D. 878. Work on the present structure was begun in 1298 and was completed around 1450, except, that is, for the spire and neo-Gothic facade, which didn't materialize until 1892.

Inside, the building is a jewel of Catalan Gothic with its vast naves and side chapels, one of which, the **Lepanto Chapel,** contains the crucifix of Don Juan's famous gallery, exquisitely carved 15th-century **choir stalls** by Matías Bonafe, and a **crypt** housing the tomb of Santa Eulalia. Don't miss the beautiful Italianate cloisters built between 1385 and 1448 with their magnolias, palm trees, and unique flock of well-fed geese—though don't let these distract you from the exceptional capitals depicting scenes from the Old and New Testaments. Outside, on the **Plaça de la Seu,** the citizens of Barcelona dance the sardana on Sunday mornings and Wednesday evenings.

Museu Frederic Marés, *Comtes de Barcelona 10. Open Tues. to Sat. 9–2 and 4–7, Sun. 9–2; closed Mon.* The museum houses the fascinating, if not a little eccentric, collection of the sculptor Frederic Marés. It ranges from polychrome crucifixes in the crypt through rosaries and crib figures, to an endless array of fans, mantillas, slippers, sewing machines, hat pins, cigarette cards, walking sticks, and playing cards on the upper floors. The highlight of the whole display, for its nostalgic value, is the small suitcase acquired by Marés in Paris in 1911, which thereafter traveled with him for the next 60 years carrying all the smaller things of the entire exhibition. The museum is enchanting, don't miss it.

Plaça del Rei. In this magnificent square it is easy to feel yourself transported back five centuries or more. Facing you is the **Palau Reial Major,** the Royal Palace, which was first the residence of the Counts of Barcelona and later, in the 13th century, the abode of the Kings of Aragón. Other buildings around the square are the 16th-century **Palau del Lloctinent** (Lieutenant's Palace), the **Saló del Tinell,** the **Capilla de Santa Agata,** and the **Palau Clariana Padellás** (see below).

Plaça Sant Jaume. This lovely square was built in the 1840s at the intersection of two old Roman roads. Today it joins two of the main thoroughfares of the Gothic Quarter, the Carrer Jaume I and the Carrer Ferran. The Carrer Ferran is one of the quarter's main shopping streets, and here you will find shops straight out of the 19th century. Note the beautiful lampposts and numerous Modernista touches. The two imposing buildings facing each other across the square are the **Palau de la Generalitat** and the **Ajuntament.** In the southwest corner of the square the narrow streets lead off into the old Jewish quarter, known as El Call.

OTHER ATTRACTIONS. Ajuntament (or **Casa de la Cuitat**), *Plaça Sant Jaume. Open during business hours.* The 15th-century palace is now the City Hall and has a splendid Gothic facade. You can visit the impressive **Saló de las Crónicas** with its splendid murals, and the famous **Saló de Cent** from where the Council of One Hundred ruled the city from 1372 to 1714.

Capilla de Santa Agata, *Plaça del Rei.* The 14th-century chapel of St. Agatha is built right into the old Roman walls. Built between 1302 and 1319, its best feature is the **altarpiece** (1464–66) by Jaume Huguet.

Museu d'Historia de la Cuitat, *in the Palau Padellás on Plaça del Rei. Open Tues. to Sat. 9–1:30 and 3:30–8:30, Sun. 9–1:30, Mon. 3:30–8:30.* Visits are free on Sundays. This museum chronicles the history of Barcelona and has an especially good section on the old Jewish quarter, El Call.

Palau de la Generalitat, *Plaça Sant Jaume. Open Sundays only, 10–2.* This 15th-century palace is the seat of the Autonomous Government of Catalunya. Its outstanding features are the beautifully balustraded Gothic stairway, the **Patio de los Naranjos,** with its fancy gargoyles and orange trees, and the ornate **council chambers** and **Capilla de Sant Jordi**—St. George being the patron saint of Catalunya.

Roman Remains. For the best view of the 4th-century Roman walls, walk along Tapinería, behind the chapel of St. Agatha, as far as Plaça Ramon Berenguer el Gran. Then visit the excavations of the old Roman and Visigoth city off the patio of the Frederic Marés Museum. Off the narrow Calle Paradis, a symbol in the paving stones marks the top of Mons Taber, the hill on which the Romans built their city.

Saló del Tinell, *entered up the stairway in the corner of Plaça del Rei.* Built in 1362, this magnificent banqueting hall is now used as an exhibition center. According to legend, it was here that Ferdinand and Isabella received Columbus on his return from his first voyage to America.

La Ribera and Ciutadella Park

La Ribera is the area between the lower reaches of the Viá Laietana and the Parc de la Ciutadella. In the 13th and 14th centuries it was the hub of Catalonia's great maritime and economic expansion. The highlights of La Ribera are the beautiful sailors' Church of Santa Mariá del Mar and the Picasso Museum, housed in two of the finest of the many nobles' and merchants' mansions of the Calle Montcada. This old part of town has undergone a revival in recent years and with its concert venues and theaters is now one of the most fashionable quarters, new bars, cafés, and restaurants opening up regularly.

Calle Argentería (Silversmiths' Street) was the main road in medieval times between the old walled city and the port, and it is a good place to begin your explorations.

MAJOR ATTRACTIONS. Museu d'Art Modern, *in Ciutadella Park. Open Tues. to Sun. 9–2, Mon. 2–7:30.* The museum occupies part of the Ciutadella Palace, built in the early 1700s as part of the city's defenses. Its excellent collection of paintings, sculpture, and decorative arts is mostly the work of Catalan artists, or those educated in Catalonia. Among leading names are works by Mariano Fortuny, Santiago Russinyol, Ramón Casas, Isidre Nonell, Joaquim Sunyer, and Antoni Tàpies. Its most famous paintings evoke the golden age of bohemianism when Picasso lived in Barcelona.

Museu Picasso, *Montcada 15. Open Tues. to Sat. 9:20–1:30 and 4–8:30, Sun. 9:30–1:30, Mon. 4–8:30.* This is one of the world's foremost museums on the artist, who spent his formative years (1895–1904) in Barcelona. The collection covers Picasso's life, from early childhood sketches done in Málaga in 1895 just prior to the family's move to Barcelona, to exhibition posters made shortly before his death. The artist lived in Barcelona during his "Blue Period," and there are sketches of the city and his menu for Els Quatre Gats (1900). One of the best rooms houses his 58 variations on Velázquez's *Las Meninas.*

Santa Mariá del Mar, *Plaça Santa Mariá. Open 8–1 and 4–7:30.* This beautiful Gothic church was built between 1329 and 1383 for the Virgin of the Sailors. It is pure 14th-century Catalan Gothic, with a wide central nave, a lovely rose window, and magnificent soaring columns. It has a simple beauty and uncluttered purity since the ecclesiastical burnings of the Civil War rid the church of its baroque trappings.

OTHER ATTRACTIONS. Fundació Maeght, *Montcada 21. Open Tues. to Sat. 10–1:30 and 4:30–8.* The Foundation is housed in the ancient **Carvello Palace** and puts on good exhibitions of contemporary sculpture and art.

La Llotja, *Passeig Isabel II.* The Stock Exchange dates from the end of the 14th century when it served as a Marine Exchange. The old Gothic Exchange, the **Saló de Contrataciones,** still serves as Barcelona's Stock Exchange and is open to visitors.

Museu d'Indumentaria, *Montcada 12. Open Tues. to Sat. 9–2 and 4:30–7, Sun. 9–2. Closed Mon.* This charming Costume Museum displays costumes from the 16th to the 20th centuries and a good collection of lace. It is well worth visiting for the building alone—a former palace. Almost opposite, don't miss the **Calle Mosques** (Street of the Flies), the narrowest street in Barcelona.

Palau de la Música, *Amadeu Vives 1, just off Viá Laietana.* Though a little above the Ribera district, this fantastic Modernista concert hall is well worth visiting. It was built in 1980 for the Orfeó Català (Catalan Choral Society) by Domènech i Montaner. Inside it is a veritable Modernista extravaganza. *Officially, visiting hours are Mon. to Fri. at 11:30 A.M., though this may depend on rehearsal arrangements.*

Parc de la Ciutadella. The Ciutadella is the city's most popular park and is at its best on Sunday afternoons. The palace now houses the **Autonomous Parliament of Catalonia.** The park was the site of the Universal Exhibition of 1888, and many of its landmarks are relics of the Fair. Features to look out for, other than the Museum of Modern Art already mentioned, are:

Castle of the Three Dragons, *Passeig del Tillers.* Designed as the restaurant of the 1888 Fair, this building now houses the **Museum of Zoology,** *open 9–2; closed Mon.*

Fountain of Aurora, *on the main lake.* This monumental cascade was the centerpiece of the 1888 Fair. The winged dragons may have been the work of Gaudí.

La Senyoreta del Paraigua. The Fountain of the Lady with the Umbrella became the symbol of the city of Barcelona and of the 1888 Exhibition.

Zoo. *Open daily 9:30–7:30.* One of the best in Spain, the zoo's most famous resident is Floc de Neu (Snowflake), the world's only albino gorilla in captivity.

Passeig del Born. Tournaments, festivals, and processions were held along this wide promenade from the 13th to the 17th centuries, and much of its old importance has now been revived. There are fashionable restaurants, exotic cocktail bars, and specialist food shops, and some of the old houses have been restored in keeping with the original 14th-century mansions. The **Born Market,** built in 1874, is now a leading venue for trade fairs, festivals, and exhibitions.

Montjüic

Montjüic, named for the Jewish community that once lived on its slopes, lies between the city and the sea, dominated by its 17th-century citadel. It was laid out as a public park at the beginning of this century, and in 1929 served as the site of the great international exhibition held alongside the one in Seville. The imposing Palau Nacíonal was Spain's leading museum. The huge fountain here, the Fuentes Luminosas, was the showpiece of the Fair and is still a very worthwhile spectacle on weekend evenings (also Thursday nights in summer). Higher up is the Olympic Stadium, built for the 1929 Fair with the intention of Barcelona hosting the 1936 Olympics—later grabbed by Berlin. Barcelona is now renovating the stadium for the Games in 1992.

Close by is the Miró Foundation and the Amusement Park and Fun Fair, whose luminous big wheel dominates the city's skyline. There are great views of the city and port from the terrace in front of the castle, and from the cafés below in the Miramar Gardens. The cluster of museums, cactus and rose gardens, and other delights merit a whole day here, if you have the time. The main means of transport to the park are the Montjüic funicular from the Paral-lel, or the cable car across the harbor from Barceloneta. Alternatively you can take buses no. 61 or no. 101 from the Plaça de Espanya.

MAJOR ATTRACTIONS. Fundació Joan Miró. *Open Tues. to Sat. 11–8, Sun. 11–2:30; closed Mon.* The Foundation was a gift from the artist Joan Miró to his native city and was completed in 1975. It holds frequent temporary exhibitions, as well as housing a small, but comprehensive, collection of works by Miró.

Museu d'Art de Catalunya, *in the Palau Nacíonal. Open 9:30–2; closed Mon. Entrance is free on Sundays.* Barcelona's number one museum contains an extraordinary collection of Catalan Romanesque and Gothic art treasures such as can be seen nowhere else in the world. In the same building is the delightful **Museu de Ceràmica** *(same hours, same ticket)* which chronicles the history of ceramics from the 13th century to the present day, with emphasis on the art in Catalonia, Aragón, and the Balearics.

OTHER ATTRACTIONS. Museu Arqueològic, *Passeig Santa Madrona. Open Tues. to Sat. 9:30–1 and 4–7, Sun. 10–2; closed Mon. Entrance is free on Sundays.* The exhibits here date from prehistoric times to the 8th century A.D. and include Carthaginian artifacts and Greek and Roman finds from Empuriés (Ampurias) on the Costa Brava. Don't miss the Roman glass room and the beautiful carved bust of the Dama de Elche.

Museu Etnològic, *Passeig Santa Madrona. Open Tues. to Sat.*

9–8:30, Sun. 9–2, Mon. 2–8:30. Entry is free on Sundays. The museum has a lively collection of exhibits from Australia, Africa, Latin America, Morocco, Turkey, and Japan.

Museu Militar, *in Montjüic Castle. Open Tues. to Sat. 10–2 and 4–8; 4–7 in winter; closed Mon.* You can reach the castle by the Montjüic funicular and cable car, or by bus no. 101 from the Plaça de Espanya and then the cable car. The Montjüic citadel was built in 1640 and has been stormed on numerous occasions. It continued as a military installation until 1960 and now houses a military museum with a well-arranged collection that includes some excellent displays of miniature soldiers—one collection alone has over 23,000 pieces.

Poble Espanyol. *Open 9–7.* This miniature Spanish village was built in 1929 by Miguel Utrillo and Xavier Nogues for the International Exhibition, the houses and plazas representing the different architectural styles of all regions of Spain. You can wander from the walls of Avila to the wine cellars of Jerez, and maybe see some glass-blowing demonstrations or a printing press in action. But watch out for the grossly overpriced souvenirs on sale. The village's buildings are home to two small museums, the **Museum of Graphic Arts** and the **Museum of Popular Arts and Crafts,** *both open Tues. to Sun. 9–2.*

The Eixample

The area known as the Eixample was the result of a mid-19th century project to extend the city. The name "eixample," or "ensanche" in Castilian, means widening or enlargement. The architect of the scheme was Ildefons Cerdá and his concept for the new town was a series of streets running parallel to the sea, crossed by streets at right angles to it. The major part of the Eixample lies between the Diagonal and the Gran Vía de las Corts Catalanes and is bisected by the lovely tree-lined avenue of the Rambla de Catalunya. To the right is the area known as La Dreta de l'Eixample, which contains the most notable buildings, while to the left L'Esquerrade l'Eixample contains the public service buildings such as the Hospital Clínico and the university.

The building was carried out at the height of the Modernismo movement, a Spanish offshoot of Art Nouveau, and its principal architects, Antoni Gaudí, Domènech i Montaner, and Puig y Cadafalch, were some of the leading exponents of this genre.

MAJOR ATTRACTIONS. Passeig de Gràcia. This elegant parade, lined with expensive stores, banks, and cafés, boasts some of the most remarkable examples of Modernismo in Barcelona.

Between Consell de Cent and Aragó, the block to your left is known as the Manzana de la Discordía, or Block of Discord. At no. 35 is the **Casa Lleó Morera** in lovely floral style by Domènech i Montaner. At no. 41 the **Casa Amatller** is by Puig i Cadafalch in a sort of pseudo Gothic style with a stepped gable decorated with ceramics. No. 43 is Gaudí's **Casa Batlló** with a mottled mosaic facade, wrought iron balconies, and ceramic roof decorated with an ornamental pinnacle.

Farther up the street, at no. 82, is Gaudí's **Casa Milá** (1910), more often known as "La Pedrera." Its remarkable curving stone facade actually ripples its way round the corner of the block. Inside, the patios and roof terrace are stunning, but permission to visit must be obtained in advance.

OTHER ATTRACTIONS. Further examples of Modernismo can be found in abundance in the Dreta de l'Eixample:

Casa Calvet, *Caap 48.* Built in 1898, this was Gaudí's first apartment building.

Casa Montaner, *Mallorca 278.* This house by Domènech i Montaner, with a charming polychrome ceramic facade, now houses the provincial government.

Casa de les Punxes, *Diagonal 416, near Bruc.* This is a striking medieval-looking building by Puig i Cadafalch.

Casa Thomas, *Mallorca 291.* The interior of this house by Domènech i Montaner can be visited.

Edificio Vidal-Quadras, *Diagonal 373,* near Roger de Lluria. **The Museu de Música** now occupies this building by Puig i Cadafalch. It has a fascinating collection of old instruments and is open Tues. to Sun. 10–2.

Escuela de Música, *Bruc, at the corner of Valencia.* The School of Music is by A. de Falguera.

Mercado e Iglesia de la Concepción, *Aragó, near Girona.* The market is an unusual metallic structure, and the adjoining church is Gothic with a beautiful 14th-century cloister.

Passatge Permanyer, *between Pau Claris and Roger de Lluria.* This alleyway is one of the jewels of the Eixample. Its vast mansions stand proudly behind front gardens.

Gaudí's Barcelona

The great Catalan genius and leading exponent of the Modernismo movement was born in Reus in 1852, and met his death in 1926 when he was run over by a streetcar. He died unrecognized in the hospital two days later. He had become a virtual recluse, spending the last 15 years of his life living in a shed on the construction site of his most famous building, the church of the Sagrada Familia.

MAJOR ATTRACTIONS. Church of Sagrada Familia (Church of the Holy Family). *This occupies an entire block of the Eixample between Mallorca and Provença, Marina and Sardenya. The site is open 8 A.M.–8 P.M. in summer, 9–6 in winter.* Gaudí was recommended as the architect for the Sagrada Familia in 1883 and now lies buried in the crypt. Far from complete on his death, work has once again begun on the church and is being carried out, amid much controversy, to Gaudí's last known plans. It is estimated it will take a further 70 years to complete.

The three portals of the church were to have been the bible of the poor, each facade to be surmounted by four towers, representing the 12 apostles. The apse was to be crowned by the Dome of the Virgin, and four large towers, dedicated to the Evangelists, were to surround the huge central cavity, the symbol of the Saviour. In his lifetime Gaudí worked only on the **Facade of the Nativity.**

Gaudí's great temple became something of a symbol to the people of Barcelona, and during the frenzy of church burning at the outbreak of the Civil War in 1936 it was the only church, other than the cathedral, that was left untouched. Today you can visit the site, see the plans and a museum, and take an elevator to the top of one of the towers for a magnificent view of the city.

OTHER ATTRACTIONS. Parc Güell, *on Mount Carmelo in the northwest of the city.* To reach the park, take subway line 3 to Lesseps and then walk (it's a steep climb), or take bus no. 19 or no. 24 from the Plaça de Catalunya. This delightful park was begun by Gaudí as a kind of garden city development to demonstrate his ideas on town planning. The project was never finished, but it constitutes a fantastic Art Nouveau extravaganza, a kind of park playground with a mosaic pagoda, undulating benches, and weird, magical architectural effects, with magnificent views over the city to the Mediterranean.

A Modernist house in the park—Gaudí's home for several years—has now been converted into a small **Gaudí museum** which is *open on Sundays only from 11–2 and 4–7.* For further information on Gaudí and permission to visit the insides of his buildings, contact La Catedrá Gaudí (Friends of Gaudí), Finca Güell, Avda. Pedralbes 7 (tel. 93-204-5250).

Excursions

MONTSERRAT. An almost obligatory side trip from Barcelona is to the shrine of **La Moreneta,** the Black Virgin of Montserrat, 50 km. (30 mi.) away, high in the legendary peaks of the Sierra de Montserrat. You can opt either for one of the organized excursions run by Juliatour or Pullmantour, or make your own way there on public transport. Buses to Montserrat (Autocares Juliá) leave from Plaça Universitat 12 (tel. 93-318-3895), or you can take one of the Ferrocarriles de Catalunya trains from the Plaça d'Espanya. Take the Manresa line as far as Aeri de Montserrat, from where a cable car runs to Montserrat (the first car up leaves around 10 A.M. and the last down at 6:45 P.M.)

The weird saw-toothed peaks of the Sierra de Montserrat have given rise to countless legends: Here Parsifal found the Holy Grail, St. Peter left a statue of the Virgin Mary carved by St. Luke, and Wagner sought inspiration for his opera. Whatever the truth of such mysteries, Montserrat is a world-famous shrine and Catalonia's spiritual heartland. A monastery has stood on the site since the early Middle Ages, though the present 19th-century building replaced the rubble left by Napoleon's troops in 1812. Today, honeymoon couples flock here in their thousands—marriage-blessing is big business in Montserrat—and twice a year on Apr. 27 and Sept. 8, the diminutive statue of Montserrat's Black Virgin becomes the object of Spain's greatest pilgrimage.

Of the monastery, only the basilica and museum are open to visitors, 6–10:30 and 12–6:30. The basilica is dark and ornate, its blackness pierced by the glow of hundreds of votive lamps. Above the high altar stands the famous polychrome statue of the Virgin and Child to which the faithful can pay their respects by way of a separate door. *(The basilica is closed to visitors during services though you are welcome to attend mass.)* At around 1 P.M. and 7 P.M. (but not in July) you can hear the famous boys' choir, the **Escolanía,** founded in the 13th century, singing the *Salve*—a memorable experience.

The **Monastery Museum** is divided into two sections: The old—**(sección antigua)** *open Tues. to Sat. 10:30–2*—contains old masters, among them paintings by El Greco, Correggio, and Caravaggio, and amassed gifts to the Virgin; the new—**(sección moderna)** *open Tues. to Sat. 3–6*—concentrates on recent Catalan painters.

But Montserrat is as memorable for its setting as for its religious treasures. The vast monastic complex is dwarfed by the grandeur of the jagged peaks and the crests are dotted with hermitages, some of which, such as Sant Joan, can be reached by funicular. The views over the mountains away to the Mediterranean and, on a clear day, as far as the eastern Pyrenees, are quite breathtaking, and the rugged boulder-strewn setting makes for some dramatic walking and hiking country.

Shopping

The area around the Gothic Quarter is the best in Barcelona for affordable shopping. The prices here are generally far less inflated than in the smarter stores of the Passeig de Gràcia and the Diagonal. Nevertheless, fashionable boutiques, jewelry stores, and antique emporiums are gradually usurping the old crafts and local produce shops that once characterized this quarter. But hunt around, and in the wealth of shops tucked away in this fascinating maze you should find something you fancy at a price you can afford.

For old-fashioned shops with typical Spanish charm, try **Carrer Ferran.** For antiques, the **Carrer de la Palla** and **Banys Nous** in the old Jewish quarter have one antique store after another, and they deal in small curiosities: books, postcards, maps, prints, etc., as well as furniture. And don't forget the **antiques market** held every Thursday on the **Plaça Nova** in front of the cathedral. You're unlikely to find any real bargains, but the prices may well be less than back home.

For young fashion stores, jewelry, and good gift shops, hunt around the area between **Caruda, Portaferrisa** (especially good), and **Boquería.** A small shopping arcade leads from Portaferrisa into the Plaça del Pi. There are two further street markets in this area; the **artists' market,** held on Saturday mornings in the Placeta del Pi, alongside the church of Sant Josep Oriol; and the **stamp and coin market,** held every Saturday morning in the **Plaça Reial.**

Finally, the central branches of the leading department stores are also close by. **El Corte Inglés** (tel. 93-302-1212) on the north side of Plaça de Catalunya is open Mon. to Sat. 10–8 (no siesta closing), and just down the street on Portal de l'Angel is **Galerias Preciadós.** Remember to ask for your foreigners' tax (IVA) refund if you are planning on spending a lot in either of these stores.

If you like avant-garde posters, prints, and art postcards, there are plenty to be found in the numerous art shops and galleries along **Carrer Montcada.** At no. 19–21 is a specialist Dalí shop, selling posters, cards, and other memorabilia connected with this Catalan artist. The **Carrer Princesa,** and streets just off it, have some interesting specialist shops such as herbalist, occult, and magic stores. The **Passeig de Gràcia** and **Rambla de Catalunya** are lined with stores and fashion houses, but the prices here are some of the highest in town and you may well want to window-shop only. If you like antiques, browse around the **Centre d'Antiquaris** at **Passeig de Gràcia 57,** next door to *British Airways*. There are some 75 stores in this antiques center, though for bargains you'd do better at the market in front of the cathedral.

Entertainment and Nightlife

To find out what's on in Barcelona, look in the daily press: *La Vanguardia, Correo Catalan,* or *Diario de Barcelona,* or better still, buy a copy of the weekly *Guía del Ocio* from any newsstand. The information office of the City Hall in Plaça Sant Jaume is also helpful in advising on exhibitions, festivals, trade fairs, etc.

MUSIC AND OPERA. Antiguo Hospital de la Santa Creu, on Carrer Hospital, just off the Ramblas, has open-air concerts on its patio in summer.

Liceo Opera House, on the Ramblas, at the corner of Sant Pau, is one of the world's most famous opera houses. The box office at Sant Pau 1 (tel. 93-318-9277) is open Mon. to Fri. 8–3, Sat. 9–1. Tickets for performances on the day are on sale in the main Ramblas entrance (tel. 93-301-6787) from 11–2 and from 4:30 onwards. The main opera season runs from Nov. through Mar., but performances can usually be seen much later into the spring. The ballet season is usually in the fall. Tickets are not expensive by international standards, and cheaper tickets can usually be obtained on the day of the performance.

Palau de la Música, Amadeo Vives 1, just off Viá Laietana. This is the main concert hall. Barcelona has a long musical tradition and best known are its Orquestra de la Ciutat de Barcelona (Barcelona City Orchestra) and the Orfeó Càtala (Catalan Choral Society). The Sunday morning concerts are a veritable institution and are often cheaper than evening performances. The ticket office is open Mon. to Fri. 11–1 and 5–9, Sat. 5–9 only. Tickets for performances on the day are available only from 5 P.M. onwards. Tickets for Sunday morning concerts can usually be bought on the day, but go early.

THEATER. Most theater performances are put on in Catalan, though a few are in Castilian Spanish. Catalonia is well known for its mime troupes (Els Joglars and La Claca), and an international mime festival is often held in March, and there is also a puppet festival. The Teatre Lliure specializes in experimental theater, and political and satirical reviews. In summer plays and song and dance performances are held at the Teatre Grec in Montjüic Park.

FILM. The majority of foreign films are dubbed into Spanish or even Catalan. However, there are some cinemas which show films in their original language. Look in the press or *Guía del Ocio* for movies marked v.o. (versión original). The Filmoteca, at Travessera de Gràcia 63, shows three films a day in their original language (often English).

JAZZ. Abraxas Jazz Auditorium, Gelabert 26 (tel. 93-230-5922). This large venue puts on live and recorded music, mostly jazz. Closed Mon. and Aug.

La Cova del Drac, Tuset 30 (tel. 93-217-5642). Located just off the Diagonal, this bar is well known for its live music, usually Catalan singing or jazz. Closed Sun.

Zeleste, Argentería 65 (tel. 93-319-8641). This is one of the best live jazz bars in town.

FLAMENCO. Barcelona is not richly endowed with flamenco spots, as Catalans are not too fond of this very Andalusian spectacle. The following tablaos are aimed right at the tourist market. The show and one drink (all you need buy) costs around 2,000 ptas.

El Cordobés, Ramblas 35 (tel. 93-317-6653). This is the one most visited by tour groups, but it's fun and colorful.

El Patio Andaluz, Ariban 242 (tel. 93-209-3378). This is slightly more expensive, but again aimed at the tourist industry. Dinner and flamenco from 9 P.M.

◆

S P L U R G E S

A Night at the Opera. Attending a performance at Barcelona's Gran Teatre del Liceo, the world's oldest opera house, is a treat you shouldn't miss even if you're not usually a devotee of opera. Ballet and opera performances are held at the Liceo year-round except for midsummer months, and frequently attract such leading Spanish lights as Plácido Domingo or Montserrat Caballé, as well as numerous international stars. The exquisite interior is gilded and has plush red velvet fittings, five tiers of horseshoe-shaped balconies, each with their own decorative motifs, and an elaborate railing around the orchestra.

For performances the auditorium is lit by the glow of the simple white lights; these date back to 1861–2 when the Liceo was rebuilt after a serious fire started by the theater's original gas lamps. Four mourning boxes are cleverly concealed on either side of the stage to shield the identity of their occupants (in the 19th century it was not considered proper for those in mourning to attend the opera). Don't miss the magnificent foyer (one floor up) with its splendid mirrors, Ionic columns, and medallions of well-known composers and singers.Seat prices vary with each performance (for ticket details, see page(149) but are generally far less outrageous than such luxuries back home at London's Covent Garden or New York's Metropolitan.

◆

ANDALUSIA— THE INTERIOR

Andalusia is Spain's most southerly kingdom. It is a magical land that really does live up to its travel-brochure image: The sun does shine almost every day, the scent of orange blossom and jasmine perfumes the air, bougainvillea clings to the dazzling white walls beneath a deep blue sky, and fountains play in vine-covered patios.

It was here that the Moorish occupation of Spain lasted longer than in any other region of the country. From 711 until the fall of Granada in 1492—the culmination of the Christian Reconquest—the Moors of Andalusia endowed this land with great buildings, showing Islamic art and architecture at their best.

The greatest legacies of the Moors, not only in Andalusia, but in the whole of Spain, are undoubtedly the region's Mezquita, or Great Mosque, in Córdoba, and the famous Giralda Tower in Seville. But the Moorish influence is not confined to these majestic structures. Andalusia's small white villages of square, flat-roofed houses, with their cool inner patios and wrought iron grilles, are just as much a Moorish inheritance. Even the cry of the Arab *muezzin* can be detected in the wailing flamenco notes of the *canto jondo,* or deep song. Moorish names, too, are still in evidence: Guadalquivir, the "great river" of the Arabs; Gibraltar, the "rock of Tarik"; and words such as *alcázar* (fortress) or *azahar* (orange blossom) all have Arabic roots.

The Christian conquerors also left their mark, in the form of great Gothic cathedrals—Seville has one of the finest in Spain—and Renaissance palaces and baroque churches, financed by the wealth that flowed in from the New World. In the long term, it was the misuse of this wealth that lead to the eventual decline of Spain; in the short term, the avenging Christians busied themselves destroying numerous magnificent Arab buildings and expelling the Moors, in the process losing their invaluable skills in agriculture and irrigation. This led to the growth of a system of land ownership that exploited the landless peasants and centered around vast *cortijos* (ranches) run by absentee landlords. Some of these are still dotted around the Andalusian landscape today. Even though a vast land reform program is now underway, one half of Andalusia's land is still owned by just 2% of its population. Unemployment, too, already high in Spain, is at its highest in Andalusia, and is one of the causes of the petty street crime that dogs the region. Nonetheless, the advent of regional government, and the obvious deep love of life of the Andalusians, gives the region an outlook that is far from gloomy.

With their great monuments and unique Hispano-Moorish beauty, Córdoba, Seville, and Granada are among the most visited cities in Spain. They have long been used to catering to visitors, so don't expect to find any real bargains here, though they all offer a wide choice of accommodations and places to eat. Remember that prices soar and rooms are hard to come by during Seville's Holy Week and April Fair, and during Granada's Music Festival from mid-June to mid-July. However, better bargains can be found in Ubeda and Baeza.

Travel within the region is relatively inexpensive, if slow. Pricewise, there is little to choose between buses and trains, but generally speaking getting from one city to another is better done by bus. Trains, other than those on direct lines to Madrid, can be very slow, and often involve tiresome changes and lengthy waits. In addition, bus terminals, unlike main train stations, usually offer baggage-checking facilities.

Baeza

The small town of Baeza, set amid the rolling hills and endless olive groves of Jaén province, is a superb example of ostentatious splendor. Of Roman origin, it was reconquered from the Moors by the Saint King Ferdinand III in 1239, and for the next two centuries stood on the frontier with the Moorish kingdom of Granada. Its greatest era was the 16th century, when it boasted a university (which survived until 1824) and a clutch of wealthy nobles all vying to outdo one another by the magnificence of their Renaissance palaces. The poet Antonio Machado came to live in Baeza in 1913 and taught in the local school, the former university, until he moved to Segovia in 1919.

Baeza is rather off the beaten track for most visitors, and offers only the simplest accommodations and eating places. But with its aura of bygone splendor and its charming unhurried atmosphere, it can make a pleasant overnight stop, or can be visited en route to Ubeda, Cazorla, or Jaén.

GETTING THERE. By Train. The nearest rail station is Linares–Baeza, 13 km. (8 mi.) away. It's located in the middle of the country on the Madrid–Córdoba and Madrid–Granada lines. Buses meet certain trains, but not at night or on weekends, so always check.

By Bus. Buses run to Baeza from Linares and Jaén (1¼ hours), and stop here on the Córdoba–Ubeda run.

By Car. Baeza is on N321 from Jaén to Ubeda, or just off N322 Bailén–Linares–Ubeda–Albacete road.

TOURIST OFFICES. Pza. del Pópulo (tel. 953-74-04-44).

WHERE TO STAY. Comercio (I), San Pablo 21 (tel. 953-74-01-00). 31 rooms. This is a very simple 2-star hostel, but all the rooms have their own bathroom and are comfortable enough for an overnight stay. It is located on the main street, close to the central Paseo.

Juanito (I), Avda. Arca del Agua (tel. 953-74-00-40). 21 rooms, all with bathrooms. This is the only place in town officially classified as a hotel. Prices are somewhat higher than the Comercio, and the hotel restaurant, which specializes in local home cooking, is one of the best places to eat; it is open to nonresidents.

MAJOR ATTRACTIONS. Ayuntamiento, *Pza. Cardenal Benavides.* This is Baeza's City Hall, an impressive building with a splendid Plateresque **facade.** It was originally used as a courthouse and prison.

Palacio de los Marqueses de Jabalquinto, *Cuesta San Felipe*

Neri. This is the most notable of Baeza's many outstanding Renaissance palaces, with a magnificently ornate **facade** dating from the 16th century. Inside, the Renaissance **patio** and **stairway,** both dating from around 1600, are very much more somber in comparison with the exuberant facade. Today, the building is used as a seminary.

Plaza de los Leones. This delightful cobbled square at the far end of the Plaza Mayor and central Paseo is the showpiece of Baeza. It takes its name from the **statue of four lions** in its center. The **Casa del Pópulo,** built around 1530, was formerly a courthouse, but today houses the tourist office. It is thought that the first Mass of the Reconquest was celebrated on its curved balcony. The **Puerta de Jaén,** marking the beginning of the Jaén road, was dedicated to the emperor Charles V, and was built to commemorate the emperor's passage in 1526 through Baeza en route to Seville for his marriage to Isabel of Portugal.

Plaza de Santa María. The square takes its name from the **fountain of Santa María** in its center. The fountain dates from 1564, and has become the symbol of the city of Baeza. The cathedral began life as a mosque, but was largely rebuilt in the latter half of the 16th century. It has some notable painted *rejas*—iron screens—by Bartolomé, and a decorative baroque **silver monstrance** which is borne in the Corpus Christi processions and kept in a concealed niche, and which will reveal itself to onlookers who insert a coin in a machine. Remains of the original mosque can be seen in the Gothic cloisters.

Cazorla

Cazorla is a remote, unspoiled Andalusian village at the end of a bumpy road in the far east of Jaén province. It is the gateway to a national park which numbers deer, wild boar, goats, royal and imperial eagles, and the rare *quebrantahuesos* (bearded vulture) among its wildlife. The pine-clad slopes and towering peaks, up to 2,200 meters (6,500 feet), of the Sierras of Cazorla and Segura rise above the village, and below it stretch miles of olive groves. Nearby lies the source of Andalusia's most important river, the Guadalquivir, which flows northwards at first into the great Tranco reservoir, with its 95-meter (300-foot) dam, before turning west towards Córdoba, Seville, and the Atlantic. In the village streets, low white houses wind their way up mountain sides, and, in spring, purple Judas trees blossom in its two picturesque squares, watched over by ruined churches, castles, and dilapidated towers.

Other than the expensive parador built originally as a hunting lodge and set some 28 km. (17 miles) up in the mountains, Cazorla offers only simple and basic accommodations, but this charming village cannot fail to enchant, and makes for a rewarding visit even if you do not have a car with which to explore the surrounding scenery.

GETTING THERE. By Bus. There are regular bus services from Jaén, Baeza, and Ubeda.

By Car. Take C325 and C328.

TOURIST OFFICES. F. Martínez Delgado 1 (tel. 953-72-00-00).

WHERE TO STAY. Andalucía (I), Martínez Ferlero 41 (tel. 953-72-12-68). 11 rooms. This simple 1-star hotel is the best bet in the village. Its rooms all have bathrooms and phones.

Guadalquivir (I), Nueva 6 (tel. 953-72-02-68). 16 rooms. You'll be hard put to it to find anywhere much simpler than this little hostel, but it is clean and fairly comfortable, and some rooms have bathrooms. There's no restaurant, but there are a number of very reasonable bars and restaurants nearby.

WHERE TO EAT. La Sarga (I), Pza. del Mercado (tel. 953-72-09-68). This is an unpretentious restaurant and one of the best places to eat in Cazorla. Try the local specialties, such as game in season, or trout from the mountain streams. Closed Tues.

La Montería (I), Generalisimo 20. Come here, to one of Cazorla's most popular *mesones,* and sample the numerous *tapas* and *raciones*— many of them specialties of the region.

Córdoba

Córdoba is one of Spain's oldest cities and was both the Roman and Moorish capital of Spain. It remains one of the most outstanding examples of the Moorish heritage in Andalusia. From the 8th to the 11th centuries, the city was one of the Western world's greatest centers of culture and learning, with Moors, Christians, and Jews all living harmoniously together within its walls.

Reconquered from the Moors by the Saint King Ferdinand in 1236, it was in Córdoba that Queen Isabella granted Columbus the commission for his first voyage to the New World, and a son of Córdoba— Gonzalo Vernández, better known as El Gran Capitán—captured the kingdom of Naples for Spain. Today, the muddy water and unkempt banks of the Guadalquivir evoke little of the city's glorious past, but the impressive Roman bridge and the old Arab waterwheel are signs of a grander era.

Córdoba's greatest drawing card is undoubtedly its beautiful 8th-century mosque, La Mezquita, one of the finest mosques ever built by the Moors. The narrow streets of whitewashed houses in the old Moorish city are well worth exploring, as are those around the synagogue and the *zoco,* a former Arab *souk.* A stroll through the warren of old streets to the east of the Mezquita is also fascinating, but be prepared for decaying houses and unsightly rubbish. The modern town offers little to lure the visitor away from the charms of the old city.

May and the fall are the most pleasant times to visit Córdoba: Avoid the sweltering heat of high summer when most places close around midday until the following morning.

For safety's sake, avoid the streets of the Old Town, other than the busy tourist route, during the deserted siesta hours. If you do go, then don't go alone, and don't carry bags and cameras when few people are around. The narrow alleyways are a mugger's paradise.

GETTING THERE. By Air. Córdoba Airport is 6 km. (4 mi.) west, near Majanaque. There are daily flights on Air Condal (tel. 957-47-78 35) from Madrid, Mon. to Fri., and flights once a week from Barcelona and Palma de Mallorca. Iberia office: Ronda de los Tejares 3 (tel. 957-47-12-27/47-26-95).

By Train. Córdoba lies on the main Madrid–Seville–Cádiz line, so there are several trains daily in each direction, as well as a daily TALGO from Valencia and Barcelona. Other services run from Granada, Málaga, Ronda, and Algeciras, some involving a change at Bobadilla junction. Córdoba station is on the Avda. de América (tel. 957-47-93-02). RENFE information: tel. 957-47-87-21. RENFE office: Ronda de los Tejares 10 (tel. 957-47-58-84).

By Bus. There is no central bus station in Córdoba. Buses arrive at different locations depending on their place of origin. It is best to check at the tourist office. Use the following only as a guide: Buses from Madrid via NIV, Ubeda, Valencia, and Barcelona (Empresa Ubesa) arrive at Paseo de la Victoria 29 (tel. 957-29-01-58); buses from Madrid via Puertollano and Ciudad Real arrive at Paseo de la Victoria 5 (tel. 957-47-75-51); buses from Seville and Jaén arrive at Avda. de Cervantes 22 (tel. 957-47-23-52); and buses from Málaga, Granada, and Badajoz (Empresa Alsina Graells) arrive at Avda. Medina Azahara 29 (tel. 957-23-64-74).

TOURIST OFFICES. Of the Regional Andalusian Government: Palacio

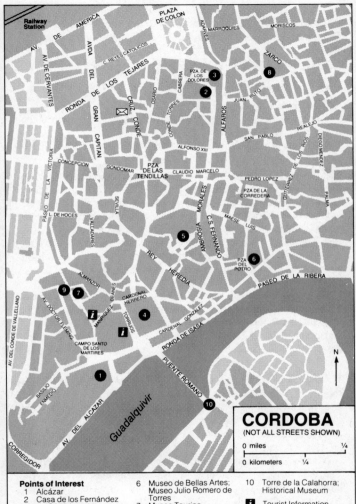

CORDOBA
(NOT ALL STREETS SHOWN)

0 miles ¼

0 kilometers ¼

Points of Interest

1 Alcázar
2 Casa de los Fernández de Córdoba
3 Cristo de los Faroles
4 La Mezquita/Catedral
5 Museo Arqueológico
6 Museo de Bellas Artes; Museo Julio Romero de Torres
7 Museo Taurino
8 Palacio de los Marqueses de Viana
9 Singagoga
10 Torre de la Calahorra; Historical Museum

i Tourist Information

✉ Post Office

de Congresos y Exposiciones, Torrijos 10, beside the Mosque (tel. 957-47-12-35). Open Mon.–Sat. 9:30–2. Municipal Tourist Office: Pza. Judas Levi (tel. 957-29-07-40). Open 8–3 and 5–7:30; 4–6:30 in winter.

USEFUL ADDRESSES. Police. Avda. Dr. Fleming (tel. 957-47-75-00).

Post Office. Cruz Conde 21.

Telephone Exchange. Pza. Tendillas.

Guides. English-speaking guides are available at the door of the Mosque, or at Torrijos 2 (tel. 957-41-06-29).

City Tours. Viajes Vincit, Alonso de Burgos 1 (tel. 957-47-23-16) runs three-hour sightseeing tours of the city by bus and on foot.

GETTING AROUND. By Taxi. Taxi stands are plentiful with the main ones in Pza. Tendillas, on the Avda. Gran Capitán, outside the Meliá Hotel, and around the Mosque. You can also hail a taxi in the street.

On Foot. Córdoba is a compact city and most of the sights are within walking distance of each other. Much of the old city is anyway only negotiable on foot, but before you set out, arm yourself with a detailed map (available from the tourist offices); it may just save you from getting lost. Public transport is by city bus, but you are unlikely to need it.

By Buggy. *Coche caballos* (horse buggies) ferry tourists around the main sights. The main hiring places are Torrijos alongside the Mosque, the Campo Santo de los Mártires across from the Alcázar, and near the Meliá Hotel on Paseo de la Victoria. They seat four, possibly five, and rides should last an hour and cost around 2,000 ptas. Always agree on the price before you set off.

WHERE TO STAY. Colón (M), Alhaken II 4 (tel. 957-47-00-17). 40 rooms, all with bathrooms. This is a recent, functional hotel tucked away at the end of a cul-de-sac just off the Avda. Gran Capitán. It is quite close to the rail station and within easy walking distance of the modern town center. It does not serve meals, but restaurants and cafés are close at hand.

Marisa (M), Cardenal Herrero 6 (tel. 957-47-31-42). 28 rooms. The draw here is a charming old Andalusian house with a great location. It's in the heart of the Old Town, overlooking the Patio de los Naranjos on the north side of the Mosque—a perfect setting surrounded by shops and some of Córdoba's best restaurants.

Riviera (M), Pza. Aladreros 7 (tel. 957-47-30-00). 28 rooms. The Riviera may be functional and rather unexciting, but it's in a reasonably convenient location in the city center, off Calle Concepción and just a 3-min. walk from the Plaza Tendillas.

Selu (M), Eduardo Dato 7 (tel. 957-47-65-00). 118 rooms. A combination of Andalusian-style modernity and a location in one of the atmospheric and narrow streets of the Old Town makes the Selu a good low-cost bet. The hotel caters to many budget tour groups, but the individual traveler will not feel out of place. Rooms are comfortable.

Alegría (I), Menéndez Pelayo 8 (tel. 957-47-05-44). 28 rooms. This simple 1-star hostel is located in a narrow alleyway between the Avda. Gran Capitán and the Pza. Aladreros, just round the corner from the Riviera (see above). It is a typical Andalusian house, charming and clean, and some of the rooms have bathrooms. It also serves both breakfast and dinner at very moderate prices.

Andalucía (I), José Zorrilla 3 (tel. 957-47-60-00). 40 rooms. The Andalucía is a long-established budget hostel in the center of town, just off Avda. Gran Capitán and Calle Concepción. Accommodations are functional but comfortable, and all rooms have bathrooms. It is located above a good-value economical restaurant which belongs to, but functions separately from, the hotel.

Boston (I), Málaga 2 (tel. 957-47-41-76). 40 rooms. Head here for a very central 2-star hostel, overlooking the Pza. Tendillas. All the rooms have bathrooms but no meals served, not even breakfast. Cafés and economical restaurants are close at hand however.

Luis de Góngora (I), Horno de la Trinidad 7 (tel. 957-29-53-99). 23 rooms. This is a typical Andalusian house with lots of charm, tucked away in the tangle of narrow streets of the Judería, just off the pleasant Pza. Trinidad. All rooms have bathrooms.

Seneca (I), Conde y Luque 7 (tel. 957-47-32-34). 12 rooms. Though only a simple, 1-star hostel, this is one of the most charming of Córdoba's good-value accommodations. Hidden away in a narrow street up the side of the Marisa Hotel (see above) and close to the Mosque, this old Andalusian house boasts one of the city's most beautiful patios. The owners are friendly, some of the rooms have bathrooms, and breakfast is served but not dinner. Rooms are often hard to come by.

Serrano (I), Benito Pérez Galdós 6 (tel. 957-47-01-42). 40 rooms. The Serrano is located in the modern town, just off the Avda. Gran Capitán and close to the station. Though unprepossessing from the outside, the hotel is built around a typical patio, and is charming and clean. All rooms have bathrooms, and breakfast is served.

El Triunfo (I), Cardenal González 79 (tel. 957-47-55-00). 26 rooms, all with bathrooms. This is the most successful, but the most expensive of the good-value accommodations, and its location is a great bonus. It is a recently modernized old Andalusian house on the south side of the Mosque, just off the Pza. Triunfo. The hostel has its own restaurant and a small patio.

WHERE TO EAT. La Almudaina (M), Campo Santo de los Mártires 1

(tel. 957-47-43-42). With an Andalusian patio and Cordoban decor and cooking, this is a most attractive place to dine at moderate prices. The restaurant is located in a charming 15th-century house and former school at the entrance to the Judería, across the square from the Alcázar.

El Churrasco (M), Romero 16 (tel. 957-29-08-19). Another well-known Cordoban tradition, in the heart of the Judería, this is an atmospheric restaurant with patio and a colorful *mesón* at the entrance. The grilled meat dishes are outstanding and the specialties are, of course, *churrasco,* a pork dish in pepper sauce, and an excellent *salmorejo*. A good selection of fish dishes is also offered. Closed Thurs. and Aug.

El Gallao Dorao (M), Cardenal Herrero 14 (tel. 957-48-01-08). For relaxed and economical dining, try this restaurant beside the Marisa Hotel. Close to the Mosque, it is popular with locals and tourists alike for its wide choice of dishes, good-value *menus turísticas,* and pleasant decor. Closed Sun. evenings.

Mesón Bandolero (M), Torrijos 8 (tel. 957-47-64-91). This beautifully decorated restaurant is located in an old Cordoban mansion. Due to its prime location beside the Mosque it caters principally for tourists and also doubles up as the restaurant for the adjacent Maimonides and Adarve hotels.

Andalucía (I), José Zorilla 3. A plain restaurant somewhat lacking in atmosphere, but its menu offers sheer good value for money. It is much patronized by locals who go there to eat on an economical everyday basis.

Las Dalias (I), Hermandades del Trabajo 5. This is a new restaurant conveniently situated close to the main square on the edge of the Judería district. It is located in an alleyway between Jesús y María and the Plaza Dr. Luque, just to the southwest of the Plaza Tendillas.

Mesón La Bodega (I), located under La Almudaina (see above), offers the typical dishes, *tapas,* and *raciones* at very reasonable prices. Closed Sun. evenings.

Mesón La Luna (I), Calleja de la Luna. A colorful *mesón* set in a lovely garden between calles Cairuan and Judíos, this used to be one of Córdoba's most atmospheric taverns. It now caters predominantly to tourists, offering several inexpensive menus and cheap *à la carte* eating. Food is not tops, but the setting makes up for it.

El Patio Arabe (I), Pza. Judas Levi. This is a delightfully decorated restaurant with dining in an outdoor patio and is located in the heart of the Judería near the Municipal Tourist Office. It is simple, and very much geared to tourists, but it is pretty and offers a choice of low-cost menus.

Los Patios (I), Cardenal Herrero 16. Aimed straight at the tourist market, Los Patios offers a fixed-price menu (around 800 ptas.), serve-yourself buffet (drinks extra), and outdoor dining in an exquisitely beautiful patio decorated with countless potted plants. It won't score many marks for *haute cuisine,* but the setting is enchanting.

El Triunfo (I), Cardenal González 87. El Triunfo is another tourist restaurant, but if an inexpensive meal somewhere close to the Mosque is what you are looking for, then it fits the bill very well. The food may be rather unexciting, but prices are low and there is a small sunny patio at the back of the restaurant. Sample the *gazpacho* or a *bocadillo,* or choose from a range of *platos combinados.*

Finally, the Calle Victoriano Rivera, just off the north side of the Pza. Tendillas, offers several inexpensive dining opportunities. The **Imperio** (I) is a typical budget restaurant with tables on the sidewalk and some good cheap menus; and next door at no. 6 is the **China Pekin** (I), a reasonably good Chinese restaurant which won't stretch the limits of your purse too far.

MAJOR ATTRACTIONS. La Mezquita (The Mosque), *tel. 957-47-05 12. Open 10–1:30 and 4–7; 3:30–6 in winter. Also open 8:30–10 A.M. to worshippers only.* Córdoba's magnificent Mosque, together with its **Patio de los Naranjos** (Orange Tree Courtyard), forms a rectangle partitioned by row after magnificent row of forestlike pillars supporting red-and-white horseshoe arches. In Muslim times the Mosque was open onto the patio.

The founder of the Mosque, Abd ar-Rahman I (756–88), incorporated into his new building marble pillars and capitals from earlier Roman and Visigoth shrines. Under Abd ar-Rahman II (822–52) the Mosque boasted possession of an original copy of the Koran and a bone from the arm of the Prophet Mohammed, and became a place of Muslim pilgrimage second only to Mecca. Al Hakam II (961–76) built the beautiful Mihrab, and the Mosque was completed around 987 by Al Mansur (976–1002).

The Mosque has been used as a cathedral by the Christians since 1236, and in the 13th century they built the **Villaviciosa Chapel,** whose Mudéjar architecture blends harmoniously with the lines of the Moorish Mosque. Not so the baroque **Cathedral-Coro,** sanctioned by Charles V in the 1520s. The belfry belongs to the same period, and was built around the original minaret. A climb to the top of it is rewarded by stunning views over the Guadalquivir and the city rooftops.

OTHER ATTRACTIONS. Alcázar de los Reyes Cristianos, *off Pza. Campo de los Mártires (tel. 957-29-63-92). Open 9:30–1:30 and 4–7; 3:30–6 in winter; closed Mon. The gardens are open and illuminated from May to Sept., 10 P.M. to 1 A.M.* Built in Moorish style by Alfonso XI in the 14th century, this *alcázar* served as a base for the Inquisition for 400 years. The buildings are not spectacular, but the view from the tower of the Roman bridge is wonderful, and the gardens and patios delightful on summer nights.

Museo Arqueológico Provincial, *Pza. Jerónimo Paez (tel. 957-47-10-76). Open Tues. to Sat. 10–2 and 5–7, Sun. 10–1:30; closed Mon.* This is an intelligently displayed archeological collection housed in a small Renaissance palace. Don't miss the superb Roman mosaics and pavements or the fascinating exhibits from the days of the Caliphate.

Museo de Bellas Artes, *off Pza. del Potro (tel. 957-47-33-45). Open Tues. to Sat. 10–2 and 5–7, 4–6 in winter; Sun. 10–1:30; closed Mon.* Make time to visit this fine arts collection that includes work by the Cordoban sculptor Mateo Inurria (1867–1924), Murillo, Valdes Leal, Zurbarán, and Goya.

Museo de Julio Romero de Torres, *opposite the Museo Bellas Artes.* This was the home of the Cordoban artist Julio Romero de Torres (1874–1930) who, with his brother Enrique, produced some fine Art Nouveau bullfight posters and paintings of languid Cordoban beauties. Some 50 paintings are on display, and *entrance is free.*

Museo Taurino, *Pza. Maimónides (also known as Pza. Bulas) (tel. 957-29-09-35). Open Tues. to Sat. 9:30–1:30 and 5–8, 4–7 in winter; Sun. and fiestas 9:30–1:30; closed Mon.* The Museum of Bullfighting is housed in the attractive Casa de las Bulas in the Judería. It contains a fascinating collection of bullfighting memorabilia, including the hide of the bull that put an end to the legendary Manolete.

Palacio de los Marqueses de Viana, *Pza. de Don Gome (tel. 957-48-22-75). Open June–Sept. 9–2; Oct.–May 10–1 and 4–6; Sun.*

10–2; closed Wed. Dating from the 14th century, this magnificent palace is known as the Museum of Patios because of its 14 galleried patios. Enjoy the numerous works of art and then wander in the beautiful gardens. In summer the patios are often open at night.

Plaza de la Corredera (or Plaza de la Constitución). The square is now sadly dilapidated, but its history is intriguing and a market is held here every morning. In days gone by there was a prison beneath the square, bullfights were staged here, and the city garrotte (which killed by strangulation) stood in its center.

Plaza de los Dolores (Square of Sorrows). The famous statue of **Cristo de los Dolores,** a Calvary scene, stands here. Take time also to look at the splendid inlaid Mudéjar doors of the 17th-century **Capuchine Convent,** and the superb Plateresque facade of the **Casa de los Fernández de Córdoba.**

Plaza del Potro. This is a picturesque square named after the **Fountain of the Colt** *(potro)* in its center. Cervantes is reputed to have stayed at an inn here, the now beautifully restored **Posada del Potro.** It is used for displays of local craftwork and painting. The **Paco Peña Flamenco Center,** where flamenco courses are held in summer, is also located in this square.

Sinagoga (Synagogue), *Calle Judíos. Open Tues. to Sat. 10–2 and 5–7, Sun. 10–2; closed Mon.* Built around 1315, this is the only synagogue in Andalusia to have survived the expulsion of the Jews in 1492. Its Hebrew and Mudéjar stucco tracery is stunning.

Torre de la Calahorra *(tel. 957-29-39-29). The tower is open Tues. to Sat. 9:30–1:30 and 5–8, 4–7 in winter; Sun. and fiestas 9:30–1:30; closed Mon.* The tower was built in 1369 at the end of the Roman Bridge, on the far bank of the Guadalquivir, to guard the entrance to Córdoba. Today it houses the city's **Historical Museum.**

EXCURSIONS. Ruins of Medina Azahara. *Open 10–2 and 4–6, Sun. and fiestas 10–1:30; closed Mon.* If you decide to visit by car, leave Córdoba along Avda. de Medina Azahara and keep heading west along C431 (Palma del Río road). The ruins are off a side road to the right. If you have no car, local buses to Palma del Río will drop you on the highway at the Medina Azahara turning. The ruins are then about a 2-km. (1½mi.) walk away. Check opening times and bus times with the tourist office *before* setting out.

Medina Azahara was founded in 936 by Abd ar-Rahman III for his favorite woman, az-Zahra ("The Flower"). It is said that it took 10,000 men, 2,600 mules, and 400 camels 25 years to erect this fantasy of 4,300 columns in dazzling pink, green, and white marble and jasper brought from Carthage. On three terraces there stood a palace, a mosque, luxuriant baths, fragrant gardens, fish ponds, even an aviary and a zoo. However, in 1013 this Moorish paradise was sacked and destroyed by Berber mercenaries, and over the next 900 years was allowed to fall into total ruin.

But in 1944 the **Royal Apartments** were miraculously rediscovered, and there followed a careful reconstruction of the **Throne Room.** The outline of the mosque has also been excavated, and there is a small display of columns, capitals, and other relics, though the most precious of these have been removed to Córdoba's Archeological Museum.

SHOPPING. Córdoba's most typical handicrafts are fine embossed leather goods, and delicate silver filigree jewelry. The first is a legacy of the Moors, the second stems from the exploitation of the silver mines of the Sierra Morena. Examples of both can be found in the tourist shops around the Mosque in the **calles Torrijos, Cardenal Herrero,** and **Deanes.**

Granada

Of all Spain's cities, none can compare with Granada. It lies in the most romantic of settings, against the unforgettable backdrop of the Sierra Nevada, and is crowned by the most glorious of all Moorish legacies, the pink-gold palace of the Alhambra. From its windows you can gaze across to the city spread way below, to the hill of the Albaicín, the old Arab quarter with its steep twisting streets of dazzling white houses, and to the Sacromonte, the highest of Granada's three hills.

After the fall of Córdoba in 1236, the Moors fled to Granada and established the Nasrid dynasty which, for the next 200 years, led Granada to the height of its glory, with commerce and industry and the arts and sciences flourishing. But in 1492 Granada, the last Moorish stronghold in Spain was weakened by internal dynastic squabbles, and the Catholic kings Ferdinand and Isabella seized this opportunity to end 781 years of Moorish rule in Spain.

Granada is also the city of Columbus, who here obtained Isabella's patronage for his voyage to the New World. It was the inspiration for Washington Irving's *Tales of the Alhambra*. And it was on a hillside just outside Granada, in August 1936, that one of the city's most famous sons, the literary genius Federico García Lorca, became one of the first victims of the Spanish Civil War.

The modern city of Granada, with its mundane thoroughfares and

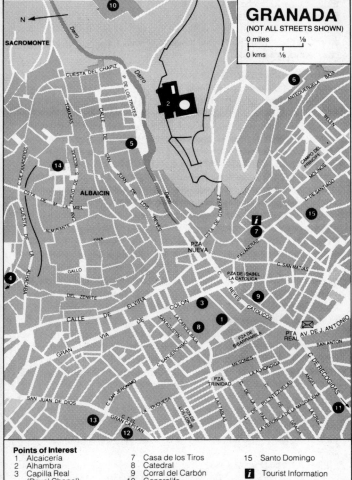

GRANADA
(NOT ALL STREETS SHOWN)

Points of Interest

1	Alcaicería	7	Casa de los Tiros
2	Alhambra	8	Catedral
3	Capilla Real (Royal Chapel)	9	Corral del Carbón
4	La Cartuja	10	Generalife
5	Casa de Castril; Museo Arqueológico	11	La Huerta de San Vicente
6	Casa de Manuel de Falla	12	San Jerónimo
		13	San Juan de Diós
		14	San Nicolás

15 Santo Domingo

i Tourist Information

✉ Post Office

— Moorish Walls

traffic-choked streets, may well disappoint, although squares like the Plaza Trinidad and Plaza Bib-Rambla are pleasant places to while away the time, and the alleyways and souvenir shops of the Alcaicería have a charm of their own. But it is first and foremost for the Alhambra that one comes to Granada, and this cannot fail you.

GETTING THERE. By Air. Granada Airport (tel. 958-27-34-00), for domestic flights only, lies 18 km. (12 mi.) to the west of the city, off N342 to Málaga, just beyond Santa Fe. There are daily flights on Aviaco to and from Madrid and Barcelona. Bonal buses (tel. 958-27-24-97) run between the airport and the city center, leaving Pza. Isabel la Católica an hour and a quarter before the flight departure time. Times are listed at bus stops. The Iberia office is at Pza. Isabel la Católica 2 (tel. 958-22-14-52).

By Train. Granada Station is on Avda. de Andaluces (tel. 958-23-34-08), off Avda. de la Constitución, about one mi. from the center. It can be reached by city bus no. 11 from the Puerta Real or Gran Vía Colón near the cathedral. Granada is on a direct line from Madrid via Linares–Baeza, and there are approximately three services a day, including a TALGO and a convenient overnight sleeper. Other services run from Algeciras, Málaga, Seville, and Córdoba, all via Bobadilla, where you may have to change. A direct service runs from Almería via Guadix. The RENFE office in town is on Reyes Católicos on the corner of Sillería, near Pza. Nueva (tel. 958-22-34-97).

By Bus. The main bus station is Alsina Graells at Camino de Ronda 97 (tel. 958-25-13-58) with services to and from Madrid, Algeciras, Málaga, Córdoba, Seville, Jaén, Ubeda, Motril, and Almería. The other main bus company is Bacoma on Avda. de Andaluces 12 (tel. 958-23-18-83) from outside the train station. It runs services to and from Murcia, Alicante, Valencia, and Barcelona. Both can be reached on the circular city bus no. 11 from Puerta Real or Gran Vía Colón.

TOURIST OFFICES. Casa de los Tiros, Pavaneras 19 (tel. 958-22-10-22). Open 9:30–2 and 5–7:30; closed Sat. afternoon and Sun.

USEFUL ADDRESSES. Police. Pza. de los Campos (tel. 958-22-49-84).

Post Office. Puerta Real.

American Express. Bonal, Avda. de la Constitución 19 (tel. 958-27-63-12).

Guides. They can usually be hired at the Alhambra ticket office just above the Puerta de la Justicia. They do visits to the Alhambra and, if required, the Royal Chapel, Cathedral, and the Cartuja.

GETTING AROUND. Transport around the city is by public bus, but most places, other than the bus and train stations, and possibly the Cartuja, can usually be reached on foot. However, if you don't fancy a steep climb, bus no. 2 will take you from the Pza. Nueva to the Alhambra, and bus no. 7 from Reyes Católicos to Calle Pages in the Albaicín. Taxis can be hailed anywhere, but main stands are in the Puerta Real–José Antonio area.

WHERE TO STAY. **América** (M) Real de la Alhambra 53 (tel. 958-22-74-71). 14 rooms. The América is a charming hostel in a former private house actually within the Alhambra precincts. Most rooms overlook the pretty patio, but some have views over the Alhambra and Generalife. Rooms with bathrooms are fairly pricey, but those without should fall well within the limits of your budget. However, the América is second only in popularity to Granada's famous parador, and it is advisable to make a reservation months ahead. Breakfast and dinner are served. The hostel is closed in winter.

Carlos V (M), Pza. de los Campos 4 (tel. 958-22-15-87). 28 rooms. This is a deluxe hostel on the fourth floor of an old house in a pleasant square in the town center. There are rooms with and without bathrooms, and meals are served.

Don Juan (M), Martínez de la Rosa 9 (tel. 958-27-15-41). 64 rooms. The Don Juan is a recent hotel in the more modern part of town between Camino de Ronda and the Pza. Gran Capitán. The rooms are functional, but comfortable.

Inglaterra (M), Cetti Meriem 10 (tel. 958-22-15-59). 40 rooms. If it's old-world period style and charm that attracts you, then this very centrally located hotel between the Gran Vía and Calle Elvira is ideal. It is close to the cathedral and shops, and several good-value restaurants and *tapas* bars.

● **Kenia** (M), Molinos 65 (tel. 958-22-75-06). 16 rooms. The Kenia is a quiet hotel in a former villa in a residential section of town, with personalized service and a large shady garden. Dinner is served. It is a little more expensive than others in this category, but the surroundings well merit spending that little bit extra.

Rallye (M), Camino de Ronda 107 (tel. 958-27-28-00). 44 rooms. The location may be dull, but this hotel is handy for the bus station and is well served by buses into town. The building itself is functionally modern, but it is comfortable and, unusually for a hotel that caters largely for tour groups, its restaurant, the Alacena, is renowned for good food, and is much frequented by locals.

Sudán (M), José Antonio 60 (tel. 958-25 -84-00). 69 rooms. With its old-fashioned rooms and aged dining room, this is a hotel that will appeal to those who enjoy a turn-of-the-century atmosphere. It's generally fairly simple. Rates in winter are better value.

Britz (I), Cuesta Gomérez 1 (tel. 958-22-36-52). 22 rooms. This is the least expensive in our Inexpensive selection, but, despite having only 1 star, it's a pleasant spot, located close to Pza. Nueva on the hill leading up to the Alhambra. Some rooms have bathrooms, but there is no restaurant.

San Joaquín (I), Mano de Hierro 14 (tel. 958-28-28-79). 26 rooms. This simple hotel with its pretty patio is located in the university area, near the Church of San Juan de Dios. There are rooms with and without bathrooms, and breakfast and dinner are both available at very low prices. Like the Britz, it is clean, but very basic.

Los Tilos (I), Pza. de Bib-Ramla 4 (tel. 958-26-67-12). 34 rooms. The hotel itself is unexciting, but it has clean, functional rooms, all with bathrooms, and overlooks a delightful central square packed with flower stalls, toy stands, and, in summer, lively cafés. It's close to the cathedral and Alcaicería, and has the further advantage of being in a traffic-free square.

➋ **Victoriano** (I), Navas 24 (tel. 958-22-54-90). 53 rooms. This is Granada's all-time best-value classic. In an old town house just off the Pza. del Carmen and Reyes Católicos, it caters to low-cost tour groups and to the individual traveler seeking great value for money. There are rooms with and without bathrooms, while its restaurant (open to nonresidents) offers an excellent *à la carte* menu and choice of very attractive *menus del día*, served with old-fashioned style.

WHERE TO EAT. Columbia (M), Antequeruela Baja 1 (tel. 958-22-74- 33). Beautifully located on the Alhambra hill, this restaurant's terrace offers magnificent views of the city, and you can often dine to live guitar music. It definitely caters to tourists, and the views may outshine the food. Prices are rather high, but the atmosphere is fun. Closed Sun.

➋ **Los Manueles** (M), Zaragoza 2 (tel. 958-22-34-15). A real traditional restaurant with ceramic tiles and smoked hams hanging from the ceiling. The prices are very reasonable, and there is good old-fashioned service.

Mesón Antonio (M), Ecce Homo 6 (tel. 958-22-95-99). This *mesón* is a simple, homey restaurant, popular with locals, in a typical Andalusian house just off the Campo del Príncipe. It specializes in roasts cooked in a charcoal oven, and there is an unusual basque influence to many dishes. Closed Sun. and July through Aug.

Sevilla (M), Oficios 14 (tel. 958-22-12-23). The Sevilla is one of

Granada's best-known restaurants and is located beside the cathedral in the Alcaicería. It is picturesque, with typical Granadino decor, if a little cramped, and there is a superb *tapas* bar at the entrance. You may need to book, and make your selection carefully if you don't want to overstep your budget.

Alcaicería (I), Oficios 8 (tel. 958-22-43-41). The delightful setting for this restaurant is the old Arab silk market, but this sometimes outshines the food. On summer evenings you can dine in a beautifully lit outdoor courtyard to the accompaniment of live guitar music. Value-for-money tourist menus are on offer alongside more pricey *à la carte* selections.

Chikito (I), Pza. del Campillo 9 (tel. 958-22-33-64). A superb selection of seafood *tapas* and good fish casseroles are on offer in this agreeable bar and restaurant. In the '20s it was a favorite meeting place of Lorca and his artistic friends, but the name and decor have changed somewhat since then.

☻El Ladrillo (I), Placeta de Fátima. This very popular bar off Calle Pages in the Albaicín is owned by a fishmonger, and the wide variety of *tapas* and fish dishes are always superbly fresh. In summer there are tables on the sidewalk for evening dining.

La Nueva Bodega (I), corner of Elvira and Cetti Meriem. Anything from a sandwich or *tapas* and *raciones* to a three-course meal can be ordered at this real budget diner. It is well known to both locals and tourists alike for its very reasonable prices.

☻El Nuevo Restaurante (I), Navas 25 (tel. 958-22-64-56). Located opposite the Victoriano hotel, this restaurant is plain and simple and much patronized by locals. It is definitely a no-frills restaurant, but it is clean, with swift, adequate service, and basic Spanish dishes at amazingly cheap prices.

☻Pizzería Verona (I), Calle Elvira. A definite favorite with the Granadinos, this traditional Italian pizzeria lies toward the northern end of the Calle Elvira.

El Polinario (I), Real de la Alhambra 4 (tel. 958-22-29-91). Lying within the Alhambra precincts, near the América hostel, this is a convenient place to have lunch while visiting the Alhambra. You can have snacks or sandwiches in the bar, or a more expensive buffet lunch in the pleasant outdoor courtyard.

MAJOR ATTRACTIONS. The Alhambra. *Open Mon. to Fri. and Sun. 9:30–6 (ticket office closes at 5:15), Sat. 9:30–6 and 8–10 P.M. Admission is free on Sun. after 3 P.M. Entrance tickets, expensive by Spanish standards, have separate tear-off sections for the Alcazaba,*

*Charles V's Palace, the Casa Real, and the Generalife. They are valid
for two days: the day of purchase and the following day. (At press time
certain sections of the complex were closed due to extensive restoration work.)*

Founded in the 1240s by Ibn el-Ahmar, or Alhamar, the first king
of the Nasrids, the Alhambra once comprised an entire complex of
houses, schools, baths, barracks, and gardens surrounded by defense
towers and mighty walls. Today, only the Alcazaba fortress and the
Royal Palace, built chiefly by Yusuf I (1334–54) and his son Mohamed
V (1354–91), remain. An intricate fantasy palace of endless patios,
arches, and cupolas, lavishly colored and adorned by geometrical
patterns of marquetry and ceramic tiles, lacelike stucco, and ornamental
stalactites, it is the last and the greatest embodiment of Moorish art
in Spain.

Although lived in for a time by Charles V, by the 17th century decay
had set in, and it wasn't until the 19th century that a restoration
program began which has continued over the last 100 years. Today,
most of the stucco and tiles adorning the walls are new.

The precincts of the Alhambra are entered through the **Puerta de
las Granadas,** a Renaissance gateway built by Charles V. Elms
planted by the Duke of Wellington adorn the slopes leading to the main
entrance, the **Puerta de la Justicia,** or Gate of Justice, built in 1340.

Beyond the ticket office, the original fortress of the **Alcazaba** is
dominated by the **Torre de la Vela,** whose summit offers an
unsurpassable view of the city. The circular Renaissance **Palace of
Charles V** stands on the site of apartments torn down by the emperor.

The heart of the Alhambra, the **Casa Real,** or Royal Palace, is
divided into three sections: the Mexuar, the Serrallo, and the Harem.
The **Mexuar** was the administrative center of the Alhambra and offers
stunning views of the Albaicín and Sacromonte. The **Serrallo** is a
series of state rooms, and centers around the famous **Patio de los
Arrayanes,** or Court of Myrtles, with its fragrant shrubs and huge
goldfish pool. In the **Hall of the Ambassadors,** with its magnificent
cedarwood dome, Boabdil surrendered to the Christians and Isabella
received Columbus. The **Harem** is reached through the **Mozárabes
Gallery,** a fine spot for photographing the famous **Patio de los
Leones,** the heart of the Harem. On the south side is the
Abencerrajes Gallery, with a stalactite ceiling of awesome beauty
and a star-shaped cupola reflected dreamily in the pool below. To the
east lies the **King's Chamber,** decorated with ceiling frescoes, and to
the north, the **Hall of the Two Sisters,** named for the two white

marble slabs in the floor, its ceiling resplendent with some of the Alhambra's most superb stucco work.

Finally, a roundabout route leads to the **Partal Gardens,** the **Apartments of Charles V,** later appropriated by Washington Irving, and to the **Arab Baths,** decorated with brightly colored tiled mosaics and lit by star-shaped pinpoints of light in the ceiling.

Avenues of bougainvillea, wisteria, neat boxwood hedges, cedars, and cypresses lead to the **Generalife,** the ancient summer palace of the Nasrid kings. Its terraces, promenades, and cypress and oleander afford a breathtaking view of the city and a perfect setting for the summer ballet and concert performances held in its amphitheater. Delicate fountains and streams cascading amid a profusion of wisteria, oleander, roses, and jasmine complete the perfection of one of the loveliest gardens in the world.

OTHER MAJOR ATTRACTIONS. Capilla Real (Royal Chapel), *entrance on Calle Oficios. Open 11–1 and 4–7; 3–6 in winter.* This magnificent chapel was begun in 1506 by Enrique Egas, and finished in 1521. With the capture of Granada in 1492 and the end of the Reconquest, Isabella decided that she and her husband Ferdinand should be laid to rest in that city. Their daughter Juana la Loca and her husband Felipe el Hermoso also lie here, and in the **sacristy** are Ferdinand's sword, Isabella's crown and scepter, and a fine collection of Isabella's paintings by medieval Flemish masters. A splendid altarpiece shows Boabdil surrendering the keys of the city to its conquerors.

La Cartuja (Carthusian Monastery), *Camino de Alfacar, in the north of town. Open 11–1 and 4–7; 3–6 in winter.* The monastery can be reached by city bus or taxi, or by a 30-min. walk from the city center. It was begun in 1506 and was moved to its present site in 1516, its construction continuing for some 300 years. It is lavishly baroque and, though splendid in its own way, may prove over-ornate to many tastes.

Cathedral, *entered from Gran Vía, the Royal Chapel, or the Pza. de las Pasiegas. Open 11–1 and 4–7; 3–6 in winter.* Adjoining the Royal Chapel and commissioned by Charles V, Granada's Renaissance cathedral was begun in 1521 by the Chapel architect Enrique Egas, but completed only in 1714.

OTHER ATTRACTIONS. Albaicín. The Albaicín is the old Moorish quarter of the city, an area of steep twisting streets and alleyways with a mixture of dilapidated white houses and luxurious villas with fragrant gardens. Many of the churches were formerly mosques, and there are numerous bars to be discovered. The view from the terrace in front of the Church of San Nicolás of the Alhambra silhouetted against the Sierra Nevada is stunning.

Alcaicería. This is the old Moorish silk exchange, bounded by the Gran Vía, Zacatín, and Oficios. The original market burned down in the 1840s, but it has been charmingly rebuilt to house arcades of souvenir shops. At night the arches and courtyards are lit by rows of white lanterns.

Casa de Castril, *Carrera del Darro 41. Open 10–2; closed Mon.* This richly decorated 16th-century palace houses Granada's **Archeological Museum,** which includes a collection of Egyptian burial urns found near Almuñécar and a beautiful Moorish room. Close by, at no. 31, are the **Arab Baths,** known as **El Bañuelo.** They are some of the best preserved in Spain, and date from the 11th century.

Casa de Manuel de Falla, *Antequeruela Alta. Open 10–2 and 4–7; 4–6 in winter; closed Mon.* De Falla's charming house contains some sketches and cartoons by Picasso, the composer's furniture, and mementos. It is located close to the Manuel de Falla Concert Auditorium.

Corral del Carbón, *Mariana Pineda, just off Reyes Católicos.* This Arab inn, the only one of its kind in Spain, was used by the Moors as a lodging house, and for storing goods. Its name means Coal Store and the Spaniards used it as such in the 19th century. Today it houses displays of expensive furniture and handicrafts.

La Huerta de San Vicente, *Calle Arabial and Vírgen Blanca. Open 10–1 and 4–7.* Lorca spent his summers in this charming house where you can now see family portraits, memorabilia, and the desk where he wrote many of his greatest works.

San Jerónimo, *Rector López Argueta 9. Open 10–1:30 and 4–7.* The Church and Convent of St. Jerome is a magnificent Renaissance building by Diego de Siloé.

San Juan de Dios, *in the street of the same name. Open 10–1 and 4–6.* The mortal remains of San Juan de Dios (St. John of God) are housed in this, the most notable baroque church in Granada.

EXCURSIONS. Fuente Vaqueros. *11 km. (7 mi.) west of Granada, between N342 Málaga road and N432 to Córdoba,* this is the village where Lorca was born in 1898. His birthplace was opened as a museum in 1986 to commemorate the 50th anniversary of the poet's death. To reach Fuente Vaqueros, contact the tourist office, or Alsina Graells (tel. 958-25-13-58) at the Camino de Ronda Bus Station. The

Museo de Lorca *is open 10–1 and 6–8, closed Mon., with tours every hour on the hour.* Víznar, where Lorca was assassinated, is just off N342 northeast to Guadix. The Federico García Lorca Park now stands on the site of the poet's assassination. Buses to Víznar leave from Arco de Elvira.

Lanjarón, Orgiva, and the Alpujarras. Lanjarón is a delightful old spa town famous for its mineral water and lies in a lovely mountain setting just off N323 Granada–Motril road. It is easily reached by bus from Granada. A little further on, Orgiva, the main town of the Alpujarras, is a good base for trips to the remote villages of the western Alpujarra. Regular buses run between Granada and Orgiva, but from there on you will have to rely on the very infrequent bus services between villages. It is a remote region with stunningly beautiful mountain scenery and was populated at one time by Moors fleeing the Reconquest. More recently, the villages were populated by Galicians who to this day continue the Moorish tradition of weaving in red, green, white, and black. Unless you are very adventurous, the once-weekly Alpujarras day-trip bus tour is the best way to visit the area; details are obtainable from the tourist office or travel agents in Granada.

Santa Fe. This village was founded in 1491 as a campground for the troops of Ferdinand and Isabella as they prepared for the siege of Granada. It is often referred to as the "Cradle of America" as it was here that Isabella and Columbus signed the agreements which led to Columbus's first voyage to the New World. It is an interesting town with several national monuments and *lies 8 km. (5 mi.) west of Granada on N342.* For details of buses to Santa Fe, contact the tourist office.

Sierra Nevada. The main and easily accomplished side trip, even for those without a car, is into the mountains of the Sierra Nevada. The ski resort itself is unspectacular, but the scenery makes for a memorable day out. However hot the weather in Granada, be sure to take a warm waterproof jacket and sunglasses—mountain weather is always unpredictable. Buses leave Granada daily at 9 A.M., including Sun., from outside the Hotel Zaida, between the Acera de Darro and the Carrera del Genil. The journey to the Solynieve resort takes about one hour and fares are low. The same bus leaves Solynieve–Prado Llano at 5 P.M. for the return journey. The bus usually continues as far as the Albergue Universitario where you can have a good lunch at very reasonable prices.

SHOPPING. Typical handicrafts of Granada are brass and copperware, a legacy of the Moors; ceramics, especially the green and blue Fajalauza pottery; marquetry—boxes, tables, chess sets, and musical boxes, made with ornate wooden patterns and inlaid with mother of pearl; and woven goods from the villages of the Alpujarras—shoulder bags, rugs, and wall hangings, in which the colors red, green, and black predominate.

Granada's main shopping streets are **Reyes Católicos, Zacatín,** and **Angel Ganivet.** The **Galerías Preciados** department store is on the **Carrera del Genil;** the **Corte Inglés** is on **Recogidas.** The **Alcaicería** beside the cathedral is a paradise for souvenir hunters, as is the **Cuesta Gomérez,** the hill leading up to the Alhambra.

ENTERTAINMENT. Flamenco. There are several impromptu—and often dreadful—flamenco displays in the gypsy caves of the Sacromonte. More often than not they are little short of rip-off tourist deals, though they do offer the chance to see the caves. Unless you know a local who will escort you to one he knows personally, your best bet is to attend a performance at one of Granada's two official flamenco clubs. Both shows cater mainly to tourists, and entrance, including one drink, costs around 1,800–2,000 ptas.

Jardines Neptuno, Recogidas (tel. 958-25-11-12). This club lies at the very bottom of Recogidas, across the Camino de Ronda. It is set in a pleasant garden with an outdoor pool, and the show is a mixture of classic Spanish dance, ballet, and flamenco.

Reina Mora, Mirador de San Cristóbal (tel. 958-27-82-28). A short drive or taxi ride up the road which leads to Murcia, the Ctra. de Murcia, will take you to this club, which is probably the better of the two. The show is a mixture of flamenco and regional dance. To make reservations during the day when it is closed, call 958-20-20-06 or 958-20-12-11.

Flamenco Mass. On the third Sunday in every month a mass, with flamenco, is held in the Church of San Pedro on the banks of the Darro River. But confirm this with the tourist office before going.

Ubeda

Standing in the heart of the olive groves of Jaén, Ubeda is a twin town to Baeza (see above), just nine km. (five miles) away. One of the first towns to be lost to the Moors, it offers little visual evidence of its Moorish past. Instead, its Renaissance splendor reigns supreme. The modern town is of little interest to the visitor, but the Casco Antiguo, or Old Town, is a superb example of a pure Renaissance town. Just follow the signs to the "Zona Monumental," and whichever of its narrow streets you wander down, you will discover innumerable Renaissance churches and palaces.

Not many tourists find their way this far east in Andalusia, and you will find a friendly welcome in this restful town. There are several low-cost accommodations, and no shortage of affordable, if not very special, places to eat. Prices may well seem low after the big cities, and there are excellent local handicrafts.

GETTING THERE. By Train. Ubeda's nearest rail station is Linares–Baeza 13 km. (9 mi.) east of Baeza, on the main Madrid–Córdoba and Madrid–Granada lines. There are several services a day and a connecting bus usually meets the trains.

By Bus. This is the most reliable way of reaching Ubeda if you haven't a car. There are regular buses from Jaén, and the journey takes around one and a half hours. Ubeda is also on the main Córdoba–Valencia route run by Ubesa. There are plenty of local buses from Linares, Baeza, and Cazorla. Ubeda's bus station is on Calle Nueva in the modern city to the west of town, just off the Baeza road, behind the Hospital de Santiago.

By Car. Ubeda lies just off N322 Bailén–Albacete road 40 km. (25 mi.) east of Bailén. (Bailén is the main junction on the NIV from Madrid, where the road splits for Córdoba or Granada.) Alternatively, if you are coming from Madrid, you could turn off NIV at La Carolina onto C3217, an attractive minor road, and Ubeda then lies 52 km. (32 mi.) to the southeast. From Jaén take N321 northeast to Baeza and Ubeda, a distance of 57 km. (35 mi.)

TOURIST OFFICES. Plaza del Ayuntamiento 2 (tel. 953-75-08-97). The tourist office is located in the City Hall in the Palacio de las Cadenas, and it can recommend walking tours taking in Renaissance mansions and churches. It can also advise on which ones can be visited and opening times.

WHERE TO STAY. Consuelo (I), Avda. Ramón y Cajal 12 (tel. 953-75-08-40). 39 rooms. Other than the rather expensive parador, the Consuelo is the only hotel in town. It's a fairly simple, but comfortable and modern 2-star establishment, and is located quite close to the bus station. The rooms all have their own bathroom, but no meals are served.

La Paz (I), Andalucía 1 (tel. 953-75-08-49). 53 rooms. This is a modern, homey, 2-star hostel. The rooms here all have bathrooms and telephone, and breakfast is served but not dinner.

Sevilla (I), Avda. Ramón y Cajal 9 (tel. 953-75-06-12). 23 rooms. The Sevilla is a simple, family-run pension with clean, pleasant rooms, some of which have their own bathroom. It is convenient for the bus station and close to the Consuelo Hotel. Breakfast and dinner are served at very affordable prices.

WHERE TO EAT. Parador Condestable Dávalos (M), Pza. Vázquez de Molina 1 (tel. 953-75-03-45). Really the only place to eat well in Ubeda; the other restaurants are good value, but nothing special. This restaurant is housed in a 16th-century ducal palace in the heart of the Old Town. A three-course dinner without wine costs around 2,000 ptas. per person and specialties include partridge *(perdiz)* casserole, and *leche frita,* a sweet custard dessert spiced with cinnamon.

MAJOR ATTRACTIONS. Plaza Vázquez de Molina. Few other squares in Spain can claim such a purity of style or such a wealth of late 16th-century Renaissance buildings. The **Casa de las Cadenas** (House of Chains) takes its name from the chains around its forecourt and is a superb example of Renaissance style. Today the palace houses the City Hall and the tourist office. Across the Plaza is **Santa María de los Reales Alcázares,** a late 15th-century church hiding behind a later, classical facade. It was built on the site of a mosque and boasts a fine painted roof and some splendid grilles, and the fine Gothic **cloisters** have some wonderful fan vaulting. Here too is Ubeda's **parador,** housed in the 16th-century **Palacio de Dean Ortega,** and close by you will find the **Sacra Capilla del Salvador,** the most elaborate and ornate of Ubeda's churches, despite being badly damaged in 1936 in the frenzy of church burning that heralded the outbreak of the Civil War. Just beyond El Salvador, the Old Town ends abruptly at the **Redonda de Miradores** which affords some wonderful views over the surrounding olive groves to the mountains of Cazorla.

OTHER ATTRACTIONS. Hospital de Santiago *is on Avda. del Cristo Rey, the road to Baeza, in the west of town.* Not far from the bus station, this huge quadrangular building is often jokingly known as the Escorial of Andalusia, but it is less solitary and severe, with a fine arcaded patio and a grand staircase decorated with frescoes. *It is currently undergoing restoration and is closed to visitors.*

San Nicolás de Bari, *in the north of the Old Town,* is a notable 15th-century church in the Isabelline style. Inside take a look at the elaborate *esparto* floor coverings for which Ubeda is famous.

San Pablo, *in the Plaza 1° de Mayo.* This church was built originally in the 13th century, but has many 15th-century Gothic additions. Like San Nicolás, it is in true Isabelline style, and inside has some interesting chapels.

SHOPPING. The Calle Valencia, outside the Old Town to the northeast, is full of stores and studios specializing in Ubeda's local handicrafts: ironwork, pottery—especially bowls and jugs colored with a deep green glaze—and the *esparto* baskets and mats woven in intricate patterns for which Ubeda is especially famous.

If you're thinking of buying some olive oil to take home, then Ubeda, surrounded by 150 million olive trees, produces its own brand: *Oro de Loma* (Golden Ridge).

◆

S P L U R G E S

Drinks at the Alhambra Palace Hotel, Granada. This is a treat which won't cost an arm and a leg, but which will offer you an unforgettable experience. Choose a fine sunny evening and go, preferably about an hour before sunset, to this flamboyant hotel built in Moorish style around 1910 and beautifully located on the Alhambra hill. With its exotic Oriental interior—even the bar is done out as a mosque—and its deep ochre facade, complete with castellations and crenellations, the Alhambra Palace is more like a Hollywood stage set than a 4-star hotel. The terrace offers the most magnificent views over the tiled rooftops of the city, and, away to your left, the peaks of the Sierra Nevada. Here, cocktail or *fino* (dry sherry) in hand, you can nibble on an olive while you watch the sun go down. It is a memorable sight.

El Caballo Rojo, Córdoba, Cardenal Herrero 28 (tel. 957-47-53-75). This is Córdoba's outstanding restaurant, winner of the National Gastronomy Prize, and famous throughout Andalusia and, indeed, all of Spain. It is ideally located in the heart of the historic center, close to the Mosque, making a visit here both a gastronomic and a visual delight. Cordoban specialties such as *rabo de toro* (bull's tail) and *salmorejo*—a local version of gazpacho, garnished with chunks of ham and egg—feature on the menu, as do Andalusian dishes and other exotic creations inspired by Córdoba's Moorish heritage. Lamb roasted in eucalyptus honey should make your mouth water, and the fish dishes are excellent, too. Though the restaurant is justly famous (you will need to book, especially at lunchtime), the prices are not exorbitant, and you will probably spend no more than you would on an average Saturday night treat at home. Pamper yourself this once. Leaving aside the beauties of the Mosque, a meal at the Caballo Rojo is likely to be the highlight of your visit to Córdoba.

If you feel like an extra-special treat while in Ubeda, then the **Parador Condestable Dávalos,** Plaza Vázquez de Molina 1 (tel. 953-75-03-45) is the place to go. Enjoy the original wooden beams and the old fireplaces, and the magnificent glassed-in gallery overlooking the central patio. Before you savor your delicious dinner, ask to visit the bodega, the atmospheric old wine cellar with wooden beams, stone arches, and enormous wine vats. After dinner, sit and relax with your coffee in one of the comfortable sitting rooms or, in winter, beside the log fire. Should you decide to really spoil yourself and spend the night here, the 26 rooms with decorated tiled floors, wooden ceilings, and deliciously big baths cost between 6,500 and 8,500 ptas. for a double.

◆

SEVILLE

Lying on the banks of the Guadalquivir, Seville, Spain's fourth largest city and capital of Andalusia, is one of the most beautiful and romantic cities in Europe. With its whitewashed houses and ocher-colored palaces, baroque facades and flower-filled patios, streets and gardens fragrant with orange blossom and jasmine, Seville is a must for any traveler to Spain.

Seville, seat of the regional government of Andalusia, and hometown of Felipe González, Spain's prime minister, has a long and noble history. Conquered by the Romans in 205 B.C., it gave the world two great emperors: Trajan and Hadrian. You can visit their birthplace at the Roman excavations at Itálica. The Moors bequeathed to this city, which they held for over 500 years, one of the greatest examples of their art in the form of the magnificent Giralda Tower.

Seville's conqueror, Ferdinand III, who retook the city in 1248, lies enshrined before the high altar of the cathedral, one of the city's greatest monuments. The rather less glorious

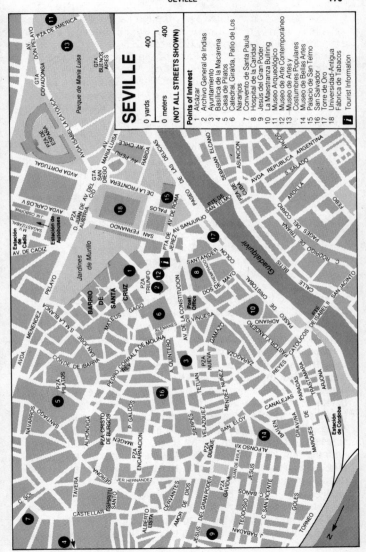

SEVILLE

(NOT ALL STREETS SHOWN)

0 meters 400
0 yards 400

Points of Interest

1 Alcázar
2 Archivo General de Indias
3 Ayuntamiento
4 Basílica de la Macarena
5 Casa de Pilatos
6 Catedral, Giralda, Patio de Los Naranjos
7 Convento de Santa Paula
8 Hospital de la Caridad
9 Jesús del Gran Poder
10 La Maestranza Bullring
11 Museo Arqueológico
12 Museo de Arte Contemporáneo
13 Museo de Artes y Costumbres Populares
14 Museo de Bellas Artes
15 Palacio de San Telmo
16 San Salvador
17 Torre de Oro
18 Universidad-Antigua Fábrica de Tabacos
i Tourist Information

Pedro the Cruel also lies here, though he nevertheless gave Seville its other great showpiece, the superb Mudéjar Alcázar Palace. A few paces away you can pay your respects to Columbus, who sailed from Palos at the mouth of the Guadalquivir. Two other great adventurers, Amerigo Vespucci and Ferdinand Magellan, set sail from Seville, and from 1503–1680 the city reaped the benefits of its monopoly of trade from the New World, filling its coffers with gold and silver and precious gemstones. In 1992 Seville will again remember its prosperous days of empire as it hosts a World Fair to celebrate the 500th anniversary of Columbus's voyage.

The showpiece of Seville is the old Santa Cruz quarter, once the home of the city's Jews, and later the setting for the antics of Don Giovanni and the nuptials of Figaro. Here, too, Rossini's Barber carried on his trade, while over the road in the splendid Old Tobacco Factory, the sultry Carmen first met Don José. Don Quijote was born in a Sevillian jail, and his creator, Cervantes, twice languished here in a debtors' prison. The great 17th-century painters Murillo and Velázquez also number among Seville's famous native sons.

The vivacity and color of Seville, immortalized by Bizet's opera *Carmen,* are no myth; they can be seen on any day and on any street, but never in greater numbers than in springtime, when Seville celebrates Holy Week and the *Feria de Abril* (April Fair). Holy Week in Seville is indeed memorable: Innumerable Christs and velvet-robed Virgins from Seville's parishes, enthroned amid white carnations and candles, are borne through the streets on floats by barefoot penitents accompanied by troupes of mummers. Two weeks later the Sevillanos, this time clad in flamenco costumes, again take to the streets to celebrate the April Fair. The spectacle began as a horse-trading fair in 1847, and horse parades, with men dressed in Andalusian riding gear and women in flounced dresses riding sidesaddle behind them, recall its equine origins. Bullfights, dancing, and the singing of *Sevillanas* accompany the night-long celebration. It is now that the true spirit of Seville and its vibrant and warm-hearted inhabitants can be seen at its best.

There is a darker side to Seville, however, for the city has developed an unenviable reputation for petty crime. Take extra-special care of your belongings at all times. *Never* leave *anything* in a parked car, and keep a wary eye on scooter riders, who are prone to smashing windshields and grabbing bags. Take only a small amount of cash and just one credit card out with you, and leave your passport, travelers' checks, and other credit cards locked in the hotel safe. If at all possible, avoid carrying purses and expensive cameras.

PRACTICAL INFORMATION
How to Get There

FROM THE AIRPORT. Seville's San Pablo Airport (tel. 954-51-06-77) is 12 km. (7½ mi.) east of town on NIV to Carmona and Córdoba. Iberia and British Airways fly here from London; some of their flights are direct, others involve one stop, either at Barcelona or Madrid. There are several flights a day from Madrid, four from Barcelona, and one or two a day from Valencia and Alicante. There are three flights a week from ·Vitoria in northern Spain. An *Iberia* bus meets most incoming flights and runs to the *Iberia* office in town on Almirante Lobo 3 (tel. 954-22-89-01). For *Iberia* information, call: 954-22-96-39.

BY TRAIN. Seville has two train stations, and both are known by two names. The Estación de Córdoba/Plaza de Armas (tel. 954-22-18-28), near the river, has several trains a day from Córdoba and Madrid, and services from Barcelona (including a daily TALGO), Zafra, Mérida, Badajoz, and Huelva. The Estación de Cádiz/San Bernardo (tel. 954-41-43-60) has trains from Jerez, Cádiz, Málaga, and Granada. Trains from these last two may entail a change at Bobadilla. The central RENFE office is on Zaragoza 29 (tel. 954-22-25-77), and is open Mon. to Fri. 9–1:15 and 4–7; closed Sat. and Sun. For train information, call: 954-41-41-11, and always double-check which station you need.

BY BUS. The principal bus station (tel. 954-41-71-11) is between José María Osborne and Manuel Vázquez Sagastizabal, not far from San Bernardo Train Station. It has services from Madrid, Barcelona, Valencia, Portugal, and all destinations in Andalusia other than the province of Huelva. Empresa Damas, Segura 16 (tel. 954-22-22-72), at the bottom of Reyes Católicos near the river, runs buses to and from Huelva. La Estellesa, Areval 7 (tel. 954-22-58-20), near the bullring, runs buses from Badajoz, Aracena, and certain destinations in Extremadura.

Facts and Figures

USEFUL ADDRESSES. Tourist Offices. The main tourist office of the regional government of Andalusia is on Avda. de la Constitución 21 (tel. 954-22-14-04), not far from the cathedral and Archives of the Indies. Its opening hours are Mon. to Sat. 9–7, and 9:30–1:30 on Sun. and fiestas. It distributes maps of the city and a useful leaflet on Seville and its province—both are free. Another free publication is the useful monthly bulletin *El Giraldillo*, which gives details of what's on in the city, and lists of restaurants and bars. The Municipal Tourist Office is at Paseo de las Delicias 7 (tel. 954-23-44-65), in the María Luisa Park, open 10–1:30 and 5–7. Free posters advertising Holy Week and the April Fair are available from the Ayuntamiento (City Hall), Pza. Nueva, though there are rarely enough to meet the demand.

Police. Pza. de la Gavidia (tel. 954-22-88-40).

Main Post Office. Avda. Constitución 32 (tel. 954-22-88-80), opposite the cathedral.

Telephone Exchange. Pza. Nueva 3. Open Mon. to Sat. 10–2 and 5:30–10; closed Sun.

Lost and Found. Almansa 21 (tel. 954-21-26-28).

American Express Agent. Viajes Alhambra, Coronel Seguí 3 (tel. 954-21-29-23).

Consulates. U.S.: Paseo de las Delicias 7 (tel. 954-23-18-85). **U.K.:** Pza. Nueva 8 (tel. 954-22-88-75).

Guides. City sightseeing tours are not as common as elsewhere, as most of Seville's sights have to be visited on foot. The guided parties you see in Seville are usually part of an all-inclusive package tour. However, if you should wish to hire an English-speaking guide to show you around—though a half-day guide fee will be quite expensive— inquire at the tourist office, or contact Guidetour de Sevilla, Cuna 41-2°-A (tel. 954-22-23-74/5); open 9–1:30 and 5–8.

Bookshops. Excellent bookshops with good travel and guidebook sections and books in English are Pascual Lázaro, Sierpes 2–4, and Libros Vértice, Mateos Gago 24.

Getting Around

BY BUS. Local buses, though you are unlikely to need them, are orange and charge a flat fee of 55 ptas. The main information office is the TUSSAM (Seville Transport Authority) *tequilla* in Pza. Nueva, where you can buy a bonobus: this is good for 10 rides at a reduced cost (around 340 ptas.) It may also supply a map of the bus routes.

Taking a bus can be confusing: Due to Seville's one-way system, many buses return along a different route from their outward journey, so always ask if you are uncertain.

BY TAXI. If you do get lost, or are feeling weary, then take a taxi—they are plentiful and not too expensive. But make sure the driver puts his meter on at the start of the ride. As a guide, prices in 1987 were as follows: The meter starts at 68 ptas., and goes up a few pesetas every 15 seconds. Supplements are 25 ptas. for suitcases; 42 ptas. for Sundays and fiestas; 42 ptas. for night fares (10 P.M.–6 A.M.). A journey to or from the airport costs 850 ptas. There is a 25% surcharge on rides during the April Fair. Taxis take up to four people.

ON FOOT. Seville, with its labyrinth of narrow streets, can be a difficult city to find your way round, and is best negotiated on foot. Fortunately, all the main sights, except possibly the María Luisa Park, are fairly close together. Arm yourself with a good city map—free from the tourist office or your hotel—and mark your hotel on it; it may not be so easy to find at the end of a day's sightseeing.

Where to Stay

HOTELS. During Holy Week and the April Fair, all Seville hotels and hostels increase their rates by 50% or more, and those that have dining rooms will probably insist on half- or even full-board terms. Many hotels are booked up at least a year in advance, and if you haven't made a reservation, be prepared for a very long, hard search.

Moderate

Ducal, Pza. de la Encarnación 19 (tel. 954-21-51- 07). 51 rooms. If it's old-fashioned comfort you're looking for, then the long-established Ducal, located just a 2-min. walk away from the Campaña and central shopping area, is the hotel for you. It serves breakfast but no other meals.

➊ Internacional, Aguilas 17 (tel. 954-21-32-07). 26 rooms. This is a beautifully maintained old Andalusian house, located in one of the typical streets of the old quarter near the Casa Pilatos Museum. It has lots of charm and is popular with Spanish guests, but serves no meals, not even breakfast.

Montecarlo, Gravina 51 (tel. 954-21-75-03). 25 rooms. Located between Reyes Católicos and Canalejas, this hotel exudes turn-of-the-century charm. A little faded in parts, its rooms are adequate if not super-comfortable, and the hotel has some exquisite ceramic tiles incorporated into its decor. Full hotel services are provided, and there is a dining room which serves both breakfast and dinner at reasonable prices.

⊖Murillo, Lope de Rueda 7 (tel. 954-21-60-95). 61 rooms. This is probably the best known of Seville's good-value hotels. Located in a fully renovated Andalusian house in the heart of the Barrio Santa Cruz, it is the only hotel in this picturesque Old Quarter. It can only be reached on foot—though porters will carry your luggage from your taxi—but its charming location more than merits the difficulty you may have in finding it. It serves breakfast but no other meals.

⊖La Rábida, Castelar 24 (tel. 954-22-09660). 87 rooms. This charming white-and-ocher painted Sevillian house halfway between Pza. Nueva and the bullring is just a 5-min. walk from the cathedral. The hotel is well maintained, with a period-style entrance hall, heavy dark wooden doors with well-polished brass fittings, and a delightful patio. The restaurant serves both breakfast and dinner.

Sevilla, Daioz 6 (tel. 954-38-41-61). 32 rooms. If it's Andalusian charm coupled with a central location you're looking for, then this delightful old hotel will fit the bill. Located in the heart of the town halfway between the Pza. Encarnación and the Pza. del Duque, it overlooks a picturesque square, and the hotel has a glass-covered inner patio and balconies decorated with flowering plants in pots. There is no restaurant, but cafés and the Corte Inglés department store are only a 3-min. walk away, and guests regularly take their meals at El Escorial restaurant (see below) just around the corner.

Inexpensive

⊖Atenas, Caballerizas 1 (tel. 954-21-80-47). 8 rooms. The Atenas is a charming old Sevillian house, close to the Internacional Hotel (see above). This small family-run hostel is well maintained and has rooms with and without bathrooms, but no meals are served.

⊖Goya, Mateos Gagos 31 (tel. 954-21-11-70). 20 rooms. This, together with the Monreal (see below), is probably the best known of Seville's budget hostels. Long a tradition with cost-conscious travelers, it has a picturesque patio and is ideally located on the edge of the Barrio Santa Cruz, just 3 min.' walk up the street from the cathedral. It serves breakfast, but you would be well advised to check whether you will be charged for it, whether you eat it or not.

Madrid, San Pedro Mártir 22 (tel. 954-21-43-06). 23 rooms. The Madrid is a deluxe hostel located only a 5-min. walk away from the Córdoba Rail Station (Pza. de Armas), and not far from the Museo de Bellas Artes. All its rooms have bathrooms, and breakfast is served. It is the most expensive in this category.

Monreal, Rodrigo Caro 8 (tel. 954-21-41-66). 18 rooms. This picturesque Sevillian house in the Barrio Santa Cruz is only 2 min. from the cathedral and *alcázar*. With its charming ocher facade, patio, and balconies bursting with flowers, it is a long-standing budget tradition, and rooms are often hard to come by. Accommodations are simple, and not all have bathrooms, but what it lacks in comfort it more than makes up in charm and ideal location. Its restaurant serves breakfast and economical meals.

Sierpes, Corral del Rey 22 (tel. 954-22-49-48). 39 rooms. Stay in the heart of the Old Town in this typical Sevillian house just 5 min.' walk from the cathedral. The hostel was extensively renovated in 1987. It has rooms with and without bathrooms, and serves both breakfast and dinner at very moderate prices. It is not easy to find at first, so take a taxi.

Simón, García de Vinuesa 19 (tel. 954-22-66-60). 47 rooms. The Simón is a simple 1-star hotel in a pretty 18th-century house painted pale creamy yellow, with iron grilles and a delightful central patio. It is located off Avda. Constitución, immediately opposite the cathedral. The management is friendly and the hotel has oodles of charm, though some rooms are faded and in definite need of renovation; inspect your room before taking it. About half the rooms have their own bathroom, and breakfast and dinner are served. This is a hotel better suited to those who prefer old-world charm to creature comforts.

Toledo, Santa Teresa 15 (tel. 954-21-53-35). 13 rooms. This very simple 1-star hostel is located in a neat white house in the heart of the Barrio Santa Cruz, halfway between the delightful Plaza Santa Cruz and the house of the painter Murillo. It has rooms with and without bathrooms, but no meals are served.

Where to Eat

Moderate

RESTAURANTS. The streets on the north and east sides of the cathedral, namely Mateos Gago, Contero, Alvarez Quintero, and Calle Alemanes, are packed with inexpensive restaurants all vying with one another to lure the cost-conscious tourist inside by offering numerous cheap *menus del día* and seemingly ridiculously priced buffets. Though most are perfectly adequate eating places, their food is generally undistinguished, and for that reason we have not listed any one of them specifically. In a few cases you should beware the all-too-cheap buffet and keep a wary eye on the standards of hygiene.

Bodegón Torre de Oro, Santander 15 (tel. 954-21-31-69). This is a long-established restaurant close to the Torre de Oro (Golden Tower). Its spacious dining room is furnished in rustic style, with huge hams hanging from the ceiling, and paintings of celebrities on the walls. In the bar, there is a good selection of *tapas* and a wide choice of wines and *finos* (sherries), and this is a popular pre-lunch gathering place for the businessmen of Seville. Specialties in the restaurant include *gazpacho, paella,* and *pollo al ajillo* (chicken in garlic).

● **Enrique Becerra,** Gamaza 2 (tel. 954-21-30-49). The Enrique Becerra is well known for quality of food and service and you may find it a little more expensive than our other listings, but it is well worth treating yourself to for something rather special. It is a small, intimate restaurant located in a picturesque Andalusian house just off the Pza. Nueva. There is an excellent *tapas* bar, and the restaurant specializes in local Sevillian home cooking. It has just eight tables, so it is advisable to make a reservation, especially at lunchtime. Closed for lunch on Sunday.

Hostería del Laurel, Pza. de los Venerables 5 (tel. 954-22-02-95). This restaurant scores most highly on its charming setting in the heart of the Barrio Santa Cruz. It has a bar and informal dining room on the ground floor and a full restaurant upstairs. In summer, tables are placed outdoors in the square, and you can enjoy the full beauty of this lovely square of ancient white and ocher houses with flower-decked balconies.

● **La Isla,** Arfe 25 (tel. 954-21-53-76). La Isla, located in the center between the cathedral and La Caridad, has long been famous for its outstanding seafood and *paellas*. Its fish and meat are superbly fresh, and though you may find it a little noisy as it is always crowded, this is one you shouldn't miss. Closed Aug.

● **La Rayuela,** Don Remondo 1 (tel. 954-22-43-52). This is a small and delightful restaurant on the corner of Argote de Molina just up from the cathedral. Its prices are a little higher than most in this category, but its intimate decor and excellent innovative cuisine are well worth splashing out on. With just nine tables and classical music to dine to, the menu offers a choice of four meat dishes and four fish dishes. The fish is brought fresh from La Cristina in Huelva province, and every day there is a special *menu de la casa* for around 1,200 ptas. Closed Sun. evening.

Inexpensive

Los Alcázares, Miguel de Mañara 10 (tel. 954-21-31-03). Located close to the Archives of the Indies and the entrance to the Alcázar, this restaurant caters largely to tourists. Its food and service are frankly not convenient location and the chance it affords to glimpse inside an old Sevillian house make it worthy of consideration.

El Bacalao, Ponce de León 15 (tel. 954-21-66-70). A 5-min. walk above Pza. Encarnación, El Bacalao serves a wide variety of fish dishes cooked in true Sevillian style. The decor is rather uninteresting, but the quality of the fish is good, and, as its name implies, the specialty is cod. Closed Sun.

☛ La Cueva del Pez de Espada, Rodrigo Caro 18. La Cueva is a colorful tavern on the corner of Pza. Doña Elvira in the Barrio Santa Cruz. It has tables outside in the square in summer, its standards are consistent, the service is friendly, and you can often dine to live guitar music.

Las Escobas, Alvarez Quintero 62 (tel. 954-21-44-79). Las Escobas claims to date from 1386 and to have fed Cervantes, Lope de Vega, and the 19th-century Sevillian poet Gustavo Adolfo Bécquer. Despite such illustrious claims, today it is a fairly ordinary *mesón,* catering to budget-conscious tourists. However, it is colorful and typical enough, and convenient if you are hungry when you come out of the cathedral.

El Escorial, Javier Lasso de la Vega 3 (tel. 954-22-59-52). This is a pleasant family-run restaurant close to the Pza. Duque shopping area. The service is friendly, and it specializes in Castilian home cooking: the *cordero asado* (roast lamb) is recommended by the owners.

☛ El Mesón, Dos de Mayo 26 (tel. 21-30-75). El Mesón is a typical Sevillian bodega, close to La Caridad Convent, which was made famous by James Michener in his massive tome *Iberia.* The restaurant has great atmosphere, with bullfight decor in the first room, including paintings by the American bullfighter-cum-artist John Fulton. The inner room is covered in photos of famous diners, Michener and numerous other Americans amongst them. On the dessert menu, the *Combinación Michener,* a plate of *membrillo* (quince preserve) with Manchego cheese, makes a pleasant change from the ubiquitous *flan.*

Exploring Seville

MAJOR ATTRACTIONS. Alcázar, *entrance in Plaza Triunfo. Open 9–12:45 and 3–5:45. Entrance is free on Sat.* The *Alcázar* can be mistaken for a genuine Moorish palace, for it was indeed designed and built by Moorish workers. But it was in fact commissioned and paid for by a Christian king, Pedro I, in the 1360s—more than a century after the Reconquest of Seville.

Pedro I, known as "the Cruel" because he murdered his step-mother and four of his half brothers, ruled Spain from Seville from 1350–69. The *Alcázar* was built on the site of a former Moorish palace, and Moorish craftsmen were brought from Granada (still under Moorish rule) to work on it. It is a contemporary of Granada's Alhambra, and the most beautiful example of Mudéjar architecture in Spain today, though its purity has been much watered down by the alterations and additions of subsequent Spanish rulers. The Catholic kings added a new wing, and the emperor Charles V added galleries to the light and airy stucco patios, and created a new wing much heavier in style, with Flemish tapestries and rich pink and ocher walls.

You enter the *Alcázar* through high sturdy Moorish walls which belie the exquisite delicacy of its interior. On the far side of the **Patio de la Montería,** the palace centers around the beautiful **Patio de las Doncellas** (Court of the Damsels). Its name perhaps pays tribute to the annual gift of 100 virgins made to the Moorish sultans. Resplendent with the most delicate of lacelike stucco and gleaming *azulejo* decorations, it is immediately reminiscent of the Alhambra. Opening off this patio, the **Salón de Embajadores** (Hall of the Ambassadors), with its cedarwood *media naranja* (half orange) cupola of ornamental green, red, and gold, is the most sumptuous hall in the palace. It was here in 1526 that Charles V married Isabel of Portugal—for which occasion he added the somewhat incongruous wooden balconies.

Opening off this hall are the **three apartments** of Pedro I's mistress, María de Padilla, and the **comedor** (dining room) of Philip II. The **Patio de las Muñecas** (Court of the Dolls) takes its name from two tiny faces carved on the inside of one of its arches, no doubt as a joke on the part of its Moorish creators. Here Pedro I murdered his guest Abu Said of Granada for the sake of his jewels. One of these jewels, a huge uncut ruby, which Pedro presented to the Black Prince in 1367, now sits among the priceless English Crown Jewels.

Having visited the bedrooms of Queen Isabella and her son, Don Juan, and walked through the wing added by Charles V, you will come out into the lovely **Alcázar Gardens.** Fragrant with jasmine and myrtle, the gardens are masterfully terraced and have ornamental baths, palm trees, and an enormous goldfish pond covered in water lilies. In the midst of this oasis of green is an orange tree said to have been planted in the time of Pedro I. A passageway now brings you to the **Patio de las Banderas** from which there is an unrivaled view of the Giralda. If you turn down the covered alley in the corner beside the palace, you will come to the Barrio Santa Cruz.

The Barrio Santa Cruz. The Barrio Santa Cruz, Seville's old Jewish quarter, is a beautifully preserved collection of twisting alleyways, cobbled squares, and whitewashed houses. Every white-washed wall is lit by a wrought iron lantern, and every balcony is bedecked with geraniums and petunias. The streets, where there are numerous bars and antique shops to be discovered, have evocative names like Agua (water), Vida (life), Pimienta (sweet pepper), Jamerdana (slaughterhouse), and Ataúd (coffin).

It was here that the painter Murillo lived and worked, and when he died in 1682 he was buried in the Church of Santa Cruz, later destroyed by Napoleon's General Soult. Nearby, in the **Calle Santa Teresa,** you can visit his house, now a small museum. The street is named after Santa Teresa, who was so enchanted by Seville that she decreed that anyone who stayed free from sin in Seville was indeed on the path to God.

The **Calle de Susana** takes its name from a sinful Jewess who, on her deathbed, asked for her body to be placed over the doorway as a warning to others. The **Callejón del Agua,** alongside the wall of the Alcázar Gardens, boasts some fine mansions, and the most delightful of the Barrio's patios.

But it is perhaps the squares of the Barrio Santa Cruz that are the most charming corners of all: The **Plaza Santa Cruz** is a tranquil delight, with its diminutive garden and fine filigree 17th-century iron cross; the colorful **Plaza de los Venerables Sacerdotes** houses a famous bar hung with hams, and the Hospital de los Venerables Sacerdotes, with its beautiful *azulejo* patio, Valdés Leal paintings, and small museum of floats from the May processions; the **Plaza de Doña Elvira** with its fountain and *azulejo* benches plays host to the young of Seville, who gather here to play their guitars. Pause a while to browse in the antique shops of the **Plaza Alianza,** and to admire the lovely blue and white tiles bearing the name of the square, framed in a profusion of bougainvillea. The Barrio Santa Cruz is the embodiment of the romance of Andalusia.

Cathedral, *main entrance on the north side in Calle Fray González, beside the Archives of the Indies; the entrance on Plaza Vírgen de los Reyes near the Giralda is also open on certain days. Open 10:30–1:30 and 4:30–6:30 in summer; 10:30–1 and 4–6 in winter; Sun. 10:30–1.* When Ferdinand III conquered Seville from the Moors in 1248, the great mosque begun by Yusuf II in 1171 was at first simply reconsecrated to the Virgin Mary and used as a Christian cathedral. But in 1401 the citizens of Seville saw fit to erect a new and more glorious cathedral, worthy of the status of their great city. They promptly pulled down all of the old mosque, except for its minaret and outer court, and set about their task with a zeal and enthusiasm unparalleled elsewhere, for this mighty building was completed in just over a century (1402–1506), a remarkable record for the time. Today, Seville's cathedral can only be described in superlatives. It is the biggest and highest cathedral in Spain, the largest Gothic building in the world, and the world's third largest church after St. Peter's in Rome and St. Paul's in London. It boasts, too, the world's largest **altarpiece.**

The exterior, with its rose window and magnificent flying buttresses, is a monument to pure Gothic beauty, but the badly lit interior, devoid of the usual central nave and transepts, can be disappointing, shrouded as it is in a gloom that belies its size and importance. Nevertheless, it is a veritable treasure house, and a shrine of Spanish history.

On either side of the **Capilla Real** stand the tombs of Alfonso the Wise (died 1248) and his mother, Beatrix of Swabia. Between his son and his wife, in a silver urn before the high altar, rest the precious relics of Seville's liberator, Saint Ferdinand, said to have died from excessive fasting. On the altar above, the **statue of the Vírgen de los Reyes,** patroness of Seville, presides, while down in the **crypt** below are relegated the tombs of Pedro I ("the Cruel") and his mistress, María de Padilla.

In the south aisle stands another flamboyant mausoleum, and scene of many a pilgrimage: the **tomb of Christopher Columbus.** His body was brought to Seville from Havana in 1899, after Cuba had gained its independence from Spain. After its trans-Atlantic wanderings—Valladolid to Santo Domingo, Havana to Seville— Columbus's body is now borne aloft by four statues representing the medieval kingdoms of Spain: Castile, León, Aragón, and Navarre. Note the other reference to the year 1492, the lance of Castile spearing the pomegranate of Granada, a symbol of the Catholic kings' triumphant conquest of that kingdom.

To the right of the entrance and Columbus's tomb lie the main treasure houses of the cathedral, containing a wealth of gold and silver, much of it from the New World, historic relics, and works by Goya, Murillo, and Zurbarán. Take the time also to visit the **Capilla Mayor,** which has a magnificently intricate altarpiece begun by a Flemish carver in 1482 which depicts some 45 scenes from the life of Christ, all lavishly adorned with immeasurable quantities of gold leaf.

The Giralda. *Opening times are the same as for the cathedral.* The Giralda, the undisputed symbol of Seville, dominates the city's skyline and can be glimpsed from almost every corner of the city. Built originally as the minaret of Seville's great mosque, it was constructed between 1184 and 1196 under the Almohad dynasty, just half a century before the Reconquest of Seville. It was crowned in 1198 by four golden balls which glinted as they caught the sun, and whose light could apparently be seen by travelers as much as a day's journey from the city. The balls crashed to the ground during an earthquake in the 13th century.

When the Christian conquerors tore down the mosque they could not bring themselves to destroy this tower of infinite beauty, and so incorporated it into their mammoth new cathedral, making it the cathedral's bell tower. In 1565–68 the Christians added a lantern and belfry to the old minaret, adding 24 bells, one for each of Seville's 24 parishes and for the 24 Christian knights who fought with Ferdinand III in the Reconquest. Also added was a bronze statue of Faith which turns as a weather vane, and from whose name, *El Giraldillo* (something that turns), we get the name La Giralda.

With its baroque additions, the slender Giralda now towers 322 ft. over the city's rooftops. In its center, in place of steps, a gently sloping ramp, wide enough for two horsemen to pass abreast, climbs to a viewing platform 230 ft. up. It is said that Ferdinand III rode his horse to the top to admire the view of the city he had conquered. If you have the energy, take advantage of the absence of steps—a stroke of Moorish genius—and follow his footsteps. The entrance ticket is inexpensive and your efforts will be well rewarded, for the view from the top (at its best in the evening) over Seville and the shimmering Guadalquivir is quite stunning. Try, too, to see the Giralda at night, when the floodlights cast a new magic over this gem of Islamic art.

Patio de los Naranjos (Court of the Orange Trees), *entered through the Puerta del Perdón in Calle Alemanes. It is usually open the same hours as the cathedral.* This patio, the outer court of the original mosque, is at its most fragrant in February and March, when the orange blossom perfumes the air. The old fountain in its center was used for ritual ablutions before entering the mosque. Two curiosities are the stuffed alligator by the Puerta del Largata in the corner near the Giralda—thought to have been a gift in 1260 from the emir of Egypt as he sought the hand of Alfonso X's daughter—and an ivory elephant tusk found in the ruins of Itálica. Across the patio, the **sacristy** houses the **Columbus Library,** a collection of some 3,000 volumes bequeathed by his son Hernando. They include Columbus's treatise to prove why his voyages to the west did not contradict the scriptures.

OTHER ATTRACTIONS. Archivo General de Indias (Archives of the Indies), *Avda. de la Constitución (beside the cathedral). Open Mon. to Fri. 10–1.* The Archives of the Indies are housed in the splendid old **Exchange Building** (Lonja) which was designed in 1572 by Juan de Herrera, the architect of the Escorial. This impressive and fascinating collection of documents relating to the discovery of the New World includes maps, drawings, trade documents, ships' logs (including Columbus's), and even the signatures of Columbus, Magellan, and Cortés. Many of the valuable 35,793 documents have not yet been thoroughly sorted and cataloged by the authorities, and the exhibits on display are constantly changed around.

Ayuntamiento (City Hall), *standing in the center of Plaza Nueva and Plaza San Francisco.* The City Hall, designed by Diego de Riaño, was begun in 1527 and completed in 1564. The ornamental exterior, particularly the exquisite **east facade** (facing Plaza San Francisco), is a fine example of the Plateresque style.

Basílica de la Macarena, *near the Macarena Gate in the north of the town. Open 9–12:30 and 5–9 (museum closes 7:30).* This church is the home of the **Virgin of Hope,** a statue more commonly known as La Macarena, the most idolized of Seville's numerous statues of the Virgin. Surrounded by candles and carnations, her cheeks streaming with glass tears, La Macarena's procession on Holy Thursday is the highlight of Seville's Holy Week pageant. She is the patroness of gypsies and protector of bullfighters, and has been granted the city's Medal of Honor along with the dubious distinction of having been made Captain General of the Nationalist forces during the Civil War.

Casa Pilatos, *Pza. Pilatos, between Aguilas and San Esteban. Open 9–6.* This is one of the loveliest old mansions in Seville. It was built by the Dukes of Tarifa, ancestors of the present owners, at the turn of the 16th century, though today it belongs to the dukes of Medinaceli. Its name—Pilate's House—stems from the popular belief that Don Fadrique, first Marqués de Tarifa, modeled it on Pilate's house in Jerusalem, where he went on a pilgrimage in 1519. It is, however, decidedly un-Roman. Rather, it's a magnificent example of Mudéjar and Renaissance architecture, and boasts a lovely patio and some superb *azulejos*.

Hospital de la Caridad, *Calle Temprado, between the Archives of* *the Indies and the river. Open 9:30–1:30 and 4–7.* An almshouse for the sick and elderly run by a religious institution, this beautiful baroque charity hospital was founded by Seville's original Don Juan in 1674. The story goes that a nobleman of licentious character, one Don Miguel de Mañara (1626–79), much given to indulging in drunken brawls and carnal pleasures, was returning one night from a riotous orgy when he had a vision of a funeral procession in which the partly decomposed corpse in the coffin was his own. Accepting the apparition as a sign from God, Miguel de Mañara renounced his worldly goods and pleasures and joined the Brotherhood of Charity. He devoted his fortune to the building of this hospital and his body is buried before the high altar in the chapel. But La Caridad's chief attractions are the fine paintings by Murillo (a friend of Mañara's) and Valdés Leal.

La Maestranza Bullring, *Paseo de Colón. Open late Apr. to early Oct. for tours at 4:45, 5:30, and 6:15. No tours on Sun. or corrida days.* La Maestranza, built in 1760–3, is the oldest, and one of the most beautiful, bullrings in Spain. There is an art gallery in an adjoining annex that is worth a visit too.

María Luisa Park. This park is one of the loveliest in Spain, with its blend of formal design, natural vegetation, and shady walkways, and was formerly the garden of the San Telmo Palace. In the burst of development and expansion that gripped Seville in the 1920s, it was redesigned to form the site of the 1929 Hispano-American Exhibition, and the impressive villas you can see today are the Fair's remaining pavilions, many of them now used as consulates or private schools.

The monumental **Plaza de España** on the northeastern edge of the park was the grandiose pavilion of Spain, the centerpiece of the whole exhibition. This vast semicircular brick building was a veritable monument to empire, a reembodiment of the Golden Age of Spain and Seville. The superb *azulejo* pictures in each of its arches represent the 50 provinces of Spain, and the four bridges over the ornamental lake the four medieval kingdoms of the Iberian peninsula.

Across the park, the **Plaza de América,** one of the loveliest spots in all Seville, is a blaze of color with its flowers and shrubs, ornamental stairways, fountains, and blue and ocher tiles, an ideal place to pass away the siesta hours.

The three impressive buildings in mock Moorish, Gothic, and Renaissance style are also remnants of the 1929 Fair, and now house the **offices of the Andalusian regional government,** the **Archeological Museum** *(open Tues. to Sat. 10–2)* with its grand collection of pre-Roman jewelry and treasures from the Itálica excavations, and the delightful **Museum of Popular Arts and Customs** *(open Tues. to Sun. 10–2)*.

Museo de Bellas Artes, *Pza. del Museo 9, off Alonso XII. Open Tues. to Fri. 10–2 and 4–7, Sat. and Sun. 10–2; closed Mon.* The former Convent of La Merced, founded in 1612, makes a beautiful setting for Seville's Fine Arts Museum, one of Spain's highest-ranking museums after the Prado. The dramatist Tirso de Molina was a friar here, and his greatest creation, Don Juan, may well have been dreamed up in the museum's halls. There are works by Zurbarán, Velázquez, Valdés Leal, El Greco, and over 50 by Murillo.

Palacio de San Telmo, *Avda. de Roma, between the Puerta de Jerez and the river.* This splendid baroque monument was built between 1682 and 1796, and was chiefly the work of the architect Leonardo de Figueroa. The fanciful Churrigueresque doorway dates from 1734. The building was once the residence of the dukes of Montpensier, and, later, also served as a naval school. Today it is used as a seminary.

Torre de Oro, *Paseo de Colón, near the San Telmo bridge.* The 12-sided Tower of Gold was built in 1220 as the last tower on the city's ramparts. It was used to close off the harbor by means of a chain stretched across the river to another tower, long since disappeared, on the opposite bank. Its name, some believe, comes from the fact that it may once have been covered in golden tiles. Others claim the tower was used as a store for gold from the New World. Its lantern is an 18th-century addition. Inside is a small, but very well laid out, **Maritime Museum,** *open Tues. to Sat. 10–2, Sun. 10–1; closed Mon.*

Universidad-Antigua Fábrica de Tabacos, *Calle San Fernando.* This is the Old Tobacco Factory (the new one is across the river), built between 1750 and 1766. A century later, it employed some 10,000 *cigarreras*. The tobacco girls, numbering among them the legendary Carmen, who rolled cigars on her thigh, constituted the 19th century's largest female work force. Immortalized by Bizet, this splendid building was once the second biggest monument in Spain after the Escorial; it is twice the size of Seville's cathedral. Since the 1950s it has been the home of Seville's university.

Excursions

Carmona. This fascinating town lies on NIV to Córdoba, 30 km. (17 mi.) east of Seville. There are several buses a day from Seville, and the ride takes around 45 min. Buses leave from the Prado de San Sebastián in front of the main bus station, but check details there or at the main tourist office.

Carmona, like Seville, was an important town under both the Romans and the Moors. In a wonderful position on a steep fortified hill, it is an unspoiled Andalusian town with a wealth of Mudéjar and Renaissance churches, and streets of whitewashed houses of clear Moorish influence, punctuated here and there by an occasional baroque palace.

The extraordinary interior of the **Church of San Pedro,** begun in 1466, is an unbroken mass of sculptures and gilded surfaces, and the church's baroque tower erected in 1704 is an unashamed imitation of Seville's famous Giralda. Nearby looms the imposing **Alcázar de Abajo** (Lower Fort), a Moorish fortification built on Roman foundations. Here the **Puerta de Sevilla** (Seville Gate), a 2nd-century Roman gateway, later altered by the Moors, leads into the Old Town.

The Gothic **Church of Santa María** was built between 1424 and 1518 on the site of the former Great Mosque (Carmona was retaken by Ferdinand III in 1247). A contemporary of Seville's cathedral, it, too, retains its Moorish courtyard once used for ritual ablutions. On the east side of town the street drops steeply down to the old Córdoba Gate, the **Puerta de Córdoba,** built by the Romans around A.D. 175 and later altered by the Moors and by Renaissance additions.

The crest of the hill is dominated by the imposing ruins of the **Alcázar de Arriba** (High Fort), erected by the Moors, again on Roman foundations, and which Pedro I (''the Cruel'') had converted into a fine Mudéjar palace. Pedro's summer residence, however, was destroyed by an earthquake in 1504, and today the *alcázar* ruins house one of Andalusia's finest paradors, which commands a splendid view over the now fertile plains where Scipio's armies once defeated Hasdrubal the Carthaginian.

But Carmona's most moving monument is its fascinating **Roman Necropolis** *(open Tues. to Sat. 10–2 and 4–6; closed Sun. and Mon.)* at the opposite (Seville) end of town. Here, in huge underground chambers, some 900 family tombs, dating from the 2nd century B.C. to the 4th century A.D., have been chiseled out of the rock. The walls of the necropolis are decorated with leaves and birds, and are pierced with niches for urns. Most spectacular of all is the **Servilia Tomb** with its colonnaded arcades and vaulted side galleries. Archeological finds from the chambers are housed in a small museum.

The Itálica Roman Ruins. *Open Tues. to Sat. 9–5:30, Sun. 10–4;*

closed Mon. Itálica lies 9 km. (5 mi.) northwest of Seville on N630 to Extremadura, and about one km. beyond the dreary town of Santiponce. Buses to Santiponce leave from Marqués de Paradas near the Estación de Córdoba approximately every 30 min., but it is best to check details with the tourist office.

The Roman colony of Itálica was founded by Scipio Africans in 206 B.C. as a home for his veteran soldiers. By the 2nd century A.D., it had grown into one of Roman Iberia's most important cities, and had given the world two great emperors: Trajan (52-117) and Hadrian (76-138). Itálica, which once had 10,000 inhabitants living in around 1,000 dwellings, has been about 20% excavated, and work is still in progress on the site.

Its most important monument is its huge elliptical **amphitheater** which once held 40,000 spectators. Here many of the seats, and a few corridors and animal dens, have been well excavated. There are traces too of the town's streets, cisterns, and the floor plans of several villas, some with mosaic floors. The best mosaics have been removed to Seville's Archeological Museum.

In Santiponce a **Roman theater** has now been fully excavated, and there is a small museum containing relics found on the site. Itálica was abandoned and plundered as a quarry by the Visigoths, who preferred Seville; it fell into decay around A.D. 700.

Shopping

The typical handicrafts of Seville consist of the things one most associates with Andalusia: castanets, fans, riding hats, embroidery, *mantillas,* tablecloths, fringed shawls embroidered with flower motifs, wall hangings, earthenware, and ceramics.

The Barrio Santa Cruz, Avda. Constitución, and the streets around the cathedral have the greatest concentration of shops selling these goods. But prices these days are generally high, and bargains hard to find. The shops listed are recommended more for their wide selection and quality than for affordability. Other than the tourist shopping areas, Seville's main shopping area is bounded by the Calles Sierpes (the main street), Tetuán, Velázquez, the Plaza de la Magdalena, and the Plaza del Duque.

The main department stores are the **Corte Inglés,** on Plaza del Duque, which stays open during the siesta hours and has a cafeteria on the top floor, and the **Galerías Preciados** on Plaza de la Magdalena. The Corte Inglés has a newer and much larger branch just a short bus ride from the center, on Luis Montoto, opposite Los Lebreros Hotel.

Ceramics. *Martian Ceramics,* Sierpes 76, at Plaza Nueva end of Sierpes, has a lovely range of plates and dishes of excellent quality. There are several ceramic shops on Mateos Gago, up from the Giralda, and a particularly good one on Romero Murube, between Plaza Alianza and Plaza del Triunfo.

Earthenware and pottery factories. If you are seriously interested in buying pottery and feel you can carry it home, you might like to try visiting some of the places where it is made. Here you may well come across some bargains, as these places sell seconds, unglazed earthenware garden pots, etc., as well as the usual range of painted plates and vases. But before you set out, do call to check these factories are open, as three of them are in the outlying Triana district, rather a long way from the center.

La Cartuja (Pickman) earthenware factory outside Seville has an outlet on Alfonso XII 25 (tel. 954-22-80-21), not far from the Museo de Bellas Artes. Try also *Cerámica Montalván,* Alfarería 23 (tel. 954-33-32-45); *Cerámica Santa Ana,* San Jorge 31, just over the Isabel II bridge (tel. 954-33-39-90); and *Mensaque Roderíguez,* Constancia 38 (tel. 45-49-04).

Fans. *Casa Rubio,* Sierpes 56; *Zadi,* Sierpes 48.

Leather jackets, belts, hats. *Artesanía Textil,* García de Vinuesa 33; *Feliciano Foronda,* Alvarez Quintero 52; *Juan Foronda,* Pza. Vírgen de los Reyes 3.

Mantillas, tablecloths, embroidered linen. *Juan Foronda,* Argote de Molina 18.

Street Markets. *Plaza del Duque,* daily craft and jewelry stalls; *El Jueves* antiques market, Calle Feria, on Thurs. mornings; *Alameda de Hercules,* craft market on Sun. mornings; *Plaza de Alfalfa,* pet market on Sun. mornings; *Plaza del Cabildo,* coin and stamp market on Sun. mornings.

Entertainment and Nightlife

BULLFIGHTS. Bullfights take place at the Maestranza bullring on the Paseo de Colón, usually on Sundays between Easter and October. Tickets can be bought in advance from the ticket windows at the ring, or from the kiosks in Calle Sierpes, though these latter ones charge a commission. Remember that *sol y sombra* tickets are cheaper than *sombra,* and that *sol* (sun) are the cheapest of all. The best fights are during the April Fair, when Spain's leading bullfighters come to Seville. Tickets for these are expensive and hard to come by, but the tourist office may be able to help.

FLAMENCO. Seville is known as the capital of flamenco, and although undoubtedly the best place to see the real thing is in the *casetas* of the April Fair, or when it occurs spontaneously in the city's bars, there are also three regular shows in the city. Though patronized more by tourists than locals, these make for a good night out, if rather an expensive one—entrance prices include one drink (all you need have) and are around 1,900 ptas. They provide the chance to see some excellent performances, interspersed with numbers of more mass appeal. Tickets are on sale in some hotels, otherwise make your reservations directly with the club. Call during the evening, as there is rarely anyone on duty before 6 P.M.

El Arenal, Rodo 7 (tel. 954-21-64-92). The well-known Tablao de Curro Vélez puts on a reasonably authentic show, probably not best suited to flamenco newcomers. Located not far from the Convent of La Caridad, and just around the corner from the Mesón Dos de Mayo, it is closed in Jan. and Feb. when the troupe travels abroad, often performing in the U.S. Usual opening times are 10 P.M.–1:30 A.M., but it is best to check.

Los Gallos, Pza. de Santa Cruz 11 (tel. 954-21-69-81). Open 9:30 P.M.–1:30 A.M., but check to be sure. This is the smallest and most intimate of the clubs, beautifully located in one of the Barrio Santa Cruz's most delightful squares. It usually puts on two shows a night of good, fairly pure flamenco.

El Patio Sevillano, Paseo de Colón 11 (tel. 954-21-41-20). Open 9:15 P.M.–2 A.M., and earlier at 7:15 when there is the demand. This one caters mainly to tour groups, and the show is very colorful and the costumes superb. The show consists of a mixture of regional Spanish dances (often performed to taped music), and pure flamenco numbers performed by some outstanding guitarists, singers, and dancers. The 9:30 and 11:30 shows are usually better bets than the ones at 7:30 or 10 P.M.

◆

S P L U R G E S

Drinks at the Alfonso XIII Hotel. Seville's leading 5-star hotel, the Alfonso XIII, is a magnificent Moorish pastiche fantasy, resplendent with *azulejos*—ceramic tile decor of Moorish inspiration—marble columns, inlaid wood, and shining brass fittings. Built in 1929 for the Spanish-American Exhibition of that year, its first guest was King

Alfonso XIII, who came to Seville to open the exhibition. Today his grandson, King Juan Carlos, stays here when he visits Seville.

The hotel is owned, but not run, by the City Hall, and is the venue for leading lights of Sevillian society. Its expensive suites are most likely beyond the reaches of even the most indulgent splurge, but a prelunch or predinner drink in the bar will afford you the chance to glimpse some of the elegant public rooms. Spending an hour at one of the tables overlooking the magnificent central patio and fountain, observing Sevillian society at large—or at least the upper echelons of it—is a delightful treat which won't stretch those purse strings too far.

Tapas at the Mesón Don Raimundo or Egaña-Oriza Restaurant. *Tapa* sampling, that most Spanish and civilized of pastimes, is particularly splendid in Seville. Though a city claiming few low-cost restaurants of great note, Seville boasts some magnificently atmospheric *tapa* bars, where infinite varieties of fish and seafood can accompany the famous fortified wines of nearby Jerez and Puerto de Santa María.

One really delightful place to indulge in this custom is the bar of the Mesón Don Raimundo restaurant on Argote de Molina 26, just a stone's throw from the cathedral, where an infinite array of these savory delicacies will titillate your taste buds. The *mesón*, located in a former convent, has lashings of Andalusian atmosphere, and has become something of an institution in Sevillian society. Reached through a small foliage-covered patio, the *mesón* is beautifully decked out with antiques and paintings collected by its owner, Raimundo Fernández.

You can dine here, but the restaurant tends to be patronized by tourists, and its prices won't let you sample the same variety as the bar. But beware: round after round of *tapas* and drinks can make that check mount up, for you can rarely tell how much a *tapa* costs, and it is decidedly un-Spanish to inquire the price before ordering. Look upon this as a real Sevillian treat, hope, as may well be the case, that you fall into conversation with other convivial drinkers, and indulge in just enough of those delicious *tapas* and glasses of *fino* to forget the time and the need for a full meal.

The Restaurante Egaña-Oriza on Calle San Fernando 41, opened early in 1987, is currently one of Seville's most "in" restaurants, though here, too, many Sevillians just go to sample the superb seafood specialties.

The decor is modern but attractive, and the bar/restaurant is situated in a prime location on the corner of the Murillo Gardens, overlooking the lovely fountain of the Four Seasons and the Old Tobacco Factory. This is a magical corner of the city, especially at night when the buildings and fountain are illuminated, and the smart, lively atmosphere of the Oriza is a little flutter well worth indulging in. The best times for *tapas* are roughly 1:30–3 and 8–9:30.

A Coche Caballo Ride. *Coche caballos,* or horse buggies, were apparently introduced to Seville by King Edward VIII of England. The present-day carriages, pulled by horses decked out in hats and plumes, ply for hire in the Plaza Vírgen de los Reyes at the foot of the Giralda. Though they are definitely a tourist gimmick, they do offer a wonderfully relaxing way to pass the lazy siesta hours after lunch. The ride should last an hour, cost around 2,000 ptas., and four to five people can fit into the carriage. Be sure to establish all these facts with the driver very clearly *before* you set out, and only pay him at the end.

The usual route, though the choice is up to you, is through the romantic, shady María Luisa Park, visiting the Plaza de América and the Plaza de España; you can then return past the El Cid and Four Seasons fountains, the Old Tobacco Factory, and the Alfonso XIII hotel. Or you could drive along Calle Betis on the opposite side of the Guadalquivir for the wonderful view of the palm-lined riverbanks and the city's impressive skyline dominated by the Giralda and Torre de Oro—this is particularly beautiful at sunset. Touristy they may be, but as a means of conveyance to some of the more outlying places, and as a welcome relaxation to foot-sore, weary sightseers, they offer a charm and romance that is uniquely Sevillian.

------------------◆------------------

THE COSTA
DEL SOL

The most famous stretch of Andalusia's coastline is that part of the Costa del Sol which stretches west from Málaga to Tarifa, Europe's most southerly point. The coast has been transformed over the past 30 years from a string of impoverished fishing villages afflicted with malaria and near starvation into the great package-tour mecca for the sun-seekers of northern Europe, and a retirement haven for Britons and Americans.

But despite the abuses of this naturally lovely area during the boom years of the Franco era, and the continuing vulgarity of many places catering to the lower end of the tourist market, the Costa del Sol still preserves some semblance of charm. It is certainly an ideal place to relax and soak up some sun after an exhausting bout of sightseeing in the great inland cities of Andalusia. It offers few sights itself, but now that the border is once again open you can always take a day trip to that fascinating anomaly—Gibraltar: visit a British pub, chat with a British policeman, and don't miss the Barbary apes! Or why not cross the Straits to exotic Tetuan or Tangier in Morocco for an exciting and different, if a little costly, excursion?

Behind the concrete monsters of the Costa del Sol—some of which are now being demolished—you will come to appreciate a more appealing side to this stretch of tourist paradise. There are still old cottages and villas set in fragrant gardens; the lights of the small fishing craft still twinkle on the sea at night; and the sun setting on the Mediterranean, silhouetting the mountains behind the coast, is still a memorable impression. On top of which the Andaluz of this region are some of the friendliest people in Spain.

On top of which the Andaluz of this region are some of the friendliest people in Spain.

Keeping an eye on expenditure will not be a burden to you either, for the resorts cater to every level of the market, from the dizzy heights of Marbella, with some of the most expensive hotels and restaurants in Spain, to Torremolinos, with some of the cheapest.

And when you've had your fill of coastal pleasures, head inland to dramatic Ronda, perched high on its rocky crag, then westwards to Cádiz, Europe's most ancient city, and then spend a morning sampling sherry in one of the famous bodegas of Jerez. The Costa del Sol and its hinterland can offer you infinite variety without breaking the bank.

Cádiz

The ancient city and port of Cádiz is built on a long narrow peninsula and claims to be the oldest continuously inhabited settlement in western Europe. It was founded in 1100 B.C. by Phoenician traders, who knew it as "Gadir;" later, it was called "Gades" by the Romans. Both Hannibal and Julius Caesar spent some time here, and the city gave Julius Caesar his first taste of public office.

Cádiz has had a rich and varied history: It was here that in 1587 Sir Francis Drake sailed into the harbor and "singed the king's beard" by burning the ships Philip II intended for the Armada, and this port that saw Villeneuve and the French fleet set sail in October 1805 for their encounter at Trafalgar with Admiral Nelson. After suffering decline over several centuries, Cádiz regained its importance after the discovery of America, becoming the base for the Spanish fleet. In the 18th century, when the river to Seville silted up, Cádiz took over the monopoly of New World trade and became the wealthiest port in Europe; most of its buildings date from this period.

In the early 1800s Cádiz successfully resisted the Napoleonic invasion, and when Ferdinand VII was taken prisoner by the French the city fathers proclaimed their own Constitution of 1812 and Cádiz became the short-lived capital of free Spain.

The Old City is African in appearance and immensely intriguing, with a luminous light and a cluster of narrow streets opening onto charming squares. The golden cupola of the cathedral looms high above the low white houses and, despite its rather seedy, dilapidated air, the district begs exploration. Indeed it is a delightful place to wander in, and you can encompass the whole of the Old Town in an hour's walk around the headlands.

Cádiz is also an important industrial port, and as such reflects some of the seamier aspects of life. There are some fine sand beaches, especially along the narrow isthmus which has now been developed as a resort—albeit rather unimaginatively—but unless you want to go for a swim, you will do better to confine your visit to the charms of the Old Town.

GETTING THERE. By Train. The station (tel. 956-23-43-01) is on Avenida del Puerto, where the isthmus joins the Old Town. Cádiz can only be reached by train from Seville and Jerez de la Frontera, and there are frequent trains from both places. It lies at the end of the direct line from Madrid via Seville, and there are some three trains a day on this route.

By Bus. Cadiz has two bus stations; the main one is on the Plaza de la Independencia (tel. 956-22-42-71), and buses arrive here from Puerto de Santa María, Jerez de la Frontera, Arcos, and Seville.There are also daily, but less frequent, services from Tarifa, Algeciras, Granada, and Almería.

The other bus station is on the Avenida Ramón de Carranza 31 (tel. 956-21-15-41) near the port, and buses arrive here from Rota, Chipiona, Sanlúcar de Barrameda, and all coastal towns west of Cádiz.

By Car. If you are approaching from Jerez or Seville, take NIV rather than A4 as this will save you the turnpike tolls. From Algeciras N340 passes through the least-developed stretch of the Andalusian coastline.

By Ferry. A ferry known as *El Vapor* crosses the harbor from the port to Puerto de Santa María four times a day. The ride takes 20 min.

TOURIST OFFICES. Calderón de la Barca 1 (tel. 956-21-13-13), on the corner of Plaza de Mina.

USEFUL ADDRESSES. Police. Isabel la Católica 13 (tel. 956-21-22-76).

Post Office. Plaza de las Flores.

Telephone Exchange. Calle Ancha 24.

WHERE TO STAY. ✆ **Francia y París** (M), Pza. Calvo Sotelo 2 (tel. 956-22-43-48). 69 rooms. Prices are a little high at this charming old-world hotel, but it is the only hotel of any note in the historic heart of Cádiz. It is located close to the Plaza de Mina.

San Remo (M), Paseo Marítimo 3 (tel. 956-25-22- 02). 34 rooms. If you want to be quite close to the beach, then this recent hotel is out along the isthmus, on its southern side.

España (I), Marqués de Cádiz 9 (tel. 956-28-55-00). 18 rooms. The España is a clean, pleasant place to stay, but prices are quite high

Imares (I), San Francisco 9 (tel. 956-21-22-57). 37 rooms. Located in an interesting old house, the Imares is just down from the Francia y París (see above). Though friendly, the hotel is generally rather run-down, and it would be advisable to check your room before you take it. Only some rooms have bathrooms.

WHERE TO EAT. Cádiz is famous for its fish and seafood: try *urta*, a local whitefish obtainable only on Spain's southern Atlantic coast. The Plaza San Juan de Dios is the heart of the restaurant area, and there are loads of *económicos*, inexpensive diners, clustered into the surrounding narrow streets.

Achuri (M), Plocia 15 (tel. 956-25-36-13). If you want good value for money, then try this excellent Basque restaurant. It is located just to the east of the Plaza San Juan de Dios.

●**Café Espagnol** (M), Duque de Victoria 6 (tel. 956-21-18-93). It is well worth trying the *urta* at this friendly, popular restaurant, but go there for the good choice of seafood anyway.

Mesón Piconera (M), San Germán 15. You will find this picturesque inn on the far side of the Plaza de España.

La Económica (I), San Fernando 2, and next door **El Nueve** (I) at San Fernando 4, are two leading *económicos* just off the Plaza San Juan de Dios. Both offer *menus del día* at real bargain prices.

MAJOR ATTRACTIONS. Cathedral, *Pza. Pio XIII. Open Mon. to Fri. 5:30–7:30 P.M., Sat. 9:30–10:30 and 5:30–8, Sun. 11–1. Opening hours can change without warning, so be sure to check.* The cathedral was begun in 1722 when Càdiz was at the height of its power; its wealth and pre-eminence are reflected in the stunning gold dome and the splendid baroque facade. The **treasury,** open 10–2, entered via Calle Arquitecto Acero, overflows with gold and silver and precious New World jewels. Among its most priceless possessions is a processional cross, the famous **Custodia del Millón,** or Million Monstrance, made of gold and named for the million or so jewels with which it is encrusted. In the **crypt** of the cathedral lies the famous Càdiz-born composer Manuel de Falla (1876-1946).

Museo de Bellas Artes, *Pza. de Mina 5. Open 10–2, closed Sat. and Sun.* The Fine Arts Museum houses an outstanding collection of superb paintings and should not be missed. Most famous of its works are those by Murillo, Alonso Cano, and, above all, Zurbarán, whose *Four Evangelists* are housed here.

In the same building is the **Archeological Museum** with a good collection of Phoenician exhibits and an especially fine 5th-century B.C. sarcophagus, unearthed in 1980.

Museo Histórico Municipal, *Santa Inés. Open Mon. to Fri. 9–1 and 4–7, Sat. and Sun. 9–1; closed Mon.* The real showpiece of the museum is a fascinating ivory and mahogany model of Càdiz made in 1779, showing in minutest detail all the streets and buildings, surprisingly little changed since then. There is also a 19th-century mural depicting the setting up of the Constitution of 1812.

OTHER ATTRACTIONS. Hospital de Mujeres, *Obispo Calvo y Valero. Open 9–6.* The building is worth visiting for its beautiful 18th-century patio decorated with ceramics from Triana in Seville. The chapel houses El Greco's fine painting of *St. Francis in Ecstasy.*

Oratorio de la Santa Cueva, *Calle Rosario. Open Tues. to Sat. 10–1 and 4–6, Sun. 4–6.* This unusual oval 18th-century chapel is visited mainly for its three paintings by Goya. If it's closed the caretaker can usually be contacted at San Francisco 11.

San Felipe Neri, *Santa Inés. Open 12–2 and 5–7; closed Sun. and July.* Spain's first liberal constitution was proclaimed in this church in 1812, and here the Cortes of Càdiz used to meet. Don't miss the *Immaculate Conception* by Murillo on the main altar. (Murillo died in Càdiz in 1682; he fell from the scaffolding in the Chapel of Santa Catalina while working on his *Mystic Marriage of St. Catherine*).

Estepona

Estepona has always been quieter and more family-orientated than its neighbors farther north. It lacks the hideous highrises of the Franco era and, though there are some fairly unattractive buildings on the main highway along the front, it is not hard to imagine the old fishing village this once was.

Its beach, over one km. (more than half a mile) long, is lined with fishing boats, and along the promenade the well-kept gardens and highly scented flowers make for a lovely evening stroll at sunset. The old Moorish village behind the Avenida de España is surprisingly unspoiled, and to wander round the old streets near the market, around the church and Plaza de San Francisco, is to leave behind the overdevelopment of so much of the rest of the Costa del Sol.

Since the reopening in 1985 of the frontier with Gibraltar, and the consequent growth in traffic using Gibraltar airport, new developments are now springing up along the coast between Estepona and La Línea, which faces the Rock. However, these *urbanizaciones* have learned from the mistakes of earlier developers, and instead of highrises typical traditional Andalusian architecture has been recreated.

GETTING THERE. By Train. Estepona is on the main Málaga–Torremolinos–Algeciras line.

By Bus. The Portillo Bus Station is on the front at Avda de España 230. Buses run between Marbella and Estepona every half an hour between 7 A.M. and 10:30 P.M. There are similarly frequent services to and from La Línea.

TOURIST OFFICES. Paseo Marítimo Gardens (tel. 952-80-09-13). It does not open during the winter months.

WHERE TO STAY. Buenavista (M), Avda. de España 180 (tel. 952-80-01-37). 38 rooms. Though an unexciting and functional hostel on the main highway facing the sea, the Buenavista does at least have the advantage of a restaurant, plus all rooms have bathrooms. Nonetheless, rooms on the front will be noisy.

Dobar (M), Avda. de España 178 (tel. 952-80-06-00). 39 rooms. Next door to the Buenavista (above), this is a similarly unexciting hotel. Only breakfast is served here.

⬤ El Pino (I), Generalísimo Franco 148 (tel. 952-80-06-96). 24 rooms. Though simple, this 1-star hostel is quieter and has much more character than the only available (M) choices. It is located one block back from the seafront in a typical Andalusian house and has a patio and budget dining room.

WHERE TO EAT. In summer there are several pleasant outdoor restaurants at the Puerto Deportivo marina to the west of town, the entrance to which is opposite the bullring.

Mesón Arni (M), Mondejar 16. While wandering in the heart of the Old Town, why not stop at this restaurant and sample some of their Mexican specialties. It opens for dinner only and is closed Wed.

Jardín (I), Almengual 10. Curry and spare ribs may not strike you as exactly Spanish, but the food in this homey spot, located in a small square between Gen. Franco and Calle del Mar, is generally good, and certainly inexpensive. There is an excellent-value *menu del día* at lunch from Mon. through Sat.

Mesón El Yunque (I), Mondejar 19. A very good value *menu del día* is on offer in this bright and cheerful mesón.

EXCURSIONS. Casares is a delightful mountain village about 20 km. (12 mi.) to the northwest of Estepona in the Sierra Bermeja. Streets of ancient white houses perch on the slopes beneath the ruins of a Moorish castle; close by, outside the village of Manilva, the ruins of a Roman bath have been unearthed. There are a couple of buses a day from Estepona to Casares and the ride is worth it simply for the superb view over the Mediterranean. An added bonus is the thriving ceramics industry you will find in the village.

Jerez De La Frontera

Jerez de la Frontera, surrounded by immense vineyards, is famous the world over for its sherry, and it is first and foremost for the sherry *bodegas* that one comes to Jerez. A visit to the huge wine cellars is an exciting experience even for those who may not care for sherry, and they are every bit as much of Jerez's heritage as its churches or convents. Names such as González Byass, Pedro Domecq, or Williams and Humbert are inextricably linked with Jerez, and the word sherry, first used in Britain in 1608, is itself an English corruption of the town's old Moorish name of Xeres.

The famous grapes of Jerez have funded a host of churches and noble mansions, and among the most outstanding are Isabelline San Miguel, Mudéjar San Dionisio, and Gothic Santiago. However, despite these notable buildings the town is sadly run down and rather dull, with only a dusty majesty about it now.

But the town's two great festivals, which draw crowds from all over Spain, turn the town into an exuberant and colorful pageant. Jerez's other great pride and joy, apart from its sherry, is its horses—very much the domain of the Anglo-Spanish aristocracy. In early May Jerez's Feria follows on from Seville's April Fair; the streets are thronged with carriages and parades of riders, and there are magnificent displays by the famous Andalusian Riding School.

September sees the celebration of the Vintage Festival. The grapes are blessed in a lovely setting on the triple stairway leading up to the Collegiate Church of Santa María. Built in the 18th century in a strangely neo-Gothic style, the church has an octagonal cupola and curious separate bell tower. Both celebrations ring to the strains of top flamenco dancers and the tragic passion of *cante jondo* singers. It is on these occasions that Jerez regains all its former splendor and color.

GETTING THERE. By Air. Jerez Airport (tel. 956-33-22-10) is 11 km. (7 mi.) from town and has direct flights from Madrid, Valencia, Barcelona, and Zaragoza. The *Iberia* office in town is on Plaza Reyes Católicos 2 (tel. 956-33-99-08).

By Train. Càdiz Station (tel. 956-33-66-82) is on the eastern edge of town, at the far end of Explanada de la Estación. Plenty of trains run from Seville and Càdiz, and there are three a day from Madrid.

By Bus. The bus station (tel. 956-34-10-63) is also on Explanada de la Estación, but is closer to town. Buses run from Seville, Càdiz, and Ronda. Local services run to Arcos de la Frontera, Rota, Chipiona, and Sanlúcar de Barrameda.

By Car. From Seville or Càdiz, avoid paying the turnpike tolls of

A6 by staying on NVI. From Ronda, N342 takes you via Arcos, a lovely old village well worth visiting for its magnificent views.

TOURIST OFFICES. Alameda Cristina 7 (tel. 956-33-11-50). Open 8 A.M.–3 P.M. The office can supply you with a free map of the location of the *bodegas* and will advise on which ones can be visited and when, along with details of possible visits to the Andalusian Riding School.

USEFUL ADDRESSES. Police. Pza. de Silos 4 (tel. 956-34-35-43).
Post Office. Cerón 1.
Telephone Exchange. Calle Eguilaz.

WHERE TO STAY. Be warned that most places will be fully booked during the May Fair and September Vintage Festival.

Nova (M), Alvar Núñez 13 (tel. 956-34-14-59). 17 rooms. Conveniently located just to the east of the center of Jerez, this friendly hotel has recently been renovated. All rooms have bathrooms.

Virt (M), Higueras 20 (tel. 956-32-28-11). 20 rooms. The Virt is the most expensive of our selections, but it is a well-furnished hostel whose rooms all have bathrooms and air-conditioning.

El Coloso (I), Pedro Alonso 13 (tel. 956-34-90-08). 25 rooms. Despite being a little shabby, this rather faded but friendly old-world hotel is perfectly adequate and all the rooms have bathrooms. It is fairly centrally located just off Gen. Franco.

Trujillo (I), Medina 33 (tel. 956-34-24-38). 17 rooms. The rooms are comfortable and clean in this well-run and recently renovated 2-star hostel.

WHERE TO EAT. Jerez has a couple of good expensive restaurants, but very few moderate eating places. Some bars serve good snacks, but there are very few worthwhile affordable restaurants.

Gaitán (M), Gaitán 33 (tel. 956-34-58-59). The Gaitán is a small *mesón,* popular with the locals—always a good sign. Closed Mon. and Aug.

San Francisco (I), Pza. Esteve 2 (tel. 956-34-12-12). You can eat a reasonable meal here at fairly moderate prices, but it's more like a cafeteria than a restaurant and lacks atmosphere.

MAJOR ATTRACTIONS. Sherry Bodegas. *Most bodegas are open to visitors Mon. to Sat 9–1, but not in August when they are busy with the grape harvest.* September is often the most interesting month to visit when they are bottling the new wine. Tours are often given in English and are in most cases—but not all—free, as is the generous

amount of sherry available for tasting at the end. You should arrange
your visit with the bodega of your choice at least 24 hours in advance.
Advice, addresses, phone numbers, and a map of locations are
available from the tourist office.

OTHER ATTRACTIONS. Museo de Flamenco, *Pza. de las Angustias
(tel. 956-34-89-93). The museum was closed at press time for
refurbishing, but is due to open sometime in 1988. Check with the
tourist office for details.* It houses fascinating displays on the history
and art of flamenco.

Recreo de las Cadenas, *Avda. Duque de Abrantes.* A 19th-
century palace that has been redesigned with the help of the Domecq
family, it now houses the prestigious **Escuela Andaluza de Arte
Ecuestre.** The Andalusian Riding School rivals the famous Spanish
Riding School in Vienna and it is often possible to watch the horses
training between 11–1, Mon. to Sat. They give a full performance of
their art on Thurs. at 11 A.M., and a special display during the May
Fair.

Málaga

Málaga, Spain's fifth largest city, claims the title Capital of the
Costa del Sol, though in reality most tourists simply use its airport and
make for the chain of resorts to the west. If you approach the city from
the airport you will first be greeted by its western outskirts, a hideous
urban sprawl of the '70s, where the highrises stretching towards
Torremolinos encroach on the traditional sugarcane fields.

But don't despair, for in its center and eastern approaches, largely
unspoiled by progress, Málaga is a pleasant enough port city with
ancient streets and lovely villas set in exotic gardens. To the east in
Pedregalejos and El Palo, once traditional fishing villages and now
residential suburbs, you can still eat wonderfully fresh fish in the
fishermen's restaurants along the beach.

Overlooking the port, the central Plaza de la Marina, with its lively
cafés and illuminated fountain, is a pleasant place for a drink. From
here you can stroll through the shady park, scene of Málaga's August
Fair, or browse in the stores on the Calle Marqués de Larios, the main
shopping street. The narrow streets and alleyways on either side of this
thoroughfare have a charm of their own, though in parts you will see
signs of dilapidation. This stems from the fact that Málaga has one of
Spain's highest unemployment and crime rates: Bear this in mind, and
always take extra care of your possessions.

GETTING THERE. By Air. Málaga Airport (tel. 952-32-20-00; 95235-17-25 for flight information) is one of southern Europe's busiest. It is connected to Málaga, Torremolinos, and the coastal resorts by a suburban train system (see *Getting Around* below). A bus runs between the airport and the *Iberia* office (tel. 952-21-37-31) on Molino Lario, but be sure you get the right stop: Vuelos Nacionales for domestic flights, Vuelos Charter or Terminal Internacional for international flights.

By Train. Málaga Station is on Calle Cuarteles, across the river (tel. 952-31-25-00). There are direct daily trains from Seville, Córdoba, Madrid, and Barcelona. From Granada and Ronda you'll need to change at Bobadilla. The **RENFE** office is on Strachan 2 (tel. 952-21-31-22).

By Bus. The main bus station for long-distance buses is Alsina Graells, Pza. de Toros Vieja 14 (tel. 952-31-04-00/04) just off Calle Cuarteles. There are daily services from Nerja, Almería, Cartagena, Granada, Ubeda, Córdoba, Seville, and Badajoz. There are baggage-checking facilities.

By Car. From Granada, the most direct route is N342 to just beyond Loja where you then follow N321 to Málaga, a total distance of 127 km. (79 mi.). Alternatively you can drop down to the coast at Motril on the mountainous and picturesque N323, then take the coastal highway west to Málaga. The third choice is the old Málaga–Granada highway, C340, via Alhama as far as Colmenar, then dropping down through the Puerto del León pass to Málaga along C345. The road surface is not always good on the latter, but the scenery is superb.

From Córdoba, take N331 to just beyond Antequera, then N321 into Malaga. From Seville, take N334 to Antequera, then N331 and N321.

On the coastal N340, especially on the western stretch between Málaga and Algeciras, take extra care at all times. Though the road is good by Spanish standards, and is currently being widened, it gets very crowded and is known locally as the *Carretera de la Muerte,* the Highway of Death. A useful tip: When you want to turn left, you do so in most cases by exiting right and looping round in a circle, often controlled by traffic lights.

TOURIST OFFICES. Marqués de Larios 5 (tel. 952-21-34-45). Open Mon. to Fri. 9–2:30, Sat. 9–1. It may also open afternoons in summer. It supplies good free maps of the city, with details of the main sights and museums. If the office is closed, the Corte Inglés department store on Avda. de Andalucía also distributes good free maps.

USEFUL ADDRESSES. Consulates U.S.: Edificio El Ancla, Ramón y Cajal (tel. 952-47-48-91) in Fuengirola. **U.K.:** Duquesa de Parcent 8 (tel. 952-21-75-71).

Police. Pintor Nogales (tel. 952-21-50-05), close to the Alcazaba.

Post Office. Avda. de Andaluces 1, across the river at the end of Alameda Principal.

Telephone Exchange. Molina Larios 11, next to Iberia. Open Mon. to Fri. 9–2 and 6–9, weekends 10–1.

American Express. Viajes Alhambra, Calle Especería, just off Pza. Constitución.

GETTING AROUND. By Train. There is a very useful suburban train service between Málaga, Torremolinos, and Fuengirola, and all intermediate resorts and the airport. It runs every half hour between 6:30 A.M. and 10:30 P.M. Its terminus is at the Málaga Guadalmedina station, just over the river almost opposite the Corte Inglés. It also calls at the Málaga RENFE station. The terminus in Fuengirola is just across from the bus station where you make connections for Mijas or any of the resorts on down the coast towards Marbella and Algeciras.

By Bus. Transport around the city is by bus and the tourist office can advise on the system. The no. 11 is the one to take for the beach and the famous *merenderos,* the popular fish and seafood restaurants.

Automoviles Portillo at Córdoba 7 (tel. 952-22-73-00) runs buses from Málaga to Algeciras and La Línea via Torremolinos, Benalmadena, Fuengirola, Marbella, Estepona, and all intermediate stops. Their blue buses run frequently and you can pick them up at any of the bus stops along the N340 coastal highway. There are also services to Mijas, Almería, Gibraltar, Cádiz, and Jerez de la Frontera.

Other small companies, mostly operating from the Alameda Principal, run services to the outlying villages, Coin, Antequera, and Ronda.

WHERE TO STAY. California (M), Paseo de Sancha 19 (tel. 952-21-51-65). 26 rooms. You won't be in the center of things here, for the California is located out beyond the bullring, but if you don't fancy the walk into the center, then you can reach it easily on bus no. 11. A '60s hotel which could do with a shot of new life, it nevertheless provides quite adequate accommodations in a city not overendowed with moderately priced hotels.

Niza (M), Larios 2 (tel. 952-22-77-04). The Niza is a well-maintained, old-fashioned hotel located on the main street just down from Plaza Constitución. It has rooms with and without bathrooms and serves breakfast but not dinner.

Derby (I), San Juan de Dios 1 (tel. 952-22-13-01). 16 rooms. Views overlooking the port are the attraction of this simple hostel right in the center of town. No meals are served, but it is right above the city's two leading cafés. There are rooms with or without bathrooms.

●**Victoria** (I), Sancha Lara 3 (tel. 952-22-42-23). 13 rooms. A recent face-lift has much improved this hotel located in an old house just off the Calle Larios. It provides excellent reasonably priced accommodations.

WHERE TO EAT. Casa Pedro (M), Quitapenas 112 (tel. 952-29-00-13). Overlooking the sea at El Palo (reached by bus no. 11), this huge dining room is one of Málaga's most famous fish restaurants. It is very popular and always crowded, especially on Sunday lunchtimes.

Guerola (M), Esparteros 8 (tel. 952-22-31-21). The menu is a little more imaginative than the usual Spanish fare here, and you can dine outside on the sidewalk in summer. Close by there are a handful of low-price *económicos:* the **Rincón de Mata, La Aldea,** and **Maite,** but this is one of the best moderately priced restaurants in the center of town.

●**Refectorium II** (M), Fernando Lesseps 7 (tel. 952-22-33- 97). For good home cooking at very modest prices visit this restaurant just off the top of Calle Nueva.

●**La Cancela** (I), Denis Belgrano 3 (tel. 952-22-31-25). Dine outdoors in a small square in summer in this delightful restaurant located just off the Plaza del Siglo.

Cortijo de Pepe (I), Pza. de la Merced 2. If you want a typical Málaga *bodega,* then make your way to this tavern-restaurant overlooking the square where Pablo Picasso was born in 1881. It serves some good, very inexpensive dishes.

MAJOR ATTRACTIONS. Alcazaba. *Open 10–1 and 5–8, 4–7 in winter; closed Sun.* The Moorish fortress dates from the 8th century when Málaga was the most important port of the Moorish kingdom. The ruins of the Roman amphitheater at its entrance were uncovered when the fort was restored. The inner palace, for a short while in the 11th century the residence of the Moorish emirs, now houses the **Archeological Museum** with a fine collection of Moorish art.

Gibralfaro. You can climb up to this 14th-century Moorish fortress through the beautiful gardens of the Alcazaba, or drive up here by way of Calle Victoria. Alternatively, a minibus leaves roughly every hour and a half from near the cathedral on Molina Lario. From the towers and ramparts of this, the highest point of the city, the views over Málaga, its port and bullring, and all along the coast are quite stunning. However, Gibralfaro is often deserted, so it is best not to carry valuables up here.

OTHER ATTRACTIONS. Cathedral. Málaga Cathedral is not one of the great cathedrals of Spain. Built between 1528 and 1782 in a mixture of styles, but principally Renaissance, it lacks a second tower to balance the single existing one, and the general aspect is rather dreary. However, the superb 17th-century **choir stalls** carved by Pedro de Mena are an outstanding work of art.

Museo de Bellas Artes, *San Agustín 6. Open 10–1:30 and 5–8, 4–7 in winter; closed Sun. P.M. and Mon.* Set in the lovely old palace of the counts of Buenavista, the collection includes works by Luis de Morales, Alonso Cano, Murillo, and Ribera, as well as a collection of 19th- and 20th-century art including Sorolla, Benlliure and Casas. There are also some childhood drawings and sketches by Málaga's most famous native son, Pablo Ruiz Picasso.

SHOPPING. Calle Marqués de Larios, lined with stylish boutiques, shoe shops, and jewelry stores, is the main shopping street. Parallel to it and a block or two to the west is **Calle Nueva,** a pedestrian shopping street with rather less expensive stores. Here you'll find numerous cheap shoe stores, small department stores, household goods, jewelry, pottery, etc. The warren of narrow streets to the northwest of Plaza Constitución—**Calle Salvago, Plaza de los Mártires,** etc.—is packed with intriguing old stores selling herbs and spices, basketware, kitchen goods, knives, old-fashioned pharmacies, etc., all making for a fascinating wander. The **Corte Inglés** department store is just across the river on **Avenida de Andalucía** (tel. 952-30-40-80), open Mon.–Sat. 10 A.M.–9 P.M. Málaga is famous for its muscatel raisins and sweet wines: *Málaga Vírgen* and *Lágrimas de Cristo* are two local dessert wines. Larios gin comes from Málaga and Bacardi rum (a good bargain in Spain) is made and bottled in the Bacardi factory just west of town (tel. 952-33-02-00 to visit). The **Casa Mira** ice-cream parlor on Calle Larios 6 is a good place to try the summer drink of *horchata*.

Marbella

Marbella does not conjure up images of a budget-holiday center with its grand hotels, smart boutiques, and luxury restaurants. Indeed, it is much favored by rock stars, moviemakers, and rich oil sheiks, and Puerto Banús, Marbella's plush marina, with its huge yachts, parade of beautiful people, and a hundred or so (expensive) restaurants, outshines even St. Tropez in ritzy glamour. However, there is another side to Marbella, and you can find good budget eating places and reasonable accommodations.

Most of the glamorous action of Marbella takes place on the fringes of the town, and once in the center you may wonder why Marbella has become so famous. The main thoroughfare, the Avenida Ricardo Soriano, is singularly lacking in charm, and the Paseo Marítimo, though pleasant enough with its array of seafood restaurants, is far from spectacular.

The real charm of Marbella is to be found in the heart of the old village, a block or two back from the main highway. Here you are in real Spain again, in narrow, whitewashed streets gathered around the central Plaza de los Naranjos, a delightful square with outdoor restaurants set amid orange trees. Marbella is not a place we can list museums and sights to see: It is a place to wander in and explore for yourself. Climb up onto what is left of the fortifications and stroll along the Calle Vírgen de los Dolores to the lovely Plaza Santo Cristo by the famous La Fonda restaurant; enjoy the geranium-bedecked windows, and the fountains; or simply sit with your drink watching two different worlds go by.

GETTING THERE. By Bus. Buses run every 30 or 45 minutes between Málaga, Torremolinos, Marbella, and Estepona. There are two or three buses daily from Algeciras, Ronda, Coin, and Ojen, and in summer, two daily from Madrid. The bus station is on the main Ricardo Soriano avenue, to the west of the center on the corner of Calle Calvario.

TOURIST OFFICES. Miguel Cano 1 (tel. 952-77-14-42) in the corner of the small park on the main highway. Open Mon. to Fri. 9:30–1 and 5–7:30, Sat. 10–1. The staff are very helpful in finding low-cost accommodations.

USEFUL ADDRESSES. Police. Calle Portada, on the corner of Lobatas.

Post Office. Alonso de Bazan 1.

Telephone Exchange. Calle Gen. Chinchilla, just off Pza. Naranjos.

WHERE TO STAY. ● **Alfil** (M), Ricardo Soriano 19 (tel. 952-77-23 50). 40 rooms. Rooms on the front will be noisy, but if you do stay in this good, moderate hotel on the main street at least you'll be in the center of things.

Lima (M), Antonio Belón 2 (tel. 952-77-05-00). 64 rooms. The Lima is a functional hotel, adequate but unexciting, but you will be in the center and just a couple of blocks from the sea. Its high-season rates may be too expensive.

●El Castillo (I), Pza. San Bernabe 2 (tel. 952-77-17-39). 27 rooms. The charm of this hostel is that it is located in the old heart of Marbella, near the Plaza de los Naranjos and the old fortifications.

Enriqueta (I), Caballeros 18 (tel. 952-77-00-58). Simple this hostel may be, but it is clean and some rooms have their own bathroom. And you'll be staying in a charming old house right in the heart of the Old Town, just above the Plaza de los Naranjos.

Finlandia (I), Calle Finlandia (tel. 952-77-07-00). 11 rooms. Tucked away in a pleasant side street, this small house is located between the main highway and the sea. Its rooms all have bathrooms, and breakfast is served. But it tends to cater for student tour groups, and you may find its rates are (M) in high season.

WHERE TO EAT. Stay away from the restaurants in the Plaza de los Naranjos unless you feel like a special treat, as they are all expensive, but explore any of the streets in the Old Town, away from the Plaza, as there are several reasonable finds hidden away here. Down on the Paseo Marítimo you can eat quite reasonably in any of the numerous pizzerias, though the other restaurants there are all quite pricey.

Balcón de la Vírgen (M), Remedios 2 (tel. 952-77-60-92). Enjoy a moderately priced meal in this picturesque restaurant located in a 17th-century house just above Casa Eladio. Closed Tues.

Casa Eladio (M), Vírgen de los Dolores 6. In a lovely street just off the Plaza de los Naranjos, this restaurant has a charming indoor patio decorated with ceramic plates. Its prices are more moderate than on the central Plaza.

Metropole (M), Ricardo Soriano 21 (tel. 952-77-77-41). Consistently good standards and fair prices have given this restaurant a good reputation. It is located close to the Alfil hotel. Closed Sun.

La Cancela (I), Misericordia 5. While exploring the Old Town pop into this extremely pretty Andalusian house for a good budget meal.

La Paloma (I), Ortiz de Molinillo. An ideal budget restaurant with low prices by Marbella standards, La Paloma exudes Andalusian atmosphere and decor.

●La Rosa de Marbella (I), Callejón de Santo Cristo. Cost-conscious visitors will love this small, picturesque restaurant located just off the Plaza Santo Cristo.

SHOPPING. Marbella's upmarket boutiques stock all the latest in designer fashion and prices, even for the scantiest bikini, are, as you might expect in this jet-set resort, astronomical. There is a branch of the **Corte Inglés** department store in the Edificio Estela 1 on Avda. Ricardo Soriano (tel. 952-82-56-60) and the money exchange office here is useful when regular banks are shut.

Mijas

The picturesque mountain village of Mijas lies only a few kilometers inland from Fuengirola and Torremolinos, and makes for a very worthwhile half-day trip. It is not a place for sightseeing, rather to wander in and enjoy the atmosphere. Though Mijas was discovered some time ago by the foreign retiree community, and the large touristy square where you arrive may well seem like an extension of the Costa's tourist bazaar, beyond this there are hillside streets of whitewashed houses and an authentic village atmosphere that has changed little since before the tourist boom of the '60s.

Make sure you find your way to the small bullring (which can be visited) and up beyond it to the charming church. From here the views over the hills to Fuengirola and the coast are quite stunning. The chapel of Mijas's patroness, the Vírgen de la Peña, on the main square, is also worth a visit and, if such things appeal, the Carromato de Max has an amazing collection of miniature curiosities from all over the world. The collection includes a Salvador Dalí painted on a pinhead and some shrunken heads. Mijas also offers some quite good souvenir shopping: look in particular for leather, woven rugs and blankets, and ceramics.

GETTING THERE. By Bus. Buses run to Mijas from Málaga, Torremolinos, and Fuengirola. In all three towns buses depart from the main bus terminal.

By Car. The quickest route (and easiest driving) is to take the road straight up through the hills behind Fuengirola. Far prettier and with some magnificent views, though it involves lots of mountain bends on a rather narrow road, is the inland route from Torremolinos via Benalmádena Pueblo. If you've been exploring further inland, the approach through the mountains behind Mijas from either Coin or Alhaurin El Grande is the most spectacular of all, and this road, though high and winding, is in quite good condition.

WHERE TO STAY. El Mirlo Blanco (I), Pza. Constitución 13 (tel. 952-48-57-00). 5 rooms. Other than the luxurious Hotel Mijas, these simple rooms belonging to the restaurant of the same name are the only accommodations in town. It is located just below the bullring.

WHERE TO EAT. El Capricho (M), Los Caños 5 (tel. 952-48-51-11).

For good, moderately priced food, make for this pleasant and atmospheric restaurant located in the shopping street, just behind the main square. Closed Wed.

El Mirlo Blanco (M), Pza. Constitución 13 (tel. 952-48-57-00). The "White Blackbird" is a Basque restaurant located in a typical village house.

Casa Jaime (I), Los Caños 3. Head for this restaurant for the best value for money on this street which has several eating places.

La Reja (I), Los Caños 9 (tel. 952-48-50-68). Only the upstairs pizzeria is (I). The downstairs restaurant is good but more expensive. Whichever you decide on you'll be able to enjoy views over the main square. Closed Mon.

SHOPPING. Most of Mijas' shops were expressly created for the tourist and the village has become a souvenir hunters' paradise. Ceramics, Lladró porcelain, Majórica pearls, leather goods, and woven rugs and bedspreads are some of the more authentic crafts on sale here. Generally speaking, the stores away from the Plaza Vírgen de la Peña offer better-quality goods than those on the square itself, so be sure to explore the side streets and don't get too caught up with the rather brash tourist wares that greet you on arrival.

Nerja

Nerja lies 50 km. (30 mi.) to the east of Málaga and is a small, though expanding, resort which so far has escaped the worst excesses of the property developers. To date its development has been confined mostly to the spread of "village" developments such as El Capistrano, one of the Costa del Sol's architectural showpieces. The villas and Andalusian-style homes here have been a big hit with the British and American retiree colonies. The town itself clusters around the old village which stands on top of a headland overlooking several small beaches and rocky coves. Swimming is pleasant enough here, though the sand is the usual gray grit.

Nerja's two outstanding features are the Balcón de Europa, a fantastic lookout place set high above the sea on a promontory just off the central square, and the famous Cuevas de Nerja, a series of huge stalactite caves, a mile or so out of town, off the road to Almuñécar and Almería.

GETTING THERE. By Bus. Buses run to Nerja village and on to the caves from Málaga (Pza. de Toros Vieja).

TOURIST OFFICES. Puerta del Mar 4 (tel. 952-52-15-31). Open during the summer only.

WHERE TO STAY. Rooms are hard to come by in high season, and it is advisable to make reservations.

Cala Bella (M), Puerta del Mar 10 (tel. 952-52-07-00). 9 rooms. Staying in this simple, old-fashioned hotel located in a charming old Andalusian house has the added advantage of stunning views over the sea. Its restaurant (open to nonresidents) has an outdoor balcony with a breathtaking view.

Portofino (M), Puerta del Mar 2 (tel. 952-52-01-50). 12 rooms. Located next door to the Cala Bella, the Portofino is equally charming, though a little more expensive. It too has a restaurant with great views (also open to the public).

Atenbeni (I), Diputación 12 (tel. 952-52-13-41). 16 rooms. If you stay in this clean, bright hostel in the center of town, you can nip downstairs to the restaurant below for good budget meals.

WHERE TO EAT. Casa Luque (M), Pza. Cavana 2 (tel. 952-52-10-04). You will find this charming restaurant just behind the church on the Balcón de Europa. Its small menu includes good pasta dishes and the prices are reasonable for the quality.

Paco y Eva (M), Calle del Barrio 50 (tel. 952-52-15-24). If fish and game dishes appeal, then try this informal *mesón*. It is central, and popular with the foreign community.

Cortijo (I), Calle del Barrio 26. The Cortijo is a small, family-run restaurant in a lovely house which dates back to the early 1800s.

MAJOR ATTRACTIONS. Cuevas de Nerja. *The caves are 4 km. (2 mi.) from the center of Nerja, off the road to Almuñécar. Open May to Sept. 9:30–9; Oct. to Apr. 10–1:30 and 4–7.* These huge caves, thought to be between 12,000 and 20,000 years old, were discovered by a shepherd boy in 1959. A kind of vast underground cathedral, they contain the world's longest known stalactite (61 m. 200 ft.) and are spectacularly beautiful, if a little overcommercialized. Part of the caves has been converted into an auditorium for concerts and ballet performances.

Ronda

Ronda, a most spectacular town set high in the mountains of the Serranía de Ronda, was the last stronghold of the legendary Andalusian bandits and the scene of the last great rising of the Moors against Ferdinand and Isabella. It is both one of the oldest towns in Spain, and one of the most dramatic. Dividing the town in two is a great ravine, El Tajo, 90 meters (300 feet) across, with La Ciudad, the old Moorish town, on one side, and El Mercadillo, the new town that grew up after the Christian Reconquest of 1485, on the other.

Spanning the gorge between the two parts of town is the Puente Nuevo, an amazing architectural feat built between 1455 and 1793, whose parapet offers dizzying views of the River Guadalevín way below. Just how many people have met their death in the gorge isn't known, but the architect of the bridge met his death while inspecting work in progress, and Hemingway refers to the throwing of people, including clergy, in the Tajo ravine in *For Whom the Bell Tolls*. Horses killed in the bullring used to be hurled into the gorge to be picked clean by vultures. Much lower down the gorge are two even older bridges, the Puente San Miguel built by the Moors, and the Puente Viejo, rebuilt in 1616 on the remains of an earlier Arab bridge.

There are some fine old mansions and churches in La Ciudad, but Ronda is visited more for its setting, breathtaking views, and ancient houses with their famous bird-cage balconies, than for any particular monument. It has long attracted writers and artists, among them Goya and Hemingway, and at the turn of the century the German poet Rainer Maria Rilke wrote many of his best works in the Reina Victoria Hotel.

The main street of the Mercadillo is the Carrera de Espinel, and the cliff-top walk and lovely gardens of the Alameda del Tajo offer magnificent views of the imposing landscape. Close by, Ronda's bullring, built in the early 1780s, is one of the oldest in Spain; indeed, Ronda is known as the cradle of modern bullfighting. A native son, Francisco Romero, invented the killing sword and cape, and his grandson, Pedro Romero (1754–1839), is said to have killed 5,600 bulls during his 30-year career. Goya's *Tauromagina* paintings were inspired by Pedro Romero, hence the Goyesca *corridas* held every September. The bullring is now owned by the famous bullfighter Antonio Ordóñez and is open to visitors. Orson Welles befriended Ordóñez and asked for his ashes to be scattered on his estate after his death. There is a bullfighting museum beneath the seats of the bullring which contains posters from the very first *corridas* held in this ring in May 1785.

GETTING THERE. By Train. Ronda lies on the line between Algeciras and Bobadilla. Ronda is also accessible from Seville, Córdoba, Granada, and Málaga by way of Bobadilla junction, though in most cases bus routes are more direct. Ronda Station is on Avenida de Andalucía (tel. 952-87-16-73).

By Bus. Ronda's bus station is also on the Avenida de Andalucía.

Buses run from Seville, Málaga, Arcos, Jerez de la Frontera, Cádiz, San Pedro de Alcántara, Marbella, and Fuengirola.

By Car. All approaches to Ronda are mountainous and involve some very winding roads. The easiest and best maintained road is C339 from the coast at San Pedro de Alcántara, though far more spectacular is C331 from San Roque near Algeciras to Jimena, then C341 via Guaquín. From Jerez, take N342 to near Algodonales, then C339; and from Seville, make for Morón de la Frontera, then C339. From Málaga, either make for San Pedro and C339, or take the scenic, but not the best maintained, C344 by way of Coin and El Burgo.

TOURIST OFFICES. Pza. de España 1 (tel. 952-87-12-72). This is in Mercadillo, just over the Puente Nuevo. Ask for a free map, and check which sights are open to visitors, and which are closed for restoration.

USEFUL ADDRESSES. Police. Vírgen de la Paz, diagonally opposite the post office.

Post Office. Vírgen de la Paz 20.

WHERE TO STAY. Though Ronda has several good budget hostels, rooms are often fully booked in high season. Weekends in winter are also often booked up as this is a popular weekend retreat for people from Seville. Though not essential, it is a good idea to make reservations. All accommodations are in El Mercadillo.

● **Royal** (M), Vírgen de la Paz 42 (tel. 952-87-11-41). 25 rooms. Stay within minutes of the famous bullring at this superior hostel that is really more like a hotel. The management is very friendly and all the rooms have bathrooms.

El Tajo (M), Cruz Verde 7 (tel. 952-87-62-36). 37 rooms. Located just off the central Carrera de Espinel, you won't be able to get a meal here, but rooms are clean and standards high.

Biarritz (I), Cristo 7 (tel. 952-87-29-10). 21 rooms. All your basic needs will be catered for in this friendly hostel. Several of the simple rooms have bathrooms, and you can eat here if you so choose.

Vírgen de los Reyes (I), Lorenzo Borrego 13 (tel. 952-87-11-40). 13 rooms. The budget-conscious traveler will be delighted to find this simple hostel located in a typical Andalusian house in the center.

WHERE TO EAT. Mesón Santiago (M), Marina 3 (tel. 952-87-15-59). On the edge of the Plaza del Socorro, this typical *mesón* has an attractive outdoor terrace and a rustic indoor dining room. Next door, and under the same management, is the cheaper **Cafetería Doña Pepa** (I).

Pedro Romero (M), Vírgen de la Paz 18 (tel. 952-87-10-61). Gaze upon the bullfighting memorabilia as you eat the good food in this colorful restaurant. It is located right opposite the bullring.

☛El Polo (M), Mariano Souviron 8 (tel. 952-87-26-69). The wood-paneled dining room of the cozy Hotel Polo serves excellent meals at very modest prices.

Hermanos Macías (I), Pedro Romero 3. A good budget find is this inexpensive restaurant located in a side street between Vírgen de la Paz and the Plaza del Socorro.

MAJOR ATTRACTIONS.
All the places listed below are in La Ciudad. As many of them are still under restoration, opening times can be erratic. For up-to-the-minute details, please check with the tourist office.

Baños Arabes. *Open Tues. to Sat. 10–1 and 4–7, Sun. 10–1; closed Mon.* The partially excavated remains of the old Arab bathhouse are a vivid reminder that Ronda was once an important Moorish capital. The star-shaped vents in the roof recall the bathhouse of the Alhambra in Granada, to which they bear a striking resemblance.

Casa del Rey Moro. The so-called House of the Moorish King is in fact an 18th-century mansion built on the remains of an 11th-century Moorish residence. The garden affords a stunning view of the gorge, and from here there is a subterranean stairway of 365 steps which descends to the river.

Palacio del Marqués de Salvatierra. *Open 10–1 and 4–7.* The house still belongs to the original family, but it is often open for visits. It boasts some splendid ceramic tiled floors and a striking Renaissance portal.

Palacio de Mondragón. The Catholic kings once resided in this early 16th-century palace which incorporates traces of the palace of Abumelik, son of a Moorish emir. From the terrace there are breathtaking views over the ravine, and its patios boast some original stucco work and a fine ceiling.

Santa María La Mayor, *Pza. de la Ciudad.* Originally the Great Mosque of Moorish Ronda, Santa María was rebuilt as a Christian church after the Reconquest in 1485. Arab traces can be seen in the 13th-century Mihrab with its stucco decoration, in the belfry which incorporates the original minaret, and in the two horseshoe arches at the foot of the tower.

EXCURSIONS.
Cuevas de la Pileta. These impressive caves are only really accessible by car, but if you're feeling energetic you can take the

train to Benaoján, and the caves are then an hour's walk along the mountainside. If you're driving, leave Ronda on C339 northwest, then branch left to Montejaque and follow the signs. The caretaker who lives down in the farm in the valley will show you round.

The caves, discovered in 1905, are thought to have been inhabited from some 25,000 years ago through to the end of the Bronze Age, making them even older than the Altamira caves in northern Spain. Nearly a mile long, some of the oldest pottery in Europe has been found here, and, along with weird stalactite and stalagmite formations, they have prehistoric wall paintings in red, black, and ocher of goats, bison, and fish.

Torremolinos

Surveying this ocean of concrete buildings it is hard to grasp that only 30 years ago Torremolinos was a poverty-stricken fishing village. It is now the mecca of self-catering apartments and package-tour operators with more than its fair share of highrises, "pubs," tawdry boutiques, and time-share peddlers. And yet, despite all this, it is not a bad place to relax after a glut of sightseeing if you enter into the spirit of things. It will certainly bring you back to earth with a bump after a trip to Granada or Seville.

Torremolinos divides distinctly into two areas: the center, with its brash Nogalera Plaza full of overpriced bars and the main shopping street, the Calle San Miguel, which leads down to what is left of the old village on a cliff above Bajondillo beach; and the much nicer Carihuela area, further west below the Avenida Carlota Alexandri. The Carihuela is far more authentically Spanish and retains many of its old fishermen's cottages and several excellent fish restaurants. A stroll along its traffic-free esplanade on a summer evening will persuade you that there is still some charm to be found in Torremolinos.

GETTING THERE. By Train. The RENFE station for the Málaga–Fuengirola suburban line is on the central Nogalera plaza. Trains run every half hour.

By Bus. The bus station is on the Calle Hoyo, the main road as you come in from Málaga. Torremolinos lies on the main Málaga–Algeciras coastal route and other services run from Mijas, Coin, Ronda, and Gibraltar.

By Taxi. Torremolinos taxis do not use meters. Either agree your fare beforehand or, if you arrive at the airport, take a look at the approved list of fares posted in the arrivals hall. As a rough guide, a trip from the airport to Torremolinos will cost around 850 ptas., and not more than 1,000 ptas.

TOURIST OFFICES. Bajos de la Nogalera (tel. 952-38-15-78).

USEFUL ADDRESSES. Police. Calle Skal, just past the Hotel Escandinavia.

Post Office. Avda. Palma de Mallorca.

Telephone Exchange. Extramuros, south of Casablanca.

British Airways. Pasaje Pizarroz (tel. 952-38-68-00/38-69-14).

WHERE TO STAY. There is no shortage of low-cost hotels in Torremolinos, though most of them are in town rather than by the beach. Expect all hotels and hostels to be booked up in July and August. Additionally many of the smaller hotels close in the winter. If you want the comfort of one of the larger package-tour type hotels with a swimming pool, your best bet will be to ask a local travel agent to book you into one as they may well obtain better rates than if you just walk in off the street.

☻**Miami** (M), Aladino 14 (tel. 952-38-52-55). 26 rooms. Surrounded by a pleasant leafy garden in one of the nicest parts of town, this hotel is located in a villa which was formerly a private residence. It is one of the gems of Torremolinos, but it is often hard to get in if you haven't made reservations. It has its own pool.

El Pozo (M), Casablanca 2 (tel. 952-38-06-22). 31 rooms. In a pleasant, modern Andalusian-style house just off the Nogalera, this is one of the best bets in the center.

Prudencio (M), Carmen 43 (tel. 952-38-14-52). 35 rooms. Although officially only a 1-star hostel, the rooms are sparklingly clean, all have their own shower, and it is located right in the heart of the Carihuela on the seafront. It has the added advantage of being above one of the best fish restaurants in Torremolinos.

Loreto (I), Calle Bajondillo (tel. 952-38-10-64). 30 rooms. A typical Andalusian house houses this pleasant hostel located at the foot of the Cuesta del Tajo, just behind Bajondillo beach. It has rooms with and without bathrooms, and meals are served.

Sola (I), Cuesta del Tajo 14 (tel. 952-38-09-17). 14 rooms. Popular because of its wonderful sea views, this picturesque budget hostel is located on the steps at the far end of the Calle San Miguel.

WHERE TO EAT. By far the best restaurants are to be found in the Carihuela along the promenade, and backing onto the streets of Carmen and Bulto. In the center, the Pueblo Blanco development off

Calle Casablanca is more tasteful than most other places and has several good restaurants.

El Comedor de la Plaza (M), in the Pueblo Blanco, is one of the more modestly priced restaurants in this pleasant development. It has tables outdoors in the square.

Europa (M), Vía Imperial 322 (tel. 952-38-09-87). The popularity of the Europa is reflected in the large number of Spanish locals who patronize it, especially on Sunday lunchtimes. It is an agreeable restaurant with a large garden, only a short walk from the Carihuela.

Prudencio (M), Carmen 43 (tel. 952-38-14-52). The specialties here are fish and seafood and standards are consistently good.

◖**El Roqueo** (M), Carmen 35 (tel. 952-38-49-46). The very best fish is served here, which is hardly surprising as it is run by a former fisherman. This is one of the Carihuela's best modest restaurants.

Florida (I), Casablanca 15 (tel. 952-38-73-66). Choose from a vast selection of mouth-watering dishes at this Danish restaurant. The fixed-price buffet is even cheaper at lunchtime than in the evening.

Pizzería La Barraca (I), on the corner of Casablanca and Fandango in the Pueblo Blanco. There is a simple charm about this informal, inexpensive pizzeria.

SHOPPING. Most of the shops are on or around the **Calle San Miguel.** Torremolinos caters almost exclusively to tourists and it often pays to ask for a discount here. This is one of the few places in Spain where shopkeepers are often willing to reduce their prices for visitors. There are also some gift shops along the **Calles Carmen** and **Bulto** in the Carihuela.

◆

S P L U R G E S

Afternoon Tea at the Hotel Mijas, Avda. de México (tel. 952-48-58-00). If you're visiting Mijas in the afternoon, this delightful treat will cause only the smallest dent in your pocketbook. At the entrance to the village (you'll pass it in your car or bus on the way in), this charming modern Andalusian hotel is set in an incomparable position overlooking Fuengirola, the ocean, and the whole coastal plain. On its terrace any afternoon between 4 and 6 you can enjoy a typically old-fashioned English afternoon tea to the strains of music from the likes of the Palm Court Orchestra. Waitresses dressed in the black uniforms, white caps, and aprons of yesteryear serve you with dainty white or brown-bread cucumber sandwiches (crusts removed, of course), buttered scones and strawberry jam, and a selection of chocolate, sponge, or traditional fruit cake. China or Indian tea is served in delicate china pots—no sign of the all-too-familiar soggy tea bag here, for leaf tea and proper tea strainers are *de rigueur* at the Mijas Hotel. This quaint ritual—which no doubt delights nostalgic expatriate British residents of the Costa—is performed in the loveliest of settings and makes an admirable and far from extravagant prelude (about 650 ptas. per person) to a stroll around the picturesque village.

Dinner at La Fonda, Marbella, Pza. del Santo Cristo 9 (tel. 954-77-25-12). Open 8 P.M. to midnight; closed Sun. Although dining at La Fonda will make a sizable inroad into your vacation budget the restaurant's blend of international chic and Andalusian charm will make it a night to remember. In the heart of old Marbella, on the charming Plaza del Santo Cristo, with its palm trees, gurgling fountain, and lovely old church, La Fonda is set in a splendid 18th-century house furnished with genuine period antiques, magnificent mirrors, and fine pictures. The picturesque Andalusian atmosphere is further enhanced by the window grilles and shutters, and an outdoor garden-patio filled with potted plants—a perfect setting for summer evening dining. It has won the National Gastronomic Prize, and its cuisine combines the best of Spanish, French, and Austrian influences with local Andalusian specialties. For dishes with a local flavor, try the *rabo de vaca a la malagueña* (oxtail Málaga style), *rape a las uvas* (monkfish in grape sauce), or *cazuela pescadores* (seafood casserole). Other treats are *pintada al hojaldre* (guinea hen in flaky pastry) or one of the delicious crêpes filled with purée of sardines or avocado and shrimps. For dessert there's *helado frito con frambuesas* (fried ice cream in raspberry sauce) or any number of delicious sweet crêpes. Reservations are strongly advised and dress is fairly formal. August is perhaps best avoided when the restaurant is overtaken by hordes of jet-setting diners.

Dinner at the Parador de Gibralfaro (tel. 952-22-19-02). If you're staying in or around Málaga it's well worth treating yourself to dinner at the Parador in the ruins of the Moorish fortress on the summit of Gibralfaro mountain, not least, for the incomparable views it offers over the city and ocean. Like parador hotels, the restaurant specializes in regional cuisine. Eat on the terrace and enjoy fish specialties like *rape a la malagueña* (monkfish grilled in garlic) or *pez espada parrilla* (grilled swordfish). Down below you is the superb vista of the bullring, the lighthouse on the Paseo Marítimo, the harbor with its visiting naval vessels, the illuminated fountain on the Plaza Marina, and the city lights stretching away to the west and Torremolinos. The view is one of the best on the Costa del Sol: On a clear day you can see as far as Gibraltar—100 km. (62 mi.) away—and if you come up here for an early predinner drink, you'll have the added delight of watching the sun set over Fuengirola way down the coast. The Parador restaurant is renowned for its fine cuisine and a set dinner here cost only 1,900 ptas. in 1987, though you should allow a little bit more for *à la carte* dining. Be sure to reserve a table, as the terrace is a popular dining venue. To reach the Parador, drive up (following the signs to Gibralfaro), take a moderately priced 15-min. cab ride, or check on the schedule of the Parador's own minibuses which run from Calle Molino Larios near the cathedral.

◆

EXTREMADURA

Extremadura (its name means "beyond the Duero river"), Spain's largest province, is one of the best budget areas in Spain. Situated in the far west, bordering Portugal, and cut off from the rest of the country by the mountains of the Sierra de Gredos to the north, and by the Sierra Morena to the south, it has long been a land remote from the traditional cultural and economic centers of Spain.

A few bus tours en route from Madrid to Lisbon, or Salamanca to Seville, stop briefly to see the Roman theater at Mérida, but otherwise most of Extremadura's visitors are the few individual travelers who come to view the great Roman ruins at Mérida, or to visit the famous monasteries of Yuste or Guadalupe, or the humble birthplace of the *conquistadores* of the New World. Some may come in search of unspoiled medieval towns like Cáceres or Trujillo, others to search out the Peninsular War battlefields where, aided by Spanish guerrillas, the Duke of Wellington sent Napoleon's armies packing between 1809–13.

With the recent opening of the National Museum of Roman Art in Mérida, and the promotion of the region's many historic paradors, national parks, and areas of great scenic beauty, tourism is now developing in this once little-known land. But it is a slow business, as the sparsity of hotels and restaurants in even the two provincial capitals shows only too clearly. But here, too, lie Extremadura's greatest charm and bargain opportunities, for the Extremeños are some of Spain's friendliest people, and the prices in this unspoiled corner of Spain are among the most reasonable anywhere.

Extremadura lies between Castile and Andalusia and shares both their culture and architecture. Its landscape is part of the great *meseta* (plateau), with vast plains and limitless horizons; the Tagus and Guadiana rivers flow across it from east to west, forming large lakes and reservoirs. The region grows wheat and tobacco, and the valleys and lower slopes are clothed in olive trees, chestnuts, and cork oaks; wildflowers abound on the hillsides, and eagles and storks are often to be seen. The summers here are ferocious, but the winters short and wild, and these lands are traditional sheep-grazing pastures, migratory shepherds from as far away as Old Castile bringing their flocks to graze on the winter hillsides of Extremadura, as they have been doing since 1273 when Alfonso X granted them special rights under the *Mesta*. Pigs are also bred here and, well-nourished on a plentiful supply of acorns, they supply some of the best sausages and hams in Spain.

Only recently have technological advances improved the quality of life here and made the farming of these lands easier. It was the traditional poverty and harshness of life in Extremadura that drove many of its natives, right up until this century, to seek their fortunes abroad, either in the New World or, in the 1950s and '60s, in Germany. Most of the *conquistadores* came from Extremadura: Hernán Cortes, conqueror of Mexico, from Medellín; Francisco Pizarro, conqueror of the Incas of Peru, from Trujillo; Pedro de Valdivia, conqueror of Chile, from Villanueva de la Serena. Another native, Vasco Núñez de Balboa, was the first man to cross the American continent and claim the Pacific for Spain, and Hernando de Soto from Jerez de los Caballeros was one of the first white men to set foot in North America.

The wealth brought back from the New World by these brave and ruthless Extremeños was often used to embellish their native towns. These grand mansions can still be seen today in villages which have changed little since the days when acute hardship drove the *conquistadores* so far from this remote corner of Spain.

Badajoz

Badajoz is the capital of Extremadura and lies on the left bank of the Guadiana river, close to the border with Portugal. Though traces of its important role in Roman and Moorish times are still in evidence, Badajoz is now a rather run-down town offering little to lure the visitor miles from his route. However, for the simply curious, or for those passing through on their way to Portugal, it justifies a visit of an hour or so, and its inhabitants are among the friendliest and most welcoming in Spain. Hotels and restaurants are very affordable.

Under Moorish rule from 1009, Badajoz was finally recaptured by Alfonso IX in 1229, but its position as a frontier town meant a continually turbulent history. The Portuguese stormed it in 1660; the European allies in the War of the Spanish Succession in 1705; the early 1800s saw numerous sieges, ending in capture by the French, followed by the Duke of Wellington's bloody attack on the town in 1812. In this century, too, it witnessed one of the first atrocities of the Civil War when, after a bitter siege, it fell to the Nationalists. Its Republican defenders tried to flee to Portugal, but were rounded up and machine-gunned to death in Badajoz's bullring.

Badajoz's two most famous sons are the painter Luis Morales ("the Divine") (1506–86) and the much despised statesman Manuel Godoy (1767–1851), favorite of Charles IV and lover of his queen, María Luisa. Today, Badajoz stands surrounded by a fertile plain irrigated by the waters of the Guadiana. Ignore the ugly sprawling modern suburbs and head for the Plaza de España in the heart of the Old Town. If you arrive by car, try to approach from the north, which gives the best view of the city's old fortifications, the Puerta de Palmas, which was once the main gateway in the city walls, and the Puente de Palmas, a bridge built in 1596 by Juan de Herrera, architect of the Escorial.

GETTING THERE. By Train. Badajoz lies on the main Madrid–Lisbon line and the journey time from Madrid is about seven hours. Badajoz can also be reached from Seville via Zafra and Mérida where you will need to change; and from Cáceres, also via Mérida. Badajoz Rail Station (tel. 924-22-11-70) is about a mile out of town, across the river over the Puente de Palmas, and there are bus connections to the city center. The RENFE office in town is on Avda. de Celada 3 (tel. 924-22-45-62).

By Bus. There are usually three services a day from Madrid to Badajoz, and the journey takes around seven hours. Buses from Seville take about five hours. There is also a daily service from Málaga and Córdoba. There are several buses a day from Mérida (one and a half hours), from Cáceres (two hours), and a couple a day from Salamanca. Badajoz has no central bus station, so check your travel details carefully with the tourist office.

By Car. Badajoz lies on the main Madrid–Lisbon highway, NV, which also passes through Trujillo and Mérida. The most direct route from Cáceres is the rather bumpy, but easily passable, N523. From Seville, take N630, then N432 west (left) to Zafra and Badajoz.

TOURIST OFFICES. Pasaje de San Juan 2 (tel. 924-22-27-63). Opening times are posted on the door, and the office is located in a pedestrian street just off the Plaza de España.

USEFUL ADDRESSES. Police. Avda. General Varela 4 (tel. 924-23-02-53).

Post Office. Paseo de General Franco (sometimes called Plaza San Francisco).

Telephone Exchange. Obispo San Juan de Rivera, just down from the Plaza de España.

GETTING AROUND. Public transport is by city bus, but you are unlikely to need this unless you arrive at the rail station, or stay at either the Lisboa or Río hotels.

WHERE TO STAY. Lisboa (M), Avda. Elvas 13 (tel. 924-23-82-00). 176 rooms. The Lisboa is a comfortable, modern hotel, a little out of town. It has good views over the river, the Puente de Palmas, and the old fortified town. Both breakfast and dinner are served.

Río (M), Avda. Adolfo Díaz Ambrona (tel. 924-23-76-00). 90 rooms. This is another modern hotel, close to the Lisboa, with a swimming pool and a terrace with fine views over the city. Breakfast only is served, but there are restaurants close by, including a good (but rather expensive) Galician fish restaurant, **La Toja,** on Avda. Elvas 21. It is about a 20-min. walk from the Río and the Lisboa into town, or you can catch a bus.

➲**Cervantes** (I), Tercio 2 (tel. 924-22-51-10). 25 rooms, all with bathrooms. The Cervantes is a comfortable 3-star hostel in one of the most pleasant squares in the old town, just a block or so down from the Plaza de España. This is the cheapest of our selections, and probably the best located unless you opt for a view of the river. No meals are served.

Conde Duque (I), Muñoz Torrero 27 (tel. 924-22-46-41). 35 rooms. If you want a modern hotel handy for Badajoz's sights, then the

Conde Duque is a good bet. It is functional but pleasant, all rooms have bathrooms and air-conditioning, and breakfast is served, but not dinner.

WHERE TO EAT. Los Gabrieles (M), Vicente Barrantes 21 (tel. 92422-42-75). If it's choice you're after, then you'll be hard pressed to decide from the wide selection of national and regional dishes on offer here. The restaurant is centrally located just a block and a half from the Plaza de España, and is very popular with the locals. Closed Sun.

● Mesón El Tronco (M), Muñoz Torrero 16 (tel. 924-22-20-76). This is one of Badajoz's most popular eating places, with an atmospheric *mesón* offering a good selection of *tapas*—which make a good (I) snack meal—and two pleasantly decorated dining rooms. It is a good place to sample the local specialties and to try some of the region's own cheeses. Closed Sun.

El Sótano (M), Vírgen de la Soledad 6 (tel. 924-22-00-19). You'll find this restaurant just around the corner from the Plaza de España, and although you may find some of its dishes just a little expensive it comes highly recommended by the locals.

Hostal Menacho (I), Abril 12 (tel. 924-22-14-46). This hostel serves good, filling, basic meals at very affordable prices.

Jamaco (I), Vicente Barrantes 5 (tel. 924-22-00-02). An ideal spot for anyone watching their pennies, the Jamaco serves very standard Spanish fare, but the *menu del día* is good value.

MAJOR ATTRACTIONS. Alcazaba. *Open 9–1 and 3–6.* The old Moorish fortress stands at the top of the city and was built around 1100. It is mostly in ruins now, but offers good views over the Guadiana River and the fertile lands around the city. The octagonal **Torre de Aprendiz** was built by the Almohades, and is more often known as the **Torre Espantaperros** or Dog-scarer Tower, "dog" being a Moorish term of abuse for Christians.

Cathedral, *Pza. de España. Open 11–1.* This severe, fortresslike cathedral was built by Alfonso el Sabio between 1232 and 1248. A Renaissance facade (1619) was added to the 13th-century Gothic interior. The **chapter house** and **side chapels** house paintings by Morales, Zurbarán, and Ribera.

Museo Arqueológico, *Pza. Alta, near the Alcazaba. Open 10–2 and 5–7, 4–6 in winter.* The museum contains archeological finds from throughout the province. Housed in a former mosque, the columns dividing its aisles are Roman, topped with Visigoth capitals.

Museo de Bellas Artes, *Meléndez Valdés 32. Open 9:30–2 and 5–7; 10–2 and 4–6 in winter.* The Fine Arts Museum displays paintings and sculpture by local contemporary artists, and works by Luis de Morales and Zurbarán, a fellow Extremeño.

Plaza Alta. Up above the town and just below the alcazaba, this old arcaded square must once have ranked high among those picturesque squares for which Spain is famous. But today it is sadly dilapidated and partially abandoned; peeling whitewashed houses and piles of rubble now surround what was once the heart of old Badajoz.

Caceres

Cáceres, in the heart of northern Extremadura and dominated by the shrine of its patroness, the Virgin of the Mountain, is one of the finest examples of a walled medieval town in the whole of Spain. Originally a Roman colony, it was later rebuilt by the Moors, who were responsible for the ramparts which encircle the whole of the Old City today.

The 9th to the 13th centuries saw constant battles between Moors and Christians until Alfonso IX retook Cáceres in 1229. On April 23 of that year, St. George's Day, it was officially joined to the Kingdom of León, an event still commemorated by its citizens when they celebrate the fiesta of their patron saint, San Jorge, in the Plaza Mayor below the Old Town.

The early Christian years were dominated by quarrels and squabbles between the town's nobles, until Ferdinand and Isabella exerted their authority. The 15th and 16th centuries saw a flurry of mansion building, much of it financed by the wealth brought back from the New World by the *conquistadores*. It is these splendid seignorial palaces, miraculously still intact today—if just a little crumbled in parts—which make up the fine Old Town which will be the highlight of your visit.

Modern Cáceres is a thriving town, seat of the region's university, and the fastest expanding city in Extremadura. The new town holds little of interest for the visitor, so head straight for the Plaza Mayor and begin your explorations there. Cáceres also makes an excellent base from which to explore other parts of the region, as it is the transport hub of northern Extremadura. Not many tourists linger long here, as you will see from its few hotels and restaurants, but this is all to the advantage of the cost-conscious travelers who should have no trouble in finding good-value accommodations.

GETTING THERE. By Train. Trains run to Cáceres from Madrid, Lisbon, Mérida, Zafra, Seville, and Badajoz. Cáceres Station (tel. 927-22-50-71) is on Avda. de Alemania, N630 to Mérida. City bus no. 1 runs every 20 min. or so from the station to the Plaza Mayor.

By Bus. Several buses a day run to Cáceres from Madrid (journey time around four hours), Plasencia, Salamanca, Trujillo, Seville, Mérida, and Badajoz. The bus station (tel. 927-22-06-00) is on Calle Gil Cordero, in the new town at the beginning of N630 to Salamanca. It is a good 20-min. walk to the Plaza Mayor, or you can take a city bus or taxi, neither of which costs very much. The bus station has baggage-checking facilities.

By Car. Cáceres lies on the north–south N630 from Salamanca to Seville, about halfway between Plasencia and Mérida. If you are coming from Madrid, take highway NV for Lisbon as far as Trujillo, then N521 west (right) to Cáceres. From Badajoz, take N523, not one of Spain's best-surfaced roads, but it is quite passable.

TOURIST OFFICES. Pza. Mayor (formerly Pza. Gen. Mola) 33 (tel. 927-24-63-47). Open Mon. to Sat. 10–2 and 5–8, Sun. 10–2; closed Sat. **P.M.** and Sun. in winter. The main thing to obtain here is a detailed (free) map of the Old City (Ciudad Monumental) which you will find invaluable in your explorations.

In summer the tourist office organizes guided tours of the Old City, along with visits to Trujillo, Guadalupe, and Plasencia. One of their guides speaks English. If an English tour of the Old City is available during your stay, it is well worth taking.

USEFUL ADDRESSES. Police. Avda. de la Vírgen de la Montaña 3 (tel. 927-22-60-00).

Post Office. Miguel Primo de Rivera.

Telephone Exchange. Antonio Reyes Huertas 40.

GETTING AROUND. Transport within the city is by bus, but you are only likely to need this for getting to and from the bus and rail stations, or possibly if you stay in the Almonte or Ava hostels. Taxis are inexpensive, and rides will only be short.

WHERE TO STAY. ➦ Alvarez (M), Parras 20 (tel. 927-24-64-00). 37 rooms. Ideally located right in the center, just two minutes from the Plaza Mayor, this friendly old hotel has comfortable, old-fashioned rooms, all with well-equipped bathrooms. The restaurant serves both breakfast and dinner at moderate prices. This is far and away the best choice, as Cáceres is short of recommendable moderate accommodations.

Ava (M), Juan XXIII 3 (tel. 927-22-39-58). 62 rooms, all with bathrooms. This 1-star hotel is rather a long way out, though handy for the bus station, and music from the adjacent bar and disco can be noisy. The service at times could be more willing.

Almonte (I), Gil Cordero 6 (tel. 927-24-09-25). 90 rooms. The least expensive of our selections, the Almonte is only a 1-star hostel but the rooms are clean and standards good for the price. There are rooms with and without bathrooms, and an adjoining cafeteria. It has a garage, and is located on the same street as the bus station, just off the Plaza de América.

WHERE TO EAT. Figón de Eustaquio (M), Pza. San Juan 12 (tel. 927-24-81-94). Regional Extremeño cooking and the meat dishes are the best bet in this colorful and very popular restaurant just up from the Plaza Mayor.

Hostería del Comendador (M), Ancha 6. Sample some good regional specialties in this atmospheric restaurant located in a Renaissance palace in the Old Town. You may find it a little more pricey than usual, but we hope you'll agree that it is a treat worth that little bit extra.

El Gran Mesón (I), Gen. Ezponda 7. This is just one of the many bars and *mesones* in this street leading out of the far end of the Plaza Mayor. It offers a good choice of snacks, *tapas,* and *raciones,* as well as a very affordable *menu del día.*

El Pato (I), Pza. Mayor 24 (tel. 927-21-35-58). El Pato offers a good range of filling *raciones* and *platos combinados,* and an inexpensive *menu del día,* as well as a regular *à la carte* menu. In summer you can eat outside on the main square.

MAJOR ATTRACTIONS. Old Walled City. The best way to enjoy Cáceres's unique medieval atmosphere (at its most beautiful at night) is to wander at whim along the cobbled streets of the Old Town, discovering as you go the golden-stoned palaces of the 14th and 15th centuries, the majestic towers, and the splendid churches.

The walls which completely encircle the Old Town were built in the 11th century by the Almohads on Roman foundations. About a dozen of the original 30 watchtowers still exist, as do many of the old gateways. The fine Renaissance mansions have changed little since the 16th century. Some of them are inhabited today, others are used as government buildings or house museums.

Enter the Old Town through the **Arco de Estrella** beside the tourist office, a gateway built in 1726. At the end of the street to your left, the **Casa de los Toledo-Moctezuma** was built by Juan Cano, a follower of Cortés. In front of you the Plaza Santa María is one of the Old Town's finest squares. The beautiful Gothic **Church of Santa María** serves as the city's cathedral and has a fine 16th-century reredos. Outside the church you can bring yourself luck by stroking the toes of the **Statue of San Pedro de Alcántara,** a much-revered local saint.

Make your way up the hill to the **Plaza San Mateo,** the highest point of the Old Town. The **Palacio de la Cigüeñas** (House of Storks), built in 1477, is the only mansion to retain the battlements on its tower, since its owners found favor with the Catholic kings at a time when they saw fit to knock the battlements off another 30 mansion towers to show the nobles just who had the upper hand. Today it houses the military. The nearby **Casa de las Veletas** (House of Weather Vanes) is built over the old alcázar, and incorporates a fine 11th-century Moorish *aljibe* (cistern) which supplied Cáceres with water right up until 1953. The building houses the city's **Museum of Archeology and Folklore.**

Three other places are worthy of mention before you leave the Old Town: the **Casa de los Caballos** houses the **Museum of Contemporary Art** which often has exciting temporary exhibitions; the **Casa del Mono** houses the **Museum of Fine Arts** which can be visited on the same ticket as the Archeological Museum; and finally the **Palacio de los Golfines de Arriba** where, on October 19, 1936 Franco was proclaimed head of state and generalísimo of all Spain's armies.

OTHER ATTRACTIONS. Iglesia de Santiago Matamoros, *Pza. de Santiago.* The Church of St. James the Moor Slayer is thought to have been the birthplace in 1170 of the medieval Order of Santiago, whose knights were charged with protecting pilgrims on their way to Santiago de Compostela. It has a remarkable altarpiece carved in 1557 by Alonso Berruguete, the famous sculptor from Valladolid.

Guadalupe

The shrine of Guadalupe lies in one of the most remote settings in Spain, high up in the mountains of the Sierra de Guadalupe in the far east of Cáceres province, near the borders with Toledo and Badajoz. Here, in 1300, a cowherd named Gil Cordero, obeying the bidding of the Virgin Mary, is said to have found the miraculous statue of Our Lady of Guadalupe, supposedly carved by St. Luke, hidden under a bush. In 1340, after the Battle of Salado, Alfonso XI erected a monastery on this site to the glory of Our Lady of Guadalupe, whose help he had invoked in defeating the Moors.

The small picturesque town of Guadalupe, with its cobbled streets and arcaded squares, grew up around the monastery, whose imposing buildings still dominate the village. Guadalupe soon became Spain's leading pilgrimage center, before whose shrine many famous people— Queen Isabella, Columbus, Cervantes—have knelt.

Guadalupe is situated in the very heart of the land of the *conquistadores,* and it was here that the documents authorizing

Columbus's original voyage of discovery were signed. Here, too, the first American Indians converted to Christianity were brought to be baptized. Columbus named an island in the Caribbean after his favorite shrine, numerous Latin American cities have taken its name, and the Virgin of Guadalupe, patroness of Mexico, is revered throughout the New World.

GETTING THERE. By Bus. There are four buses a day from Talavera de la Reina in Toledo province (journey time around two hours). There are also two daily buses from Navalmoral de la Mata (three hours), and one a day from Cáceres (four hours) via Trujillo (three hours).

By Car. The approach to Guadalupe involves some mountain driving, but on well-surfaced roads. There are three main access routes: from Talavera de la Reina take C401 southwest via La Nava de Ricomalillo and Puerto de San Vicente, and Guadalupe is reached after 104 km. (65 mi.); from Trujillo take C542 southeast from NV to near Zorita where it joins C401 east to Guadalupe, a distance of 78 km. (49 mi.); from Navalmoral de la Mata (this is the most winding mountainous approach) head south along the unclassified road which crosses the Valdecañas reservoir on the Tagus river to Bohonal de Ibor, and keep following this road for 75 km. (47 mi.) until you reach Guadalupe.

WHERE TO STAY. Hospedería del Real Monasterio (M), Pza. Juan Carlos I (tel. 927-36-70-00). 46 rooms. This hostelry, the alternative to the expensive parador, is located in a converted wing of the monastery, and offers comfortable, atmospheric accommodations. All the rooms have bathrooms, and the hotel has a good (M) restaurant (see below). Its bar, in the superb setting of the Gothic cloisters, is a good place to sample the local homemade *Licor de Guadalupe,* brewed from herbs by the monks. Closed mid-Jan. through mid-Feb.

Cerezo (I), Gregorio López 12 (tel. 927-36-73-79). 15 rooms. The Cerezo is a clean, simple, 1-star hostel. The rooms have their own bathroom; no meals are served.

WHERE TO EAT. Hospedería del Real Monasterio (M), Pza. Juan Carlos I (tel. 927-36-70-00). The two dining rooms of the monastery's hostelry specialize in serving local dishes such as *migas a la extremeña,* a kind of fried bread-crumb soup, or dishes based on hams and sausages from the village of Montánchez. To drink, you can sample the local Cañamero wine or the *Licor de Guadalupe.* Closed mid-Jan. through mid-Feb.

Mesón el Cordero (M), Convento 11 (tel. 927-36-71-31). This cozy *mesón* is family-run and serves good home cooking. Partridge stew, roast lamb, or goat often feature on the menu, as do *migas* and *arroz con leche,* a kind of rice pudding. Closed Mon. and Feb.

MAJOR ATTRACTIONS. Church. *Open all day.* The church, *approached up a flight of steps from the main square,* dates from the end of the 14th century. Its beautiful grilles were made by two ironsmiths from Valladolid in the early 16th century, and the ornate **retable** is the work of Giraldo de Merlo and Jorge Manuel Theotocópulos, son of El Greco. From her niche above the altar, the cause of all this splendor peers out from the depths of her sumptuous cape and veil, a diminutive Virgin, carved of oak and darkened by the candle smoke of many centuries.

Monastery. *Open 9:30–1:30 and 3:30–7. Guided tours only.* The Gothic monastery, with its towers and turrets and fortified walls, was constantly adorned and embellished from its foundation in the 14th century right through to the 18th century. Its architecture and adornments are the work of the greatest craftsmen of those times, and were financed by donations from the millions of faithful who flocked to worship within its walls. Originally a Hieronymite monastery, it was sacked by the French in 1809 and later abandoned from 1835 until 1908 when the Franciscans moved in.

Outstanding amongst its numerous treasures are the vast Mudéjar **cloisters,** built between 1402 and 1412: Two stories of brick horseshoe arches surround a patio with a unique 1405 *templete,* a central fountain surmounted by a kind of pavilion topped with a spire. The **sacristy,** the most ornate and sumptuous room in the monastery, was built expressly to house a collection of eight portraits of the Order's most famous monks, painted by Zurbarán between 1638 and 1647. This classical architecture with lavish baroque additions is a perfect setting for the works—even the window frames echo the adornment of the picture frames.

The climax of the visit is when you ascend to the **Camarín,** a small and much adorned chapel behind the high altar of the church. Here a somewhat vulgar device revolves the gaudy enameled throne and enables you to come face to face with the miraculous bejeweled Virgin herself. Don't leave without a visit to the **relicario,** which houses the Virgin's elaborate wardrobe and the precious jeweled crown which she wears only in the most solemn processions.

Mérida

Mérida, now a rather unprepossessing town, was founded by the Romans in 25 B.C. and became the capital of the Roman province of Lusitania. It was embellished with splendid villas, temples, a circus for chariot races, a magnificent theater, aqueducts, and a truly monumental bridge over the Guadiana. After the Romans, the city fell into decay and many of its buildings were dismantled by the Moors, who used the stones to build their great mosque at Córdoba. But despite such plundering, Mérida still boasts the finest collection of Roman ruins in Spain today, and the new National Museum of Roman Art is an exciting treasure house of all the greatest Roman finds in Spain.

The center of modern Mérida is the Plaza de España with its numerous outdoor cafés. Traveling to or from Mérida is relatively easy as the city is the crossroads of Extremadura, lying at the junction of the Salamanca–Cáceres–Seville road, and the main Madrid–Badajoz–Lisbon highway. Hotels and restaurants, however, tend to be more expensive here than in other parts of the region. A stay of a day and a night should enable you to see all the sights at your leisure.

GETTING THERE. By Train. Mérida Station (tel. 924-31-20-05) is in the north of town at the end of Calle Cardero. There are several trains a day from Madrid, Badajoz, and Cáceres, and daily services from Zafra, Seville, and Portugal.

By Bus. The bus station (tel. 924-25-86-61) is on Marquesa de Pinares 9, not far from the train station. There are several buses a day from Madrid and Trujillo, Seville, and Badajoz, and a couple of services a day from Cáceres, Salamanca, Zafra, Córdoba, and Málaga.

By Car. Mérida lies on the main NV highway with Madrid and Trujillo to the east, and Badajoz and Lisbon to the west. It also lies on N630, the main north-south road crossing Extremadura from Salamanca via Cáceres and Mérida to Seville.

TOURIST OFFICES. Calle del Puente 9 (tel. 924-31-53-53), just off the southeast corner of Plaza de España, in the street leading down to the Roman bridge. The staff gives out free information on the Roman monuments, and can give help with questions and tickets for the summer Drama Festival in the Roman theater.

USEFUL ADDRESSES. Police. Rambla de Sta. Enlalia.

Post Office. Pza. de la Constitución.

WHERE TO STAY. Emperatriz (M), Pza. de España 19 (tel. 924-3131-11). 41 rooms. The Emperatriz is located in the 15th-century Burnay Palace, on the corner of the main square. All rooms have bathrooms, and there is a pleasant café-terrace on the square. This is about the only affordable (M) hotel in town, though its rates are higher than our usual selection.

Nueva España (I), Avda. Extremadura 6 (tel. 924-31-33-56). 9

rooms. One of half a dozen inexpensive 1-star hostels near the train and bus stations, the rooms at the Nueva España are modern and spotlessly clean, and all have bathrooms. No meals are served.

If you have a car, there are two roadside hotels just out of town whose rates fall more within our usual price range:

Zeus (M), at km. 341 on NV (tel. 924-31-81-11). 44 rooms. A comfortable, functional 2-star hotel on the road out to Madrid, the Zeus serves breakfast but not dinner.

Los Milagros (I), at km. 278 on N630 (tel. 924-31-76-61). 17 rooms. This is a recent, functional roadside hostel and restaurant a couple of miles from the center, on the road to Cáceres just beyond the aqueduct of Los Milagros. The rooms are clean, and good-value meals are served in the restaurant.

WHERE TO EAT. There are few inexpensive fully-fledged restaurants in Mérida, but no shortage of bars with a few tables set aside for diners at meal times. Look in any of the streets around the Plaza de España or along calles Sagasta and J. Ramón Mélida near the Roman theater.

Mesón El Emperador (M), just off the Plaza de España. Adjoining the Emperatriz hotel, this atmospheric *mesón* offers a choice of regional specialties, as well as dishes from Asturias in northern Spain.

Nicolás (M), Félix Valverde Lillo 13 (tel. 924-31-96-10). The menu here is a little wider-ranging than many, but the food and service do not always live up to the decor of this elegant restaurant in the center of town.

Britz (I), Félix Valverde Lillo 5. This is a bar-cum-restaurant serving staple Extremeño food such as rabbit or lamb stew. Its *menu del día* is satisfying and good value.

MAJOR ATTRACTIONS. **Museo Nacional de Arte Romano,** *Calle J. Ramón Mélida, opposite the entrance to the Roman Theater. Open 10–2 and 4–6; closed Mon. and Sun. P.M.* This exciting new building was finished in 1986, and the plan is to house major Roman artifacts from all over Spain here to form the National Roman Collection. A Roman road, discovered when the foundations of the museum were dug, has been imaginatively incorporated into the display. There are some excellent and enormous mosaics, as well as a good collection of artifacts from Mérida's Roman sites—among them several busts of Augustus, the city's founder.

Roman Theater and Amphitheater. *Open 8–8 in summer, 8–7 in winter.* The Roman theater and arena *(anfiteatro)* are situated side by side and can be visited on the same ticket. The great theater is

Mérida's finest monument, and one of the best-preserved Roman theaters anywhere in the world. It was begun in 24 B.C. by Agrippa, who gave it as a gift to the citizens of Mérida (then called August Emerita). Its great granite blocks hold together without mortar, and its tiers of semicircular seats, built for an audience of 6,000, face a stage with an impressive backdrop of marble columns. The theater makes a superb setting for the city's summer Drama Festival.

The adjacent **arena,** or **amphitheater,** was used for chariot races, gladiator fights, and mock naval battles for which the entire arena had to be flooded. It dates from around 8 B.C., when it could hold 14,000 spectators. The *vomitoria,* or covered tunnels through which the audience left the arena, are especially well preserved.

OTHER ATTRACTIONS. Alcazaba, *alongside the river, by the Roman bridge. Open 8–1 and 4–7.* This solid octagonal fortress was built by the Moors around 835, on the site of both a Roman and Visigoth fort, to guard the bridge across the Guadiana. Its Moorish builders incorporated into it blocks of granite from the Roman Theater up the road, as well as Corinthian columns and Visigoth friezes from other ruins around the town. After the defeat of the Moors in 1228 it was taken over by the Knights Templar and became a residence for the knights of the Order of Santiago. Gutted by the French in 1808, it has now been partially restored. Its greatest treasure is its *aljibe,* a cistern built first by the Romans, then much restored by the Moors.

Aqueduct of Los Milagros. The best preserved of Mérida's aqueducts lies to the north of town, just across the railroad. Its triple tier of red brick arches once brought water into the city from the reservoir of Proserpina, 5 km. away.

Roman Bridge. This splendid granite bridge spanning the Guadiana was built during the reign of the emperor Trajan. It is the longest known bridge—792 m. (2,575 ft.) and 64 arches—ever to have been built by the Romans. It was repaired by the Visigoths in 686 and again in 1610 by Philip III, and today carries traffic on a major highway.

Roman Circus. Part of the central racetrack and the spectator stands still remain of the Circus Maximus. It once held a crowd of some 30,000 who would pour into the stadium to cheer on their favorite chariot drivers as they careened around the course.

Trujillo

Cradle of the *conquistadores,* the little town of Trujillo, 48 km. (30 miles) east of Cáceres, is the showpiece of Extremadura. Altogether some 600 sons of Trujillo sought their fortunes in Peru, Bolivia,

Amazonia, and Paraguay, and the town gave its name to no fewer than three cities of the New World. The proud mansions of Trujillo, some still inhabited by descendants of the *conquistadores,* are a little later (mainly 16th and 17th century) than those of Cáceres and have more ornamentation and distinctive features.

Ignore the dull streets of the new part of town and head straight up the hill to the magnificent Plaza Mayor. The Moorish castle, now in ruins, and the old streets of Trujillo, lined with countless noble palaces, fine churches, and four of the original seven gates of the city, will carry you back to the days when gold and silver in abundance flowed in from Peru.

GETTING THERE. By Bus. Trujillo Bus Station (tel. 927-32-12-02) is on the Ctra. de Badajoz, just off the main Cáceres–Madrid road, the Calle Encarnación. There are regular buses each day from Madrid, Cáceres, Badajoz, and Mérida, and just one a day from Guadalupe and Plasencia. It is about a 15-min. uphill walk from the station to the Plaza Mayor.

By Car. Trujillo lies on NV, the main Madrid–Mérida–Badajoz highway. From Cáceres, take N521 48 km. (30 mi.) east, and from Plasencia, C524 80 km. (50 mi.) south.

TOURIST OFFICES. Plaza Mayor 18 (tel. 927-32-06-53), under the arcades on the west side of the square. The opening hours are a little erratic, but when she is there the lady is helpful. Ask about visiting the palaces and churches because some of them are kept locked and you may need to know where to obtain the key. Take a look at the wall map of the New World which charts the routes of Trujillo's native sons and the places they appropriated.

USEFUL ADDRESSES. Police. Just off the west side of Plaza Mayor.

Post Office. On the corner of Encarnación and Pardos.

Telephone Exchange. In the park on Ramón y Cajal on the way out to Cáceres.

WHERE TO STAY. Las Cigüeñas (M), at km. 253 on N-V (tel. 927-32-12-50). 78 rooms. Located on the edge of town on the road to Madrid, this is a functional, but comfortable, roadside hotel. It has an old and a new wing and full restaurant service. Its prices are rather high, but other than the parador (which is expensive), this is the only hotel in town.

Pizarro (I), Pza. Mayor 13 (tel. 927-32-02-55). 5 rooms. You will get a wonderful view over the Plaza Mayor if you stay in this small 1-star hostel. It has spotlessly clean rooms and is located above an excellent (I) restaurant. None of the rooms have bathrooms, but a shower is available at no extra charge.

WHERE TO EAT. Fonda La Troya (I), Pza. Mayor 11 (tel. 92732-41-56). Eating in La Troya is an experience in itself. Generous portions of simple home-cooked food are heaped before you. You won't get much choice as this is more like eating with a family, and there is no printed menu as such, but the price for a three- or four-course meal of this wholesome fare is simply incredible. It is an experience to be treasured, if maybe a little daunting for those with no Spanish.

Pizarro (I), Pza. Mayor 13 (tel. 927-32-02-55). For sheer good value and good, basic home cooking using fresh produce from the market, it is hard to beat the restaurant of the Hostal Pizarro. Its restaurant has been lovingly run by the same family for over 60 years.

MAJOR ATTRACTIONS. Plaza Mayor. Trujillo's irregularly shaped Plaza Mayor, surrounded by fine Renaissance palaces and arcaded walkways, is one of the finest in Spain. At its most beautiful at night, the square is dominated by a powerful **statue of Pizarro** on horseback. The statue, made in 1929 by the American sculptors Charles Rumsey and Mary Harriman, was a gift to the town by the Rumsey family and a duplicate statue stands in the Plaza de Armas in Cuzco, Peru. Of the many fine buildings in the square, the following are the most notable (start on the north side and work round clockwise):

Casa de las Cadenas (House of Chains). The chains on the outside of the house are said to have been placed there by Christians freed from Moorish slavery. Philip II guaranteed the right of sanctuary to anyone reaching these chains.

Church of San Martín. This building, crowned with the nests of innumerable storks, dates back to the 15th century, though it has many 17th-century additions. Inside, its nave is paved with the tombstones of many of Trujillo's illustrious families, and the organ is especially fine. *You may need to seek out the caretaker to open the church.*

Palacio de los Duques de San Carlos. *Open 9–1 and 3–6.* This beautiful 16th–17th-century palace is now inhabited by cloistered nuns. Ring the bell and one of them will show you round. The visit takes you to the inner patio surrounded by an arcaded gallery of granite columns, and a fine unusual 17th-century winding staircase. A donation will be appreciated.

Palacio del Marqués de la Conquista. This superbly decorated 16th-century palace was built by Hernando Pizarro, the only legitimate brother of the five Pizarros who conquered Peru. To the left of the window is a bust of Francisco Pizarro and his wife, an Inca princess, and to the right one of his half brother, Hernando, and his wife. The palace is not open to the public and can only be viewed from the outside.

OTHER ATTRACTIONS. Moorish Castle. The castle was built by the Arabs in the 11th century on the site of a former Roman stronghold. A second line of fortifications was built in the 15th century, and much of the castle has recently been well restored. There are spectacular views over Trujillo and the surrounding plain.

   Palacio Orellana-Pizarro, *Pza. Juan de Tena 2, just behind the Palacio de la Conquista.* The building is used as a school, but it is open for visits. A Renaissance doorway gives access to a beautiful Plateresque patio decorated with the coats of arms of the Pizarro and Orellana families.

   Santa María la Mayor, *Pza. Sta. María.* Trujillo's finest Gothic church, built on the site of an Arab mosque, is now sadly in a poor state of repair. *It is usually closed, but the key can be obtained from the caretaker, Sra. Tomasa, opposite.* Inside, beneath a big rose window, are the two stone seats where Ferdinand and Isabella sat to hear mass. The church boasts a beautiful reredos by Fernando Gallego, inspired by the Flemish school, and many notable tombstones. Outside the church, the **Calle de las Palomas,** leading down from the Plaza Santa María, is one·of the oldest and prettiest streets in Trujillo.

SHOPPING. Trujillo is a good place to purchase local Extremeño handicrafts. **Cerámicas Conchi,** Pza. Mayor 18, has a good display of local pottery. Woven goods—blankets, rugs, and local costumes—in vivid colors are on sale at **Maribel Vallar,** on Domingo Ramos and the corner of Juana Bazaga. Typical jewelry of filigree silver and gold is sold in the **Chanquet** studio on Calle San Francisco, and **Domingo Pablos Barquilla** on Pza. San Judás specializes in basketwork, though much of this is large pieces of furniture.

Yuste

   If you want to see the isolated monastery of Yuste, where Charles V, weary of the responsibilities of empire, spent the last 18 months of his life (February 1557 to September 1558), you will have to venture into one of the most remote corners of Extremadura. Your nearest budget accommodations will be one of the hostels in Jarandilla de la Vera, or one of a handful of inexpensive hostels in the charming market town of Plasencia, some 48 km. (30 miles) to the west. If you don't have a car, the only means of reaching the monastery is to take the early morning bus from Plasencia to Cuacos, the nearest village, then walk the two km. up the wooded hill to the monastery. There is an afternoon bus back from Cuacos to Plasencia.

Monastery. *Open 10–1 and 4–7 for guided tours only.* Before setting off for somewhere so remote it is best to check these opening times with the tourist offices in Cáceres or Plasencia (in the Casa de Cultura, Trujillo 17 (tel. 927-41-27-66).

The monastery was founded in 1404, but was all but gutted during the Peninsular War and fell into further ruin with the suppression of the monasteries in the 1830s. Today it has been restored and is run by Hieronymite monks, but it is nevertheless rather gloomy and does not entirely do justice to its illustrious past.

You can visit the church in whose **crypt** you will see the first coffin of Charles V, where his body lay for 16 years before being taken to lie in splendor at the Escorial; the **dining-hall;** the Gothic and Plateresque **cloisters;** and the **royal apartments** with the bedroom where Charles V died. Here everything is draped in black and remains, supposedly, just as it was when the great man passed on. You can see the special chair in which the old gentleman was brought to the monastery, a footrest designed especially for his gout-ridden legs, and the bed in which he died. Next to his bed a specially built door opens onto an adjoining chapel; this enabled the ailing emperor to hear mass from his bed.

Back on the main road, the picturesque village of **Cuacos** lies in the heart of tobacco-growing country, and you will see the leaves draped to dry over the ancient balconies of 16th-century wooden houses. The overhanging roofs supported by rough wooden pillars give a veritable medieval air to the whole place. Here Charles's illegitimate son, Don Juan of Austria, lived while visiting his father at the monastery. You can visit his house, the **Casa Jeromín,** whose upper story has been well restored.

Zafra

Zafra is a delightful small town in southern Extremadura, well worth visiting on your way to Badajoz, Mérida, or Seville. Its greatest attractions are its two beautifully restored arcaded squares, the Plaza Grande and the Plaza Chica, and its splendid 15th-century castle, now a parador. With its cobbled streets and typical buildings, Zafra has a charm of its own, part Andalusian, part Extremaduran.

GETTING THERE. By Train. Zafra can be reached by direct trains from Badajoz, Mérida, Seville, and Huelva.

By Bus. There are regular services to Zafra from Badajoz, Mérida, and Seville.

By Car. Zafra lies 73 km. (46 mi.) southeast of Badajoz, just off N432, close to the junction with N630, the Mérida–Seville road.

TOURIST OFFICES. Pza. de España (tel. 924-55-10-36), in the parador.

WHERE TO STAY. Parador Hernán Cortés (tel. 924-55-02-00) and the **Huerta Honda Hotel** (tel. 924-55-08-00) are the only hotels as such. Both are excellent, but expensive (5,500 ptas. and up). For very simple accommodations you could try:

Arias (I), at km. 72 on N432 (tel. 924-55-07-55). 34 rooms. This is a basic roadside hostel on the edge of town, by the gas station on the road to Badajoz. Some of its rooms have bathrooms, and you can have both breakfast and dinner here at reasonable prices.

Pensión Rafael (I), Vírgen de Guadalupe 7 (tel. 924-55-20-52). 12 rooms. This family-run boardinghouse has some rooms with bathrooms, and you can eat here too.

WHERE TO EAT. There is very little choice in Zafra, and if you want to be economical it is best to stick to meals in your budget accommodations. But if you want to splash out a bit, try the following:

Parador Hernán Cortés (M), Pza. Corazón de María 7 (tel. 924-55-02-00). A meal in the dining room of this splendid parador will be fairly pricey, but not prohibitive. Regional specialties served are *caldereta* (Extremeño stew), and for dessert the *brazo de gitano* (literally gipsy's arm), a kind of cake roll filled with custard. Wines are from the Zafra cooperative.

Posada del Duque (M), López Asme 30 (tel. 924-55-08-00). Located beside the Huerta Honda Hotel, this restaurant is decorated in Andalusian style and has an attractive outdoor patio.

MAJOR ATTRACTIONS. Parador Hernán Cortés. This impressive castle with its mighty walls and eight towers was the ancestral seat of the dukes of Feria and was built in 1437 by Lorenzo de Figueroa. Hernán Cortés, a protegé of the Duke of Feria, lived here for some time before his expedition to Mexico. Even if you are not a guest of the parador, you can go inside for a coffee or a drink in the bar, and see the beautiful marble **patio** attributed to Juan de Herrera, architect of the Escorial, the **Sala Dorada** (Golden Room) with its stunning red and blue Mudéjar ceiling, and the **chapel** with its Gothic octagonal dome.

Plaza Chica. Meaning "Little Square," the Plaza Chica is the real showpiece of Zafra. In Moorish times, when Zafra was an important commercial center, it was used as a *zoco* where fairs and markets were held. Have a look for the groove cut into the stonework of one of the columns; this was once used as a yardstick by the market traders. Notice, too, the patterned paving and the grilles over the windows. A 500-year-old palace stands on one side of the square, and there are a couple of *tapas* bars beneath the arcades.

Plaza Grande. Slightly newer than its neighbor, the Plaza Chica, the Plaza Grande, with its fountain and palm trees, is over 200 years old and was once used as a bullring. The balconies and window grilles have straight, unadorned ironwork bars typical of the Extremadura style. Both squares were skillfully restored in the mid-1970s.

OTHER ATTRACTIONS. Candelaria Church. The church was built by the Duke of Feria in 1546. It has a red brick belfry, and its most notable feature is its **altarpiece** with nine paintings done by Zurbarán in 1644.

Santa Clara Convent, off the Plaza España. Built in the 15th century, the convent houses the pantheon of the dukes of Feria, the Figueroa family. Here you can see the alabaster **tombs** of the first duke and his wife.

SHOPPING. Typical pottery is on sale in the shop just across from the parador, and the **municipal market** often sells good handmade articles.

◆

S P L U R G E S

Dinner at the Parador Vía de la Plata, Pza. de la Constitución 3 (tel. 924-31 38 00). Mérida's parador is one of the oldest and most beautiful of the chain. It is located in the baroque monastery of San Francisco, constructed by knights of the Order of Santiago in the 16th century from the ruins of a palace which once housed Roman guards and later a Visigoth governor. The low white building, with its patio of rounded arches and ancient columns, is beautifully decorated, and a meal in its superb dining room is a treat you will enjoy both for the lovely setting and for the fine quality of the food and service. The prices are extremely reasonable for such a popular place, and if you order with care you won't spend much more money than in many of Mérida's other restaurants, and certainly not as much as you would in a comparable restaurant back home.

The menu specializes in a wide range of local cooking, offering all the traditional meat dishes like *caldereta extremeña* (a classic extremeño stew), *conejo guisado a la emeritense* (Mérida rabbit casserole), and more unusual choices like *zorongollo extremeño* (braised red pepper salad) and *tencas escabechadas* (pickled lake fish). For dessert be sure to try *repápalos con leche,* a local specialty of fritters filled with custard and sprinkled with cinnamon. It is wise to make a reservation, as this is a very popular parador, and the locals come here to eat, too.

◆

Index

Index

Map page numbers appear in **boldface**

FODOR'S TRAVEL GUIDES

Here is a complete list of Fodor's Travel Guides, available in current editions; most are also available in a British edition published by Hodder & Stoughton.

U.S. GUIDES

Alaska
American Cities (Great Travel Values)
Arizona including the Grand Canyon
Atlantic City & the New Jersey Shore
Boston
California
Cape Cod & the Islands of Martha's Vineyard & Nantucket
Carolinas & the Georgia Coast
Chesapeake
Chicago
Colorado
Dallas/Fort Worth
Disney World & the Orlando Area (Fun in)
Far West
Florida
Fort Worth (see Dallas)
Galveston (see Houston)
Georgia (see Carolinas)
Grand Canyon (see Arizona)
Greater Miami & the Gold Coast
Hawaii
Hawaii (Great Travel Values)
Houston & Galveston
I-10: California to Florida
I-55: Chicago to New Orleans
I-75: Michigan to Florida
I-80: San Francisco to New York
I-95: Maine to Miami
Jamestown (see Williamsburg)
Las Vegas including Reno & Lake Tahoe (Fun in)
Los Angeles & Nearby Attractions
Martha's Vineyard (see Cape Cod)
Maui (Fun in)
Nantucket (see Cape Cod)
New England
New Jersey (see Atlantic City)
New Mexico
New Orleans
New Orleans (Fun in)
New York City
New York City (Fun in)
New York State
Orlando (see Disney World)
Pacific North Coast
Philadelphia
Reno (see Las Vegas)
Rockies
San Diego & Nearby Attractions
San Francisco (Fun in)
San Francisco plus Marin County & the Wine Country
The South
Texas
U.S.A.

Virgin Islands (U.S. & British)
Virginia
Waikiki (Fun in)
Washington, D.C.
Williamsburg, Jamestown & Yorktown

FOREIGN GUIDES

Acapulco (see Mexico City)
Acapulco (Fun in)
Amsterdam
Australia, New Zealand & the South Pacific
Austria
The Bahamas
The Bahamas (Fun in)
Barbados (Fun in)
Beijing, Guangzhou & Shanghai
Belgium & Luxembourg
Bermuda
Brazil
Britain (Great Travel Values)
Canada
Canada (Great Travel Values)
Canada's Maritime Provinces plus Newfoundland & Labrador
Cancún, Cozumel, Mérida & the Yucatán
Caribbean
Caribbean (Great Travel Values)
Central America
Copenhagen (see Stockholm)
Cozumel (see Cancún)
Eastern Europe
Egypt
Europe
Europe (Budget)
France
France (Great Travel Values)
Germany: East & West
Germany (Great Travel Values)
Great Britain
Greece
Guangzhou (see Beijing)
Helsinki (see Stockholm)
Holland
Hong Kong & Macau
Hungary
India, Nepal & Sri Lanka
Ireland
Israel
Italy
Italy (Great Travel Values)
Jamaica (Fun in)
Japan
Japan (Great Travel Values)
Jordan & the Holy Land
Kenya
Korea
Labrador (see Canada's Maritime Provinces)
Lisbon
Loire Valley

London
London (Fun in)
London (Great Travel Values)
Luxembourg (see Belgium)
Macau (see Hong Kong)
Madrid
Mazatlan (see Mexico's Baja)
Mexico
Mexico (Great Travel Values)
Mexico City & Acapulco
Mexico's Baja & Puerto Vallarta, Mazatlan, Manzanillo, Copper Canyon
Montreal (Fun in)
Munich
Nepal (see India)
New Zealand
Newfoundland (see Canada's Maritime Provinces)
1936 . . . on the Continent
North Africa
Oslo (see Stockholm)
Paris
Paris (Fun in)
People's Republic of China
Portugal
Province of Quebec
Puerto Vallarta (see Mexico's Baja)
Reykjavik (see Stockholm)
Rio (Fun in)
The Riviera (Fun on)
Rome
St. Martin/St. Maarten (Fun in)
Scandinavia
Scotland
Shanghai (see Beijing)
Singapore
South America
South Pacific
Southeast Asia
Soviet Union
Spain
Spain (Great Travel Values)
Sri Lanka (see India)
Stockholm, Copenhagen, Oslo, Helsinki & Reykjavik
Sweden
Switzerland
Sydney
Tokyo
Toronto
Turkey
Vienna
Yucatán (see Cancún)
Yugoslavia

SPECIAL-INTEREST GUIDES

Bed & Breakfast Guide: North America
Royalty Watching
Selected Hotels of Europe
Selected Resorts and Hotels of the U.S.
Ski Resorts of North America
Views to Dine by around the World

AVAILABLE AT YOUR LOCAL BOOKSTORE OR WRITE TO
FODOR'S TRAVEL PUBLICATIONS, INC., 201 EAST 50th STREET, NEW YORK, NY 10022.